A PALACE FIT FOR A LAIRD

Rowallan Castle
Archaeology and Research

1998–2008

Archaeology Report no 1

A PALACE
FIT FOR A LAIRD

Rowallan Castle

Archaeology and Research 1998–2008

Archaeology Report no 1

Gordon Ewart and Dennis Gallagher

with contributions from
Thomas Addyman, Ciara Clarke, Amanda Clydesdale, Clare Ellis, Julie Franklin, John Harrison, Nicholas Holmes, William McQueen, Ann MacSween, Kath McSweeney, John Sanders, and Patricia Vandorpe

Illustrations by
David Connolly, Andrew Dunn, Andrew Hollinrake, Angus Mackintosh and Sylvia Stevenson

HISTORIC SCOTLAND

First published by Historic Scotland 2009

ISBN 978-1-84917-015-4

Cover photo by David Henrie, Historic Scotland; with inset
of oak door from Rowallan Castle now on display in the
Museum of Scotland © National Museums of Scotland.
Licensor www.scran.ac.uk

CONTENTS

LIST OF ILLUSTRATIONS

ABSTRACT

The programme of archaeological excavation and survey at Rowallan Castle commenced in 1998 with excavation within the late medieval tower, itself placed on a natural mound. This revealed a Bronze Age burial pit, a series of timber structures and a stone platform. The burial pit contained a layer of cremated human bone and a Food Vessel of c 2300/2100–1700 cal BC. Traces of at least three episodes of timber building pre-dating the stone tower were revealed, and radiocarbon dating from contexts associated with two of these structures has suggested construction dates of c 100 BC and 300 BC respectively. This excavation, combined with subsequent comprehensive analysis of the upstanding building, has demonstrated the medieval and post-medieval development of the site beginning with a tower house of mid 13th- to 15th-century date. The S range of the courtyard was established in the late 15th–early 16th century and construction of the Great Hall is identified as the work of Mungo Mure (1513–47). His successor, John Mure, was responsible for the remarkable fore work of the castle, as well as the construction of the gallery, woman house and back work.

Historical research has shown that, contrary to generally accepted history, Rowallan was held by the Comyn family in the mid 13th century, not becoming a Mure possession until the latter part of the century. An account is given of the owners of Rowallan, its setting, and the economy of the estate.

ACKNOWLEDGEMENTS

Gordon Ewart and Dennis Gallagher would like to acknowledge and thank the following people:

- Doreen Grove, Richard Fawcett, Richard Strachan and Peter Yeoman of Historic Scotland, and Geoffrey Stell of Stirling University, for their support and advice during the fieldwork and reporting process. Peter Yeoman served as managing editor of the volume.

- the excavation staff – David Connolly, Andrew Dunn, Andrew Hollinrake, Alan Radley, Paul Sharman, David Stewart and Jon Triscott

- the staff of the Historic Scotland Monument Conservation Unit based at Glenluce who assisted the excavation staff

- Loy Associates, under the direction of Ross Dallas, who completed the survey

- Thomas Addyman, John Harrison, William McQueen and John Sanders for their respective chapters

- Ciara Clarke, Amanda Clydesdale, Clare Ellis, Julie Franklin, Nicholas Holmes, Ann MacSween, Kath McSweeney and Patricia Vandorpe for their specialist reports in the excavation chapters

- Thomas Whalley for his assistance in compiling and editing the final document

- David Connolly, Andrew Dunn, Andrew Hollinrake, Angus Mackintosh and Sylvia Stevenson for the various illustrations throughout the report

- East Ayrshire Council www.futuremuseum.co.uk <http://www.futuremuseum.co.uk/> , RCAHMS, the National Library of Scotland, and Historic Scotland for providing illustrations

- Jackie Henrie for copy editing

Thomas Addyman would like to thank Duffield Morgan Ltd for funding the fieldwork which resulted in his paper, and for permission to use it within this publication.

1 INTRODUCTION

Gordon Ewart

It [Rowallan] has been a delightful mansion-house, having a very pleasant situation in a well-timbered park on the banks of the Carmel, a clear flowing stream which is here increased by the waters of a small burn.

(MacGibbon and Ross 1887–92, ii, 375)

Rowallan Castle (Illus 1) had for centuries been the home of one family, the Mures of Rowallan, but, in the 18th century, the heiress of Rowallan married the son of the Earl of Loudoun and the lands became part of the Loudoun estate, the house no longer serving as the principal family home. Thereafter the building was neglected and the estate grounds, known mainly for its fine trees, became a place of recreation for the local populace who, according to Adamson (1875, 124) 'enjoy themselves beneath the spreading trees in front of the castle, and merrily foot it upon the green sward'. Adamson described the castle at that date:

The oldest and most dilapidated seems to have been erected on top of a rock, or crag. The ground chambers of this portion only remain, and are in a very ruinous and crumbling condition, portions of their roofs having fallen in . . . The more modern building faces south and is divided from the older by a loopholed wall some forty feet long. In it is an ornamented gateway, above which the date 1666 is still legible. The front of the building has a very imposing appearance, and bears many sculptured devices. To the principal door – which is of oak, and studded with iron, there is a flight of broad stone steps. . . Near the centre of the court grows a sombre yew tree, which accords in a manner with the ruinous and deserted appearance of the building. The first indication that the place is partly inhabited is a neatly whitened step in front of a finely-carved oaken door. This is the entrance to the apartments occupied by the keeper and, in point of fact, to the interior of the castle. A few relics of past greatness have been preserved. In the old dining-room there is an elaborately carved sideboard and an old arm chair which bears the date of 1617. These are of oak and very interesting. In a small room, called, Lord

1 General view of Rowallan from the SE, prior to conservation works (*Royal Commission on the Ancient and Historical Monuments of Scotland © Crown Copyright*)

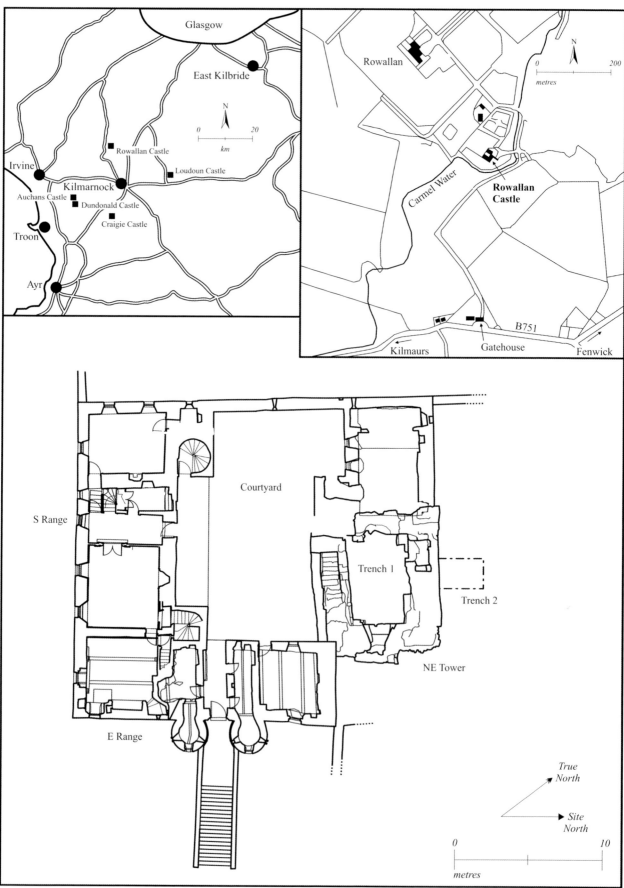

2 Site location

3 Aerial view of Rowallan Castle (*Royal Commission on the Ancient and Historical Monuments of Scotland © Crown Copyright*)

Loudoun's sleeping apartment, there is a beautifully carved wardrobe in oak. The room door and panelling are of the same material. The next room of interest is at the top of the building, and is called 'the auld kirk.' Here are some several fragments of kirk stools, which are for the most part moth-eaten and rotten. In this room the distinguished William Guthrie of Fenwick is said to have occasionally preached, and the pious Sir William Mure to have met with his tenantry to worship the God of their fathers. In almost all the rooms throughout the building every available space on the walls is covered by names and addresses . . . At the back of the castle is an old garden, which does not contain anything of historical interest

Adamson (1875, 113)

The castle (Illus 2) lies N off the B751, 3km NE of the village of Kilmaurs (NS 4347 4242). It is set within the designed landscape of the Rowallan estate and is approached today from the SE, the main entrance to the estate, through a gatehouse built in the Baronial style at the beginning of the 20th century as part of the upgrading of the estate by Robert Lorimer on behalf of the new owner, Cameron Corbett, Member of Parliament for Tradeston in Glasgow. This work included the construction of Rowallan House – which replaced the castle as the focus of the estate. It lies to the NW of the old castle and was built on the site of the former Rowallan Mains (1860 OS ed). The designed landscape of Rowallan extends today over 205 acres (83ha), including c 24 acres of parkland and 60 acres of woodland (Land Use Consultants 1988, 359).

The road through the estate progresses more or less straight to the NW of the gatehouse, with trees planted on either side forming an avenue, again apparently dating from the Lorimer reworking of the estate. The road then turns sharply NE to skirt the Holmepark Plantation which, although dating from an earlier plan, was largely replanted during the early 1900s. From this point the road passes by the old castle, which lies in a generally level area defined on the S and E by a steep bend in the Carmel Water, near its confluence with the Balgary Mill Burn and Gardrum Mill Burn. A small stone bridge leads to the entrance to the old castle (Illus 3).

The entrance to the castle's outer courtyard is by means of a gateway of 1661. Few traces of courtyard buildings survive, and the present survey did not include any investigation of this area. The castle is laid out in quadrangular form, with ranges on the N, E and S sides of an inner courtyard. The W side is closed by a stretch of curtain wall. This inner courtyard is entered via a finely constructed flight of stone steps leading to a gatehouse within the E range, flanked by twin towers. This configuration has created a courtyard level well above the surrounding ground level, the result of substantial infilling

The importance of Rowallan Castle as a historic building was emphasised in the late 19th century by the seminal work of MacGibbon and Ross (1887–92, II, 375–89) which described not only the structure of the building but also its ornate woodwork and other internal fittings, the panelling and doors in particular. Neglect continued, as shown by photographs of the interior taken in 1941. One of these shows the ornate door of the aumbry lying detached and covered in graffiti (RCAHMS AY688/4). When the castle was passed into State care by Lord Rowallan in 1950, it was in very poor condition, requiring a very substantial programme of repair which was undertaken over several years. This included major works to make the buildings wind and watertight, re-roofing of the E and S ranges and the installation of new windows and conservation heating. Inevitably this weatherproofing exercise affected the archaeological record of those parts of the castle.

Kirkdale Archaeology was invited to carry out a project that combined documentary research, the recording and analysis of the standing building, and archaeological excavation within the NE tower, to present a description of the development of the site from prehistory to the present day. The recent detailed survey was intended to record these interventions as well as to integrate features from the unrepaired areas of the castle with new below-ground archaeological findings. In addition, an illustrated record was prepared for the castle as a whole. This involved scale drawing, photography and descriptions of key features for all the standing elements of the castle. As part of a programme of repair and consolidation on the fabric of the monument by Historic Scotland, the ruined structure forming the NE corner of the quadrangular plan was fully excavated internally. Once the tower was emptied of debris, each internal elevation was recorded. The excavations began with a small-scale trial excavation (undertaken in August 1998) on the ruined structure which forms an element of the N range of the castle. This building (the NE tower) was cleared and recorded in advance of a comprehensive programme of consolidation and repair presently underway on parts of the castle fabric. Other than the fact that the NE tower had apparently been reduced in height and filled with rubble, the original form of the structure and its building history were unknown prior to the recent survey. The work was completed over three main programmes of excavation, starting in October 1998 and culminating in September 1999.

This report presents an amalgamation of the excavation and standing building recording evidence.

ARCHAEOLOGY AND SURVEY

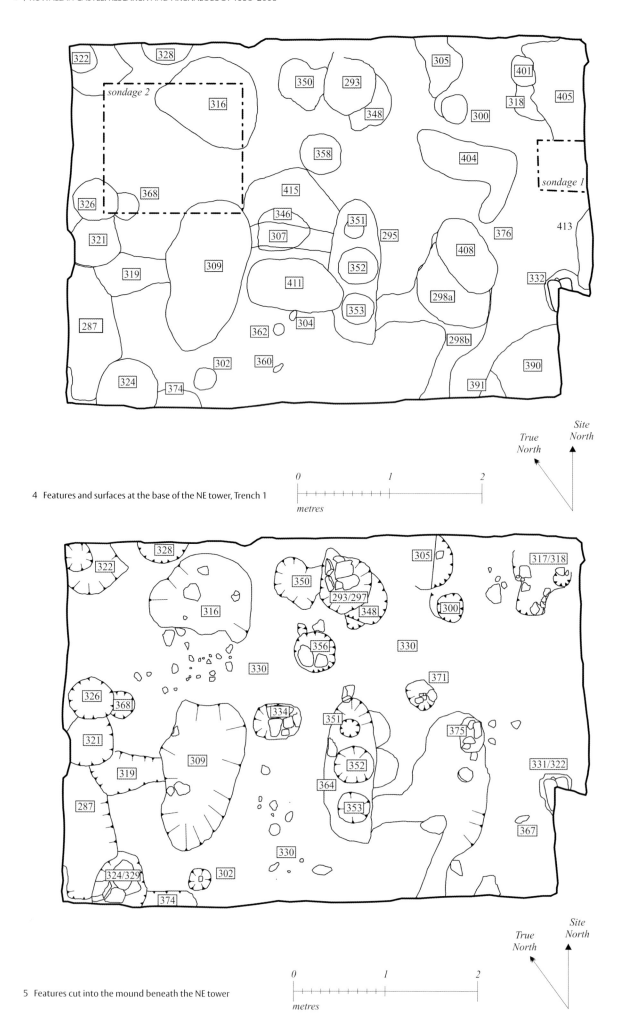

4 Features and surfaces at the base of the NE tower, Trench 1

5 Features cut into the mound beneath the NE tower

2 PREHISTORIC FINDINGS

Gordon Ewart

Introduction

Following the excavation of the NE tower of Rowallan Castle (see Chapter 3), a return to the site saw the excavation of prehistoric features. The area available for excavation, while comprising the entire internal space at the base of the tower, measured only 5.7m E–W by 4m N–S. The tower interior, below the medieval and later deposits, consisted of an almost level layer of pink-brown clays and silts (F330). This featured intermittent, ephemeral and localised fine spreads of truncated occupation and general trampled deposits, both sealing and cut by a series of negative features (Illus 4).

An examination of the cuts in the truncated earlier ground surface within the tower (F330) revealed a total of 35 identifiable features consisting of 17 post-pits, four large shallow depressions and 14 other cuts (Illus 5, 6 and 7). These were grouped into a series of types on the basis of size, structural characteristics and limited stratigraphic association. The truncation of the mound, however, damaged the archaeological evidence for any detailed interpretation of such a palimpsest. This, coupled with the relatively restricted view of the potential mound summit, has resulted in a necessarily general review of the structures revealed.

Subsoil

A 0.9m deep sondage was dug against the inside face of the E wall in an attempt to locate bedrock below the tower walls. Analysis of the soil profile within the pit defined a succession of gravel and silt layers, but generally showed that the mound was largely natural.

A 1.5m² square area in the NW quadrant of the trench was dug to a depth of 0.3m to identify any buried features below the general (F330) horizon, but none was found.

The Late Bronze Age Cremation

One feature was a subrectangular pit (F408). This measured 0.9m by 0.6mm with a depth of 0.25m and contained a layer of burnt human bone (F407). The bone was notable for its lack of charcoal. A food vessel was buried on its side in the S end of the cremation pit. This was two-thirds intact; its upper side had been damaged during the process of lowering the tower floor to accommodate the new vault in Period 3. There was no identifiable cut for the deposition of the burnt bone or the food vessel (Illus 8). The pit was cut by a shallow depression (F298) of probable medieval date.

The Stone Platform

A stone structure (F405) was located in the extreme NE corner of Trench 1. This comprised subrectangular paving, 1.12m long by at least 0.6m wide, defined by vertical-set side slabs and filled by 80mm of small, rounded stream pebbles. The full depth of this feature was approximately 0.14mm. The stone platform was cut by post setting (F401), part of Timber Structure 2, but it is not known if it was contemporary with either the earlier Iron Age timber structures or the cremation burial.

Timber Structure 1

The fragmentary remains of a timber building aligned N/W S/E consisted of a single post or group of posts (F396) and two slots, approximately 0.25m wide and 0.12m deep (F298 and F404) (Illus 9). These narrow slots are interpreted as wall lines of relatively light construction, possibly of wattle or plank. It is possible that the distinctive clay-rich fill of the slots is indicative of a daub wall fabric, and that post (F396) is an example of a small wall post. This group cut the cremation pit (F408).

Timber Structure 2

This structure consisted of a series of earth-fast posts (F293/297, 322, 332, 320/321 and 401) alongside complex slot (F287, 295, 307, 319 and 411) and slot-and-post elements (F346, 348, 350, 351, 352 and 353 which together appear to form part of a straight-sided timber building, probably aligned N–S (Illus 10). The post settings were characterised by the use of yellow sandstone for both packers and post pads, which were still *in situ*. They appeared to reflect a post of 150–200mm in diameter. Their depth varied from 100mm to 350mm.

The use of slots along with posts to form wall lines suggests evidence of wall fabric and load bearing, rather than sill beams, which generally imply lighter constructions, perhaps internal partitions. The F295 and F351/352/353 complex along with F307 and F346 may be evidence of a partition towards the N.

Radiocarbon dating from contexts associated with Timber Structures 2 has suggested a construction date of 120–55 BC.

Timber Structure 3

This structure consisted of three postholes (F324, 326

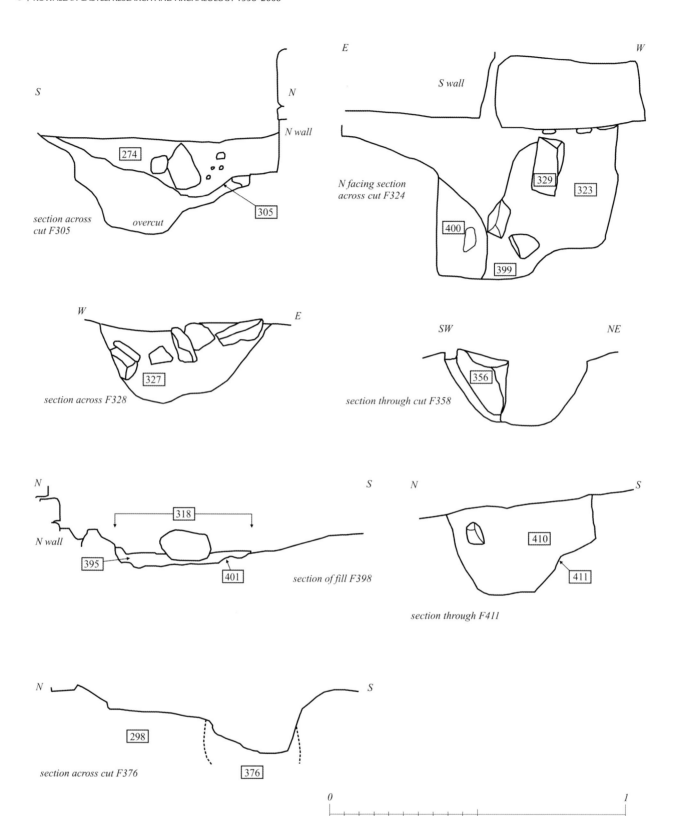

6 Sections of post-pits and slots

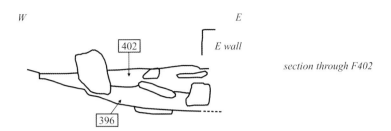

W · E

402

E wall

396

section through F402

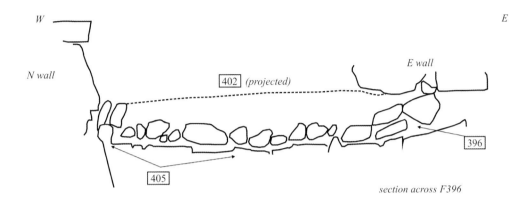

W · E

N wall

402 *(projected)*

E wall

396

405

section across F396

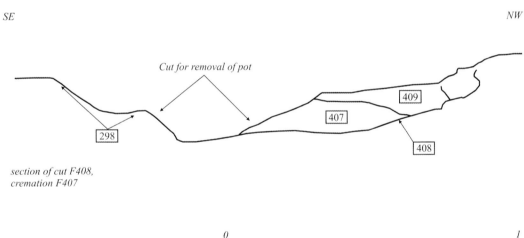

SE · NW

Cut for removal of pot

409

407

298

408

*section of cut F408,
cremation F407*

0 · 1

metre

7 Sections of prehistoric features

8 Bronze Age Food Vessel *in situ*

and 328) all in excess of 300mm in diameter and with depths ranging from 220mm to 350mm. Only one example (F324) retained evidence of its packers *in situ*. The latter were a mixture of stone types, sandstone and local dolerite, retaining a characteristic mixed fill, featuring burnt clay flecks as well as significant deposits of charcoal. The presence of burnt clay was also noted in the other two examples, but the packers did not survive. F326 and F324 were cut over shallower precursors, F368 and 374 respectively, which lay slightly to the E of the main pit. These truncated features were smaller (c 200mm in diameter)

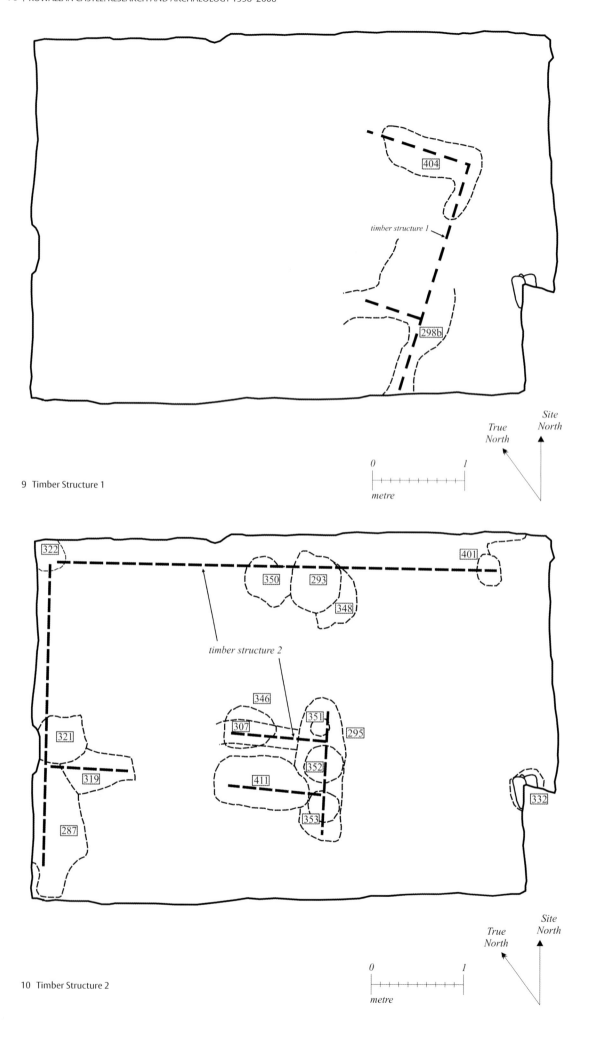

9 Timber Structure 1

10 Timber Structure 2

and shallower (c 250mm) and their respective fills did not feature any burnt clay (Illus 11). The large size, spacing and line of the Type 6 posts suggest a series of major posts on a curving alignment (Illus 12). They appear to be sealed by Timber Structure 2 features, but are themselves multi-phase, apparently enclosing Timber Structure 1 as well as features F408 and F405.

Radiocarbon dating from contexts associated with Timber Structure 3 has suggested a construction date of 300 BC. A single grain of *Triticum* (wheat) from a sample taken from the basal fill of a posthole (F324) yielded a date of 2215±55 BP (AA–45640), placing it in the first millennium BC.

11   View of pits in Trench 1, from SE

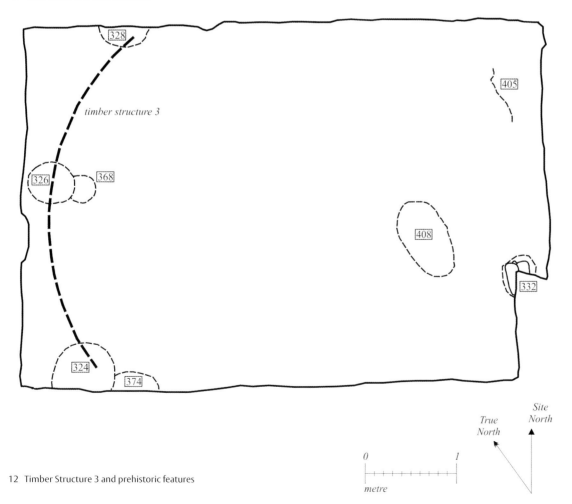

12   Timber Structure 3 and prehistoric features

THE FOOD VESSEL

Ann MacSween

Description

A bipartite Food Vessel (Illus 13) was recovered from F380. The profile is complete over half of the vessel. Over the other half of the vessel, the upper portion of the vessel is missing. (A few sherds, including several from the rim, were found during excavation of the interior contents in the conservation laboratory at AOC Archaeology.) The dimensions are as follows: external diameters – rim 155mm, shoulder 175mm, base70 mm; average wall thickness 9–10mm; height 148mm.

The rim is slightly splayed to the exterior and has an internal bevel. Around the shoulder are stops, probably originally six in all. The fabric is fine clay with c 10 per cent rock fragments which has fired hard and is reduced (grey) with oxidised margins (red/brown). There is no sooting on the outside and only light sooting in the interior – it appears that the vessel has not been used for cooking.

The vessel is extremely finely decorated over the exterior surface, and on the interior of the lip, with intricate, thin bands of decoration, impressed into a smooth slip. The two decorative elements used are impressed triangles and comb-impressed oblique lines (sometimes the comb-impressed lines have been incised to further emphasise them). The triangular impressions always occur in a double band of opposing triangles creating a zig-zag in false relief. The oblique lines are arranged either in a single band, the individual lines sloping from upper left to lower right, or in two or four bands together, forming a herringbone pattern.

The following is the scheme of decoration:

- rim bevel: a band of incised oblique lines bounded at each side by a band of opposed triangles;
- flat exterior lip: a double band of oblique lines;
- collar (from top): a double band of oblique lines, a band of opposed triangles (repeated three times);
- shoulder: upper carination – double band of oblique lines, one on the upper angle and one on the lower angle of the carination; lower carination – single band of oblique lines;
- body – band of opposed triangles, band of oblique lines (repeated six times);band of opposed triangles; two double bands of oblique lines, forming a herringbone pattern.

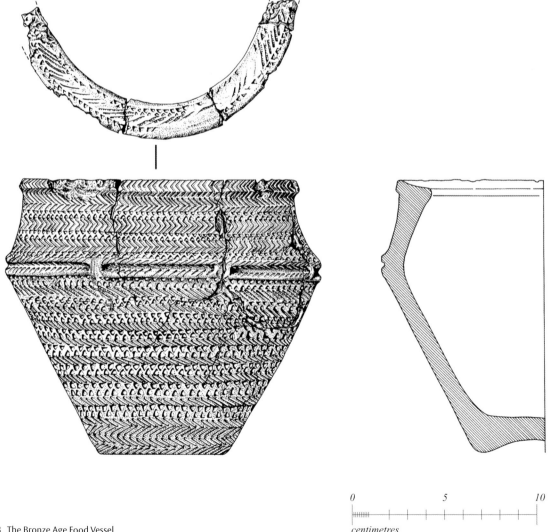

13 The Bronze Age Food Vessel

0   5   10

centimetres

Comment

The Food Vessels from SW Scotland known up to the mid 1960s were published by Simpson (1965) and those up to 1970 by Morrison (1971). Consideration of the illustrations of these vessels highlights the wide range in form and decoration covered by the term 'Food Vessel' and consequently the difficulties in achieving a meaningful typological classification, even within a restricted geographical area.

In the absence of a systematic study of Food Vessels from Scotland, only a few general points are made here. In terms of decoration, the Rowallan vessel has similarities to other Food Vessels from the region, most strikingly to one from Maybole (Morrison 1971, 13) which also has all-over comb-impressed decoration and bands of false relief, although in terms of shape it is a tripartite vessel. A vessel from Ayr (Morrison 1971, 13) is closer in terms of shape, being a bipartite vessel with stops around the shoulder, this time decorated all over with comb-impressed decoration and incision. Ritchie and Shepherd (1973, 25) suggest a combination of outer influence and indigenous development for both Beakers and Food Vessels from the SW, and the sharing of many decorative traits between the two traditions is apparent. The arrangement of decoration in horizontal bands is, for example, strong in the Beaker tradition.

Sheridan (1997) has summarised the radiocarbon dates for Food Vessels up to 1997. Relatively few dates are available but they lie between 1800 and 1400 bc; c 2300/2100–1700 cal BC (Sheridan 1997, 39), overlapping with Beakers which have a time span of 2600–1800 cal BC for their main period of use (Kinnes *et al* 1991).

CREMATED BONE

Kath McSweeney

Background and Methods

The cremated bone material from Rowallan Castle originated from three different contexts. The bulk of the remains came from a layer of burnt human bone (F407) within an oval pit. A few fragments of bone (F409), according to the data structure report, came from a deposit of 'mid brown silty clay sealing F407'. The third group of remains (F380) came from a food vessel found on its side at the S end of the cremation pit. The contents of the pot were subsequently excavated in spits and a small quantity of bone from each of these spits was bagged separately. In addition, further small amounts of bone material were marked 'E', 'W', 'S' and 'scatter'. The association of these deposits of bone with the pot is not made clear in the data structure report, although, as the pot had been damaged by subsequent disturbance, it is possible that they are thought to have originated from the pot. The bone material from each of these contexts was examined and is reported separately, although any possible relationship between them is discussed below.

Description of the remains

A total of 378 bones or fragments of bones from F407 were identified to either a specific or general anatomical area. There was only one identified fragment from F409, and 18 from F380. General methods of ageing and sexing used are those outlined in Bass (1987), Brothwell (1981) and Breathnach (1965). The identification and assessment of age of the dental remains is based on van Beek (1983).

Condition of the remains

The condition of the remains was generally quite poor. The largest fragments were about 65mm for long bone shafts and there was a number of cranial fragments of about 45mm. In general, however, fragment size was considerably smaller than this. There were no complete bones, apart from a few almost complete hand phalanges and several vertebrae that had survived with bodies intact.

The Rowallan Castle cremated material displayed considerable splintering, distortion and splitting of layers of bone as a result of burning. The colour of the bone was generally light beige. There were a few fragments of the cranium, long bones and spine which were a darker blue-grey in colour, suggesting that these areas were less well calcined, and there were a few chalky-white fragments. Surprisingly, several vertebrae had survived almost intact. This is quite uncharacteristic of cremated bone; normally one would expect to find a marked absence of softer cancellous bone, such as that found in vertebrae, the pelvic bones and the ends of long bones; such bone tends to disintegrate at high temperatures. However, in this case, with the exception of a few hand phalanges, which often tend to remain intact during the cremation process, vertebrae were the most undamaged of all of the surviving bones.

A total of 64 per cent of the total bone weight was identified to at least a general anatomical area.

Number of individuals

There was no evidence for the presence of more than one individual. The bulk of the examined remains came from F407. From this context there were no duplicated bones and no indication of any variation in robustness and no inconsistency in age indicators. The remains from F409 and F380 consisted of a few cranial fragments, some non-specific long bone fragments and several tiny unidentified fragments. There was no indication that any of these bones from these latter two contexts were from an individual other than that represented by the remains in F407; none of these fragments was markedly different in colour, texture or robustness, and did not duplicate any of the bones from F407.

Completeness of the remains

Bones from all skeletal areas were identified from the material from F407. The identified fragments include numerous pieces of cranium, part of the jaw, several teeth without enamel, a few fragments of clavicle, scapula and ribs, a substantial part of the spine, some fragments of the pelvis, part of all of the six major long bones of the body, largely pieces of shaft, several almost complete hand phalanges, as well as numerous incomplete phalanges which may have belonged to the hand or foot. As previously mentioned, the remains from both F409 and F380 consisted of a few cranial fragments, some non-specific long bone fragments and several tiny unidentified fragments. As the identified fragments from these deposits were largely undiagnostic, it was not possible to determine whether they were part of the skeleton from F407, or from one or more other individuals.

The total weight of the bone fragments from the main bone deposit (F407) was 1005g, 1081g if the bone from F409 and F380 is included. Using the study of modern cremations by McKinley (1993, 284) as a guideline, the total weight of the Rowallan Castle cremated material could represent the full remains of a single individual.

Age at death

The state of tooth development and epiphyseal fusion indicates that this individual was at least 25 years of age. All cranial sutures were unfused. This can indicate that age was not advanced. However, several lumbar vertebral bodies displayed a moderate degree of marginal osteophytosis. This is a normal process of ageing and can start to develop as early as the thirties, especially if the individual is involved in a heavy occupation. It is likely therefore that this individual was at least 35 at the time of death.

Sex

With most cremated material, the assessment of sex is very problematic. This is because the most reliable areas for sexing, such as the pelvis or cranium are usually either missing, unrecognisable, or too fragmented to enable sex to be assessed with any great degree of reliability. In this case there was very little on which to assess sex. A fragment of frontal with fairly pronounced brow ridges, and the head of a humerus, which appeared large but was not measurable, may be indicative of male sex, although as the evidence is very tenuous, it must be concluded that the sex of this individual cannot be assessed.

Pathology

A few pathological lesions were identified. Some very fine pitting was noted on the external surface of several fragments of parietal bone. It is thought that cranial surface pitting can signify iron deficiency anaemia during childhood. However, the degree of bony reaction is not marked and the pitting may be of little significance here. A small round smooth cavity on the mesial surface of the crown of a third molar is indicative of a carious lesion at the point of contact between the third and second molar. The healed socket for the left canine, with the bone slightly sunken on the external surface of the mandible, indicates that this tooth

was lost during life. Moderate marginal lipping was present on the bodies of two lumbar vertebrae. The full extent of this spinal degeneration could not be assessed because not all of the vertebrae had survived. Degeneration of the spinal column is a normal process of ageing, although it can also be precipitated or exacerbated by hard physical work or trauma. Some degree of spinal degeneration is normally present by middle age, but can commence as early as the mid thirties. It is quite possible that such a degree of deterioration was completely asymptomatic and that the individual suffered no pain.

Cremation Technology and Burial Practice

The bones had been subjected to a fairly marked degree of cracking, twisting and curved lateral splintering. In addition, many cranial fragments had warped, causing the inner and outer tables to separate, in some cases completely reversing the natural curve of the cranium, so that the inner surface bowed outwards. Ubelaker (1978, 35) suggests that curved lateral splintering and marked warping can be indicative of the body being burnt while still 'fresh', ie soon after death. Mays (1998, 207) proposed that fragmentation and distortion are most likely to be the result of rapid water loss during the cremation process.

In general, the Rowallan Castle cremated bone fragments were light beige in colour, with a few fragments with dark-grey/blue areas of colouration; this was particularly evident on the internal surface of the cranium and the shafts of larger long bones. Several fragments were white in colour and chalky in texture. It has been well established that the colour of bone changes with increasing temperature (Ubelaker 1978, 34; Mays, 1998, 217). Burnt bone can vary in colour, from shades of red, brown, black, blue, grey, yellow, to white. Although there are some slight differences in reported results, in the main, the higher the temperature, the lighter the colour. Light grey or white colouring occurs with temperatures in excess of 645°C (Mays, 1998, 217). Shipman et al (as cited by Mays) found that white or light-grey colouring occurred with temperatures of 645–940°C, while Mays' experiments showed no change in colour over 645°C. Wells (1960) found that black colouring occurs with temperatures of less than 800°C, while temperatures above 800°C produced calcined bone, which ranged in colour from blueish-grey to white. Furnaces in modern crematoria were said to operate at between 820°C and 980°C (Wells 1960, 35). In view of the general colour of the Rowallan Castle cremated remains, and the above-mentioned reported results of experimentation, it is clear that temperatures of at least 645°C must have been achieved during the cremation process and, for this to be achieved, cremation technology must have been well understood.

Just as the colour of cremated remains can give an indication of the temperatures reached during burning, variations in the colour of bone fragments can be suggestive of uneven burning of the body. Several fragments of bone were considerably darker than the rest. This was particularly evident among some cranial and some long bone fragments. Of significance in this case is the survival of several vertebrae, particularly from the lumbar region. These factors suggest that burning may not have been even throughout the body. Less well-burnt fragments in the skull and the larger long bones are commonly found; these areas consist of more dense bone that requires longer firing. However, it is unusual to find such good preservation of the bones of the spine in relation to the rest of the body, and it is very likely that in this case the spine was at the periphery of the fire, and that the body was positioned on its side during burning.

POSSIBLE WORKED BONE

Amanda Clydesdale

A small fragment of burnt bone showing apparent incised decoration, in the form of parallel banding, was identified during the assessment stage. Microscopic examination of the bone indicated that the apparent incisions were in fact heat fractures and not deliberate anthropogenic decoration.

PLANT REMAINS

Patricia Vandorpe

Objective and Methods
Following assessment, one sample (F399) was selected for full macro plant analysis. The aims of the analysis were to investigate the nature and provenance of the charred macro plant remains. Identifications were carried out using a low-powered binocular microscope and were checked against the modern seed reference collection at AOC Archaeology (Loanhead). A standardised counting method was used, counting the embryo ends for cereal, and whole seeds for all other. The botanical nomenclature follows Stace (1991).

Samples
The sample was taken from the basal fill of a posthole (F324) initially considered to relate to the medieval occupation of the site, but subsequently a single grain of *Triticum* (wheat) yielded a date of 2215±55 BP (AA–45640), placing it in the first millennium BC.

Results
One hundred and twenty charred plant macro remains were counted. Poor preservation and distortion of the plant remains prevented identification to species level for most grains. The plant remains consisted predominantly of cereal grains, possible rye (*Secale cereale*) and wheat (*Triticum*), a few barley grains (*Hordeum vulgare*), one emmer grain (*Triticum dicoccum*) and a single oat grain (*Avena*). Only two

wheat glumes (*Triticum* sp) were recovered and two seeds of wild plants, namely knotgrass (*Polygonum* sp) and sedge (*Carex* sp) (Illus 14).

Species	No. of items
Polygonum sp.	1
Carex sp.	1
cf *Avena*	1
Hordeum vulgare	5
Hordeum sp.	2
cf *Secale cereale*	23
Secale/Triticum	34
Triticum sp.	2
Triticum sp. (glume)	2
Triticum cf dicoccum	4
Cerealia indet.	45

14   Table showing botanical remains from F336 and F399

Discussion
The botanical remains were part of a secondary deposit retrieved from the mixed fill of posthole F324 containing burnt clay flecks and charcoal. Because of the high degree of distortion of the grains, it is thought that they were subjected to high temperatures before being deposited in the fill of the posthole. In addition to this, the poor preservation of the grains suggests that they were exposed for some time before being deposited. The cereals represented, wheat and barley, are widespread in Scottish first millennium BC contexts. Rye is not very common in the first millennium BC, and although it was never an important crop, there is only evidence for its cultivation in Scotland from the first millennium AD onwards (Dickson and Dickson 2000). Therefore, the grains identified as possible rye in this context probably did not reach site as a crop but more likely as a crop contaminant.

The composition of the sample is not significant enough in quantity and variety of plant remains to enable us to relate it to a specific activity. Nevertheless, the plant macro remains are most likely the product of human waste material such as debris from floor sweepings and cooking activities.

RADIOCARBON DATING

Ciara Clarke

Results
The results of the radiocarbon exercise were unanticipated in that they demonstrate a first millennium BC presence at the site. Rowallan was considered to be important as a late medieval courtyard castle with elements of early medieval occupation, in turn raised over the truncated remains of a Bronze Age ritual site. The radiocarbon results indicate that prehistoric activity at the site was more extensive than previously acknowledged (Illus 15).

Context	Material	Radiocarbon Age bp	Lab Code
F323	Carbonised grain: *Triticum* sp	2245±55	AA-45639(GU-9602)
F333	Charcoal: *Corylus avellana*	2005±45	AA-45643(GU-9606)
F335	Charcoal: *Corylus avellana*	2070±50	AA-45642(GU-9605)
F399	Carbonised grain: *Triticum* sp.	2215±55	AA-45640(GU-9603)
F400	Carbonised grain: *Triticum* sp.	2290±60	AA-45641(GU-9604)

15   Table showing results of radiocarbon dating programme

Discussion

Statistically the radiocarbon dates fall into two distinct groups (see A5.9: Composite radiocarbon calibration plot).

- F323, F399 and F400 comprising one group;
- F333 and F335 comprising the second group.

However, the calibration relationship is not constant and all periods between 400 BC and 800 BC have more or less the same radiocarbon age. Baillie and Pilcher (1983) describe this as the first millennium BC radiocarbon disaster. The dates from Rowallan fall within this bracket and, while statistically the two groups of dates are distinguishable, the characteristics of the calibration curve at this time should be taken into account. It is more accurate to say that the groups *may* be discrete.

SOIL MICROMORPHOLOGICAL ANALYSIS

Clare Ellis

Objectives

Eight undisturbed block samples were collected from sediments relating to the mound at Rowallan Castle to address four research questions:

1   What were the formation processes leading to the presence of an artificial mound?
2   What activities have contributed to sediment accumulation?
3   What is the evidence for mound truncation?
4   How has the mound been modified through time?

Geology and geomorphology

Rowallan Castle is located at approximately 95m OD at the confluence of Balgray Mill Burn, Gardum Mill Burn and Carmel Water. It sits upon modern alluvium and basaltic lavas of Upper Carboniferous Troon Volcanics. The surrounding drift comprises predominantly till. To the W of the castle is Monkcastle Sandstone, sandstones and limestones of the Upper Limestone Formation and Lower Carboniferous Limestone Coal formations comprising cyclic sandstones, siltstones and mudstones with coal. To the E are Troon Volcanics, Lower Coal Measures comprising interbedded sandstones, siltstones and mudstones with thick coals and Bauxite Clay, the latter produced by the contemporaneous weathering of the lavas. Immediately to the N is a area of undefined pyroclastic rock. The valley in which Rowallan is located was the focus for glacial meltwater channels, especially on the W side.

Three samples (48, 49 and 50) were taken from a consecutive vertical sequence in Trench 2, E-facing section. Five samples (57.1 to 57.5) were taken from Sondage 2, E-facing section. Full descriptions of the samples are given in the Archive Report. Common or notable characteristics of specific samples are summarised here. The sediments range from silt to sands, all the contexts contain small stones or grit. Sorting ranges from poor to moderate. The microstructure of the finer contexts is generally massive or granular and those dominated by sand generally exhibit either pellicular or interaggregate structure. Dipping laminations (35–45°) occur in many of the samples, although these are often poorly defined.

The matrices are generally dark-brown, colloidal organic matter masking much of the mineral component. The matrix material often exhibits a weak grain or pore anisotropy. The mineral component is dominated by subangular to subrounded quartz. The rock fragments all appear to be derived from the surrounding geology, basalts, cherts, and quartzite, with occasional bauxite clay clasts. Many are stained by ferrous irons.

Discussion

The precise mode of formation of the 'mound' has not been ascertained. There are three possible modes of sediment accumulation:

- the sediment is an anthropic dump of alluvial material;
- the sediment is part of an alluvial terrace;
- the sediment is a colluvial deposit which has undergone some soil pedogensis.

The overlying sediment is similar, although there are possible remnants of mortar within the matrix. The uppermost is interpreted as a dumped deposit (but again an anthropic or natural agency cannot be determined), but it has mortar rubble inclusions.

The lower sediment is microlaminated. The sand layers are well sorted and could be wind-blown or fluvial in origin. Other layers may have been dumped by natural agencies (ie fluvial or colluvial) or by human activity. However, anthropogenic dumps are usually heterogeneous, with a poor structure, low intra-ped porosity and commonly contain coarse fragments of charcoal (Courty *et al* 1989), therefore the evidence strongly indicates a natural origin for the mound. It is clear that whatever the means of accumulation, deposition was rapid.

The majority of the sediment examined appears to have been derived from an alluvial source. There was little evidence for anthropic-derived material (ie charcoal, bone fragments, pottery, etc), the exception being Sample

48 which contained charred wood fragment, rare bone fragments and the remnants of mortar.

The coal fragments are entirely natural in origin and would have been a natural component of the alluvial deposits. Fragments of micrite, some with pieces of chert attached, and other clasts containing rock fragments occur in Samples 49 and 48. These are likely to be the remnants of mortar and presumably relate to a destruction phase of the castle. Chert fragments occur in the majority of samples and most of these are likely to be derived from limestone in which the calcium carbonate has been replaced by silica; these chert inclusions were a component of the alluvial deposits. Those in Samples 49 and 48 could also be the remains of limestone that was not completely transformed to quicklime in the burning process. Clay clasts, possibly derived from a clay-bonded wall, were observed in Sample 49.

No firm evidence for mound truncation was observed in any of the micromophology samples, but the upper sediment has been modified through human action, predominantly in the form of the addition of mortar rubble and minimal refuse material. There is no clear anthropic modification of the remaining sediments within the 'mound'.

All the sediments have been affected by post-depositional processes. Soil ripening, in this context the incorporation and breakdown of organic matter and bioturbation, has occurred in all the samples, but is more abundant in the upper samples. All the samples have also been affected by the post-depositional downward movement of porewater laden with silt and clay particles. The illuviated silt and clay has settled out of solution within pores and voids and around inclusions. The crescentic, laminated nature of many of these coatings is indicative of episodic, perhaps seasonal, periods of wetting and drying. In addition, the sediments have been subject to post-depositional bioturbation, mostly comprising the earthworm activity. Biological activity continued to occur after the cessation of clay coat accumulation.

DISCUSSION OF THE PREHISTORIC FINDINGS

Gordon Ewart

The interpretation of the excavation is necessarily inconclusive due primarily to the small scale of the area examined and the effects of truncation. However, most of the features so far revealed can be grouped typologically and can therefore be interpreted as elements of a series of building activities

Analysis of the mound showed that it is a largely natural formation over a bedrock outcrop. The bedrock seems to be one of a series of low ridge-like formations, defining the higher ground S of the river line, which delimits the S edge of the castle complex. The outcrop may have been extended southwards from an early date, culminating in the raising of the castle courtyard. The post typology suggested a relatively small enclosure, reflecting in turn, a limited building platform. The features associated with the cremation and stone platform (F405) have suffered from truncation in the later medieval period. The stone platform is undated, but was disturbed by a post setting (F401) and may have been augmented by a further, much eroded cut (F318). This may indicate association with Timber Structure 1 or 3.

The features associated with the cremation and Food Vessel proved to be very rudimentary, with burnt human bone located towards the S end of a shallow subrectangular pit. There was no identifiable cut for the deposition of the burnt bone or the Food Vessel, and it may be that the fill of the pit, along with its associated burnt bone, were laid around the vessel, rather than the vessel being placed at a later date. Excavation confirmed the presence of the Type 3 slot cut across the general fill of the cremation pit, as well as a shallow cut (F396), seen as part of the Timber Structure 1 series.

The cremation burial may have been part of an extended cemetery. Another cremation urn was found on the Rowallan estate in the 19th century (Smith 1895, 96). There is a great variation in the form of burials of this period found in SW Scotland; some have cists and others are protected only by a cairn or mound. The use of natural mounds as sites for cremation burials is not uncommon in the Ayrshire area. Examples have been found at Bennan Hill (NS 3792 0337) and Genoch (NS 3904 0110). It is not known if the stone platform (F405) is contemporary with the cremation or with the Iron Age timber structures, but it is possible that it formed part of a Bronze Age ritual complex. A cist containing probable Food Vessels was found in the early 19th century at Ardeer Mains, Stevenson, in association with a 6m-long causeway and a standing stone (Morrison 1978, 128–9) A similar vessel, discovered at Culzean Castle (on the Kennel Mount site), in association with a severely truncated mound featuring a stone kerb, may also offer a reasonable parallel (Ewart 1996).

Truncation during the construction and conversion of the medieval stone tower removed much of the contextual evidence for the activities represented by the range of timber features and the burial. The grouping of the features into discrete structural types, however, has been borne out by radiocarbon dating evidence. This evidence is in turn more indicative than conclusive as the samples gave dates for only a single pit from each of Timber Structure 2 and Timber Structure 3. Therefore they cannot be considered as anything other than general contextualisation for all the possible related pits in either putative structure. Nonetheless, this evidence confirms activity clearly outwith the earliest medieval occupation and the Bronze Age burial activity. The dates suggest that the large earth-fast posts lying in a wide arc (Timber Structure 3) date between 265 and 340 BC, while the truncated posts and slots of Timber

Structure 2 may be somewhat later (120–55 BC). The two structures do not appear to have stood together, in that the W side of Timber Structure 2 overlies the assumed line of the Timber Structure 3 arc. Neither is associated necessarily with the Bronze Age cremation, and of the groups of features revealed in total, the combination of slots and posts in Timber Structure 1 and Timber Structure 2 appear to reflect straight-sided buildings rather than a circular construction (as is the case with Timber Structure 3). The complexity of the small area exposed is indicative of the concentration of activity on the mound, the full extent of which is unclear. The presence of crude stonework to the S of the NE tower may represent some form of structure set on the southern limits of the mound. This might imply a building platform roughly twice the size of Trench 1. However, it is equally possible that since perimeter features from both the Timber Structure 2 and Timber Structure 3 groups are evident, the available building platform may not extend far beyond the S wall of the NE tower. The impression certainly is one of sequential building over virtually the same footprint, the top of the mound itself.

Timber Structure 3 may be either some form of house or enclosure, with posts 1.8m apart describing a diameter of around 5m. The limits of Timber Structure 2 are not so easily defined, but it is a minimum of 5m long and 3.6m wide, and could extend a further 1–2m on its long axis and 1m on its shorter side. The context and associations of the stone platform are unknown at present. Due to the absence of any structural detail other than under the broadest of categories (rounded and straight-sided plans), the most useful approach to these features is in terms of their precedent on similar castle sites.

Natural mounds are common in the glaciated landscape of Ayrshire and the excavated timber structures, whether for ritual or defence, emphasise how such features of the landscape were exploited, obvious foci of human activity. Timber structures have been noted on several early medieval fortified sites, (eg at Peebles Motte (Ewart and Murray 1978–80), Dundonald Castle (Ewart 1992), Cruggleton Castle (Ewart 1985)) and the Rowallan example conforms generally to this type of timber building, featuring earth-fast posts for its long walls. The Ayrshire sites of Dundonald Castle (Ewart 1992), Auldhill, Portencross (Caldwell *et al* 1998), and Courthill (Scott 1989) all featured timber halls in association with prehistoric occupation, comparable with Rowallan, and much of the prehistoric activity was in turn associated with burials.

3 EXCAVATION OF THE NE TOWER

Gordon Ewart

Introduction

The NE tower of Rowallan Castle stands between 3m and 7m above existing ground levels. Externally the remnant N and E walls appear to be abutted by an earth bank with a regular sloping profile on the N side, and a stepped profile on the E side. The heavily restored and more substantial S wall forms part of the N side of the internal courtyard of the present castle. The W wall is now an internal wall within the extended N range. Before excavation commenced, the ground within the tower comprised of a bowl-shaped depression occupying the E end of the interior, surrounded by heavily overgrown walls and wall heads. This hollow was the result of earlier clearance and robbing of the W and the E walls, the former having been partially cleared, apparently as part of the consolidation work on the W end of the N range (Illus 16).

The main excavated area (Trench 1) was within the NE tower. A smaller trial trench (Trench 2) was dug against the external face of the N wall of the tower. Initial work concentrated on excavating several metres of collapsed vault and wall masonry from the interior of the tower in order to reveal and record the structural elements of the building prior to consolidation of the masonry. In addition, an opportunity was afforded to study the lowest levels of the tower, including early floor levels and evidence of structures pre-dating the existing tower. The last phase of works in June 1999 consisted of the removal of all debris from the tower interior. The floor level of the tower had been lowered by 0.3m in the 17th century in order to provide more space for a newly created vaulted chamber. The surviving occupation deposits proved to be shallow, ranging from 10 to 150mm in depth, and yielded late 17th-century finds from the lowest levels.

Trench 1

The area available for excavation, the entire internal space at the base of the tower, measured only 5.7m E–W by 4m N–S. The infill of the tower consisted of a series of demolition rubble and debris spreads which had accumulated after the vault collapsed and the walls were robbed of stone. The

16 Excavation in progress

surviving N and S walls stood approximately 1.25m above the infill level, although the inner faces of the tower walls were obscured. The inner facing masonry of the N and S walls had been robbed away to a level of approximately 2m below the outer facing masonry, leaving a mass of wall-core stonework sloping towards the centre of the tower. Also, the depth of infill deposits completely filled the centre of the tower and much of the wall heads were buried under a blanket of grass-covered debris leaving only the tops of the outer wall faces as exposed stonework (Illus 17).

Within the tower, the features contemporary with the occupation of the medieval tower included three large shallow depressions, two of which lay towards the W of trench with the other lying towards the E of the area. All three features had been damaged by later medieval activity, in that occupation debris had contaminated the upper fills of these features. However, in the light of later discoveries regarding the scale and scope of timber features within the tower footprint, these features are best seen as evidence of shallow settings for robbed-out stonework, possibly as part of renovations. Their position towards the central axis of the tower basement suggests that they held a series of padstones connected with the construction of a new vault in the 17th century.

A 0.9m deep sondage was dug against the inside face of the E wall in an attempt to locate bedrock below the tower walls. Analysis of the soil profile within the pit defined a succession of gravel and silt layers, but generally showed that the mound was largely natural. An area was excavated in the NW quadrant of the trench in an effort to identify any buried features below the general horizon, but none was found.

THE BURIED TOWER STRUCTURES

The Intramural Stair

An intramural stair was located in the W end of the S wall. A through-passage between two doorways (F244 – N and F247 – S) joined the tower interior to an external entrance at the W end of the S wall. This passage had a blocked-off section running into the core of the wall. The material filling the stair space was a very loose deposit (F245) of sand, stones and mortar waste. This material was revetted at its W end by loose red masonry blocks, put in place during a recent period of landscaping when the doorway (F247) was opened up and the passage partially cleared. The surviving stair consisted of seven grey sandstone steps (F268) rising to the E. Evidence of a complete rebuild of the outer face of the S wall suggests that the fill of the stair (F245) could have been deliberate packing rather than collapse debris. A coin of 1741 was found in this material.

The steps terminated at a height of 1.6m above the paving of the passageway (F280), and at a distance of 2m. At this point the imprint of a further five robbed-out steps (F269) could be seen, rising up for a further 1.2m to the wall head.

The side walls to the stair were extremely badly robbed, but there was some evidence of how the vault noted in the main tower excavation was inserted against the stair construction. The new vaulting had weakened the N wall of the stair, necessitating a repair (F282).

17 The trial trench across the infill of the NE tower

The Passage

The narrow (1.1m wide) passage ran between the inner doorway (F244) to the N and the outer doorway (F247) to the S, a distance of 2.4m. The floor of the passage was formed of worn white and red sandstone slabs (F280) covered with a thin coal trample. The N end of the passage showed evidence of rebuild associated with the remodelling of the inner doorway (F244). The doorway originally featured a 0.12m step up from the paving of the passageway into the interior of the tower, which in turn was reduced to its footings when the floor of the basement room in the tower was lowered at the time that the vault was inserted.

A series of photographs taken by the Department of the Environment in 1972 provides valuable documentation of the site before more recent clearance (Historic Scotland photography archive A3148/5–7). They show the sequence

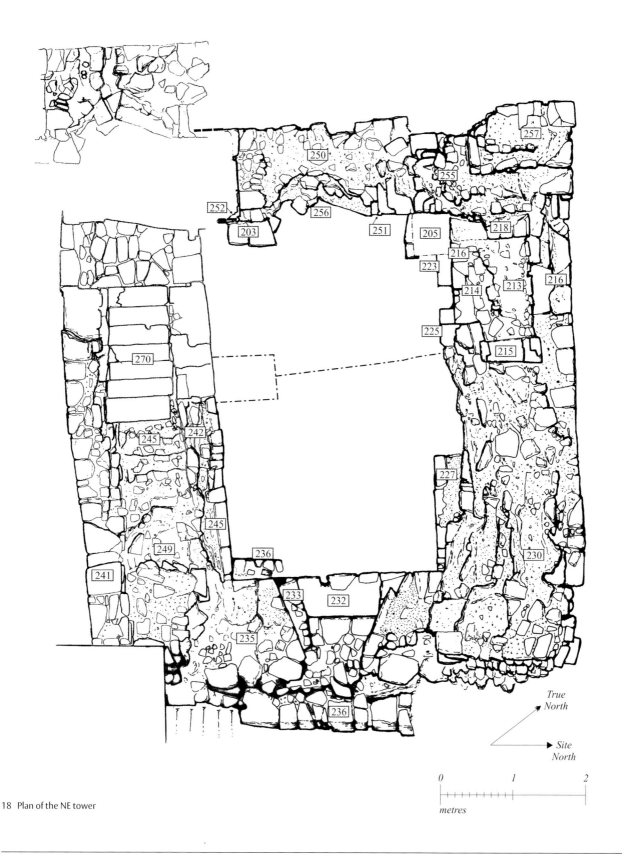

18 Plan of the NE tower

of building within the E wall of the NE tower over a cleared, levelled bedrock eminence. The foundation masonry comprises a steeply battered wall face, built directly over the bedrock platform. This walling (presently buried) appears to be bonded into the masonry of the N wall (F230). The upper exposed walling forming the E wall overlies the battered primary build, and is clearly part of the walling excavated as F235. In addition to these two elements, there appears to be a residual section of original upper E face overlying the battered basal wall. This fragment of wall defines the extreme southern limit of an upper E wall face for the NE tower, clearly built over by the N wall of the present E range.

A small area of the mound was excavated immediately N of the tower. The exposed surface at this point comprised an area 12m E–W by 3m N–S, standing some 4m above the general ground surface to the N and E. Within this area, Trench 2 measured 3m N–S by 2m E–W and ultimately reached a depth of 2m against the base of the N wall.

Bedrock was located at a depth of 0.1m below present turf level and appeared to be made up of a hard but heavily fractured dolerite-like material. This same material just to the W of the tower was seen to weather into red grit, in which selective decay of the rock had left substantial rounded boulders, which were used in the footings of the tower. The base of the tower N wall at the S end of Trench 2 consisted of a chamfer course of red sandstone sitting on a undefined depth of split dolerite boulders (F508), identical to those seen in the interior of the tower (F383), comprising the lowermost 0.3m of masonry.

Trench 2 revealed a succession of debris levels interspersed with natural accumulations, sloping gently towards the edge of the mound. Uppermost was 0.12m of topsoil, sealing a thick layer (0.6m deep) of stone and mortar demolition debris from the decay of the N wall. This in turn sealed a thin light-brown sandy soil, possibly a natural soil accumulation which covered a deposit of broken, burnt handmade bricks, many of which featured an oval maker's stamp. The brick debris lay over 0.3m of reddish silty sand, in turn sealing two coal-rich midden deposits. These layers sealed the natural hillside profile of compacted, orange-brown sandy clay.

The basal masonry of the N wall of the tower comprised of broken and split boulders with surviving traces of mortar pointing. The wall was 1.2m high with a pronounced batter. The surviving remnant of walling presently defining the SW corner of the tower was not investigated due to its unstable condition. There was evidence, however, of a complex doorway arrangement on the S side of the tower. The main access into the tower was at one time via a (now restored) doorway, the threshold of which lies at present some 1.5m above the internal courtyard surface. This outer doorway led to an inner doorway 2m to the N, implying a narrow intramural space between the outer S wall and the S wall of the tower interior (Illus 18).

INTERPRETATION

Trench 1

The interpretation of the features excavated within the early ground surface is necessarily inconclusive due to the small scale of the area examined and the effects of truncation. Those dating to the pre-medieval activity on the site are discussed in a separate report, but some related to the medieval stone tower.

The need for temporary support during the centring process when a new vault was inserted is reflected by at least one group of features. The comprehensive reconstruction of the tower in the early 17th century to create a larger basement at ground level saw the insertion of a simple barrel vault in place of a timber floor (Illus 19, 20 and 21). The span of the vault (4m) required support during construction until the stones could be keyed in place. It is postulated that the features are evidence of supports for temporary centring resting on a series of pad stones roughly along the central axis of the basement area.

19 Interior of W wall of NE tower

20 NE tower and NW range from the S

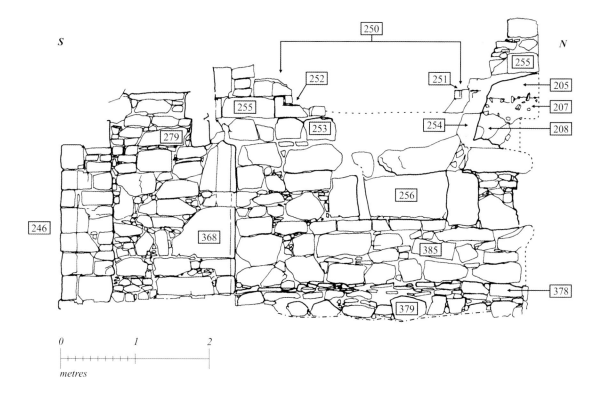

21 Elevation of the W wall of the NE tower showing inserted vault

Trench 2

The present shape of the N side of the mound is the result of successive periods of accumulation and landscaping which have widened its sides by at least a metre. Further landscaping in the 1970s has removed the top of the slope and replaced it with a flat artificial surface, probably created simply to expose the bottom sandstone masonry of the wall.

The tower N wall was built directly on the surface and is presumed to have been intended to be exposed. There is no foundation cut for this wall and it seems likely that a stepped platform on which to place the foundation masonry was cut into the mound. The earliest excavated horizons in this trench comprised 0.42m of soil and domestic waste, sealed by the brick debris. This represented both occupation and clearance from the last use of the tower.

It is now clear that the tower was not built on a pre-existing flat-topped feature as it appears today, but was in fact built on the edge of a small hill or ridge. Its walls were built over the edge of the slope to the extent that the base of the interior foundations of the N wall is 0.9m higher than the base of the outer foundations. This indicates a slope of about 30°, similar to the exposed sloping profile noted in Trench 2.

THE FINDS
Julie Franklin

Introduction

Most of the finds came from the occupations layers within the vault of the NE tower and most were very tightly datable to the late 17th to mid 18th century when the castle was in decline. These included several wine bottles, clay pipe fragments, coins and other copper alloy objects and probably represent occasional use rather than permanent occupation. The finds relating to the building fabric were more scattered. Window glass, fire bricks and door hinges were found in the rubble from the collapse of the vault and in Trench 2, outside the castle.

Pottery

The pottery numbered only 26 sherds, all of which were post-medieval in date. Most were of locally made post-medieval Reduced Ware. This is found in large quantities on both the W and E coasts, beginning possibly as early as the 16th century, and continuing until the early 18th century. Two conjoining sherds (F207 and F212) from a green glazed jug belly were marked with a large incised arrow. Similar marks are seen on the bases of some French vessels, where, incised post-firing, they are assumed to be merchants' marks. Here, incised before firing, the arrow may be a maker's mark or simply a decorative device, though an unusual one.

Two sherds of tin-glazed earthenware were found,

one a rim sherd from a bowl or porringer. Both sherds are unpainted. Tin-glazed pottery was produced in Britain and northern Europe from the first half of the 17th century until superseded by harder wearing types in the 18th century (Jennings 1981). The only other sherd was of a brown glazed red earthenware of 17th-century or later date.

The pottery assemblage, though similar in date to the glass bottle collection, differs in terms of completeness of vessels. The scattered sherds have possibly been redeposited from elsewhere, or from slightly earlier in the castle's history, though they are of a similarly utilitarian nature.

> 1 Post-medieval Reduced jug belly sherd. External green glaze. Incised, pre-firing, with a large arrow, apparently pointing down, though orientation not certain. F207, F212 (Illus 22).
>
> 2 Tin-glazed earthenware bowl/porringer rim. F212 (Illus 22).

Vessel Glass

The 88 sherds of vessel glass were all from green glass wine bottles, ranging in date from 1650 to 1800. The best of these, including one complete profile, were from the occupation layers of the vault. These bottles may well have contained wine consumed on site, or may have been reused to carry water or other liquids.

The importance of drinking in whatever activities were taking place on site should not be overplayed. The minimum vessel count for the vault is only eight bottles, which could all have been deposited over two or three different nights spanning a century. For the courtyard, the count is only five, conceivably all deposited at the same time. Interestingly, those from the vault were found around the edges, avoiding the central area, suggesting at least a cursory attempt to keep the place tidy. The following identifications are with reference to Hume (1961) and Leeds (1941) and are grouped by context in approximate order of deposition.

> 3 Bottle neck and shoulder, olive-green glass; c 1680–1720; F290 (Illus 23).
>
> 4 Bottle base and shoulder, olive-green glass; c 1650–70; F264 (Illus 23).
>
> 5 Bottle neck and shoulder, olive-green glass; c 1680–1710; F264 (Illus 23).
>
> 6 Bottle base, olive-green glass; c 1740–70; F264 (Illus 23).
>
> 7 Bottle neck and shoulder, sea-green glass; c 1750–70; F283 (Illus 23).
>
> 8 Bottle, complete profile, amber-green glass; c 1750–70; F278 (Illus 23).

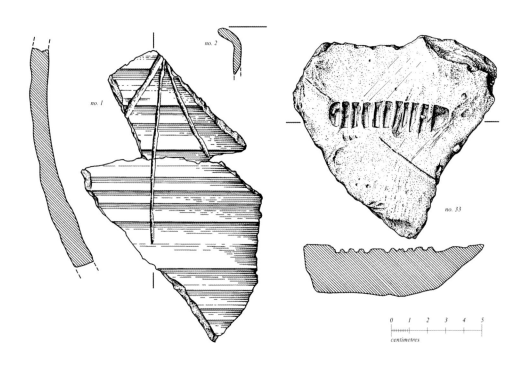

9 Bottle neck, olive-green glass; mid–late 18th
century; F278 (Illus 23).

10 Bottle neck, amber-green glass; c 1770–1800;
F101/F102 (Illus 23).

11 Bottle base, olive-green glass; c 1770–1800; F101/
F102 (Illus 23).

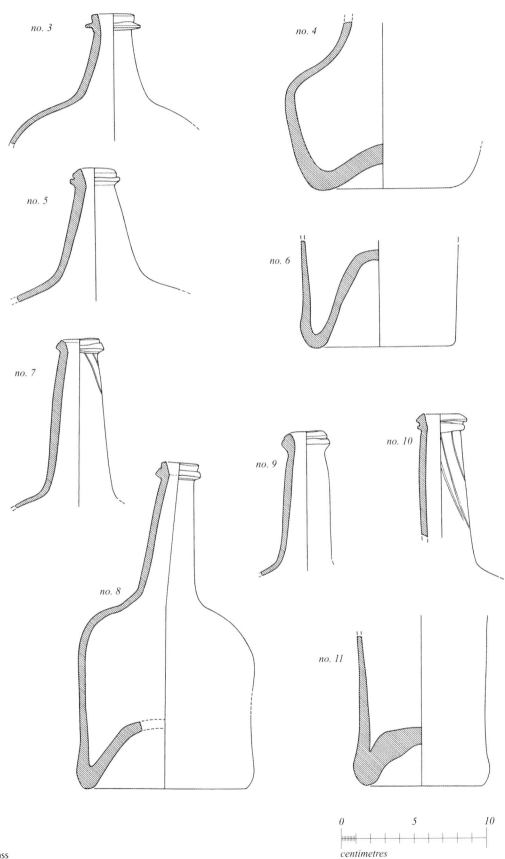

23 Vessel glass

Copper Alloy

24 Buckle. Cast double-D framed buckle with decorative knops at outer edge of each loop and at either end of the bar, pin missing; length 46mm, width 30mm. F264 (Illus 24).

An almost identical buckle from Basing House, Hampshire, was dated to the first half of the 17th century and compared to similar buckles from Jamestown, Virginia (Moorhouse 1971, 58, no 169). Whitehead dates all such buckles to the period 1550–1650 (1996, 65). Though a similar buckle from Sandal Castle was found in deposits dating from 1270 to 1400 (Goodall 1983, 233), an early 17th-century date seems most likely.

25 Suspension chain. Twelve links from a chain made with D-sectioned wire. Each link is figure-of-eight shaped, with wire coiled five times around the centre. The bottom link is broken. The top is joined to a 'T-bar', made from a length of wire bent to form a central loop to link to the chain, and two side loops. Length 175mm, width of T-bar, 28mm. F286 (Illus 24).

A chain from Coventry, dating to the mid 16th century has a similar 'T-bar' attachment to no 25. Here it is interpreted as

a piece to hook into a buttonhole, to suspend important and often used items, such as a seal or bunch of keys (Woodfield 1981, 94, no 39). The links of the Rowallan chain are, however, of a different type. Only one parallel could be found for links formed in this way, an unfortunately unstratified example from Colchester (Crummy 1988, 10, no 1412).

26 Wire pin. Coiled wire head soldered or stuck to shaft. Length 60mm. F276 (Illus 24).

27 Domed stud, with integral rivet, possibly a fitting from a piece of furniture. Diameter 13mm. F294 (Illus 24).

28 Hinge strap. Tapering strip, with wider rounded terminal with large hole. Other end broken, with a long lateral slit, possibly accidental, possibly for fixing. Length 144mm, max width 26mm. F264 (Illus 24).

Iron

All the iron is structural in nature and relates to the fabric of the building. This includes three hinges from two different doors. The largest of these was a single hinge strap with a loop at the end. From its length and remaining nails, the door had to be at least 820mm wide and 320mm thick. Some wood still adheres to its back, with the grain running laterally, implying this was fixed to the inside of the door. The

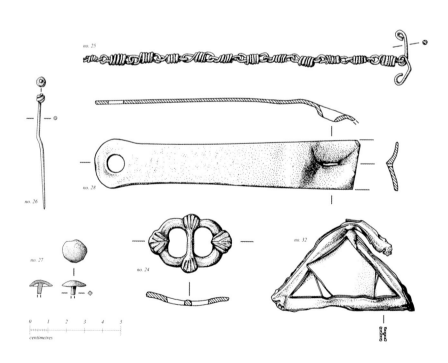

24 Copper and lead artefacts

smaller pair of hinges has wood grain running transversely. They are from a door of minimum width 195mm, and of thickness 270mm, possibly a cupboard, shutter or chest. Another strip has a shaped terminal with nail hole and is possibly also from a hinge strap. But for a handful of nails, none of the other iron objects were recognisable, though three strips from the vault occupation layers, of approximate width, 20mm, all slightly curving, may be from barrel hoops (F264 and F276).

29 Hinge strap. Loop and tapering strap from a hinge. Widens slightly at the end to form a terminal. Evidence for 10 fixing nails, more closely spaced towards the pivot. Length 880mm, max width 45mm. F212 (Illus 25).

30 Hinge. Most complete of a pair of rod pivot hinges. Hinge strap, tapers at a shoulder near the pivot, two nail holes at the wider end, one at the narrow end. End appears to be broken off. Vertical fixing plate with four nail holes still connected with pivot. Length 195mm, width at pivot 47mm. F212 (Illus 25).

31 Strap, possibly from a hinge. Strip with crown-shaped terminal. Broken at other end. Nail hole in terminal and possibly another in centre. Length 92mm, width 32mm. F290 (not illus).

Window Glass and Lead

There were 42 pieces of window glass. Several of these are painted, with certain areas appearing redder than others, but their condition is such that no designs are apparent. None of the other sherds appear to be coloured. The nine sherds from outside the tower (F503) are associated with lead cames, with one small pane being broken but still complete, held together by its surrounding lead. Unfortunately, not enough survives to suggest what the windows of the castle windows may have looked like. The glass must date to the building fabric, before the tower began its decline, probably the 16th century or earlier.

32 Window pane, complete, with lead cames. Length 77mm, width 60mm. F503 (Illus 24).

Ceramic Building Material

Two fire bricks (F203 and F262) were found, both of similar proportions, 210mm by 100mm by 70mm. Both showed signs of heating and one was partially covered in a slag deposit.

A coarse floor tile (F314) with some slag deposited on its edge was also found. This is made of badly wedged clay, giving an orange and white marble effect in its core. It is 31mm thick, 92mm wide, and slightly domed in the centre.

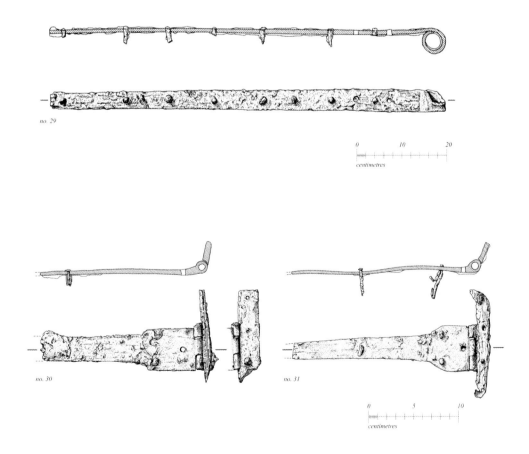

no. 29

0   10   20
centimetres

no. 30   *no. 31*

0   5   10
centimetres

25 Iron artefacts

Striations on the top surface show where it has been roughly smoothed off. It has no signs of glaze and was probably for use in a forge as with the fire bricks above.

Another large fragment is probably from another coarse floor tile (F503). It has no complete dimensions but is of a fine orange sandy fabric, with patches of grey in the core. A large striped ovoid impression in the surface appears to be intentional and is possibly a maker's mark, though no parallels for this could be found.

> 33 Floor tile/Brick. One fragment of edge but no complete dimensions. Orange sandy fabric with occasional large quartz inclusions and patches of grey in core. Impressed mark on surface. 105+mm x 105+mm x 28+mm. F503 (Illus 22).

Clay Pipe

The 23 clay pipe finds are all stem sherds. All have a wide bore (7–9/64") indicating a date from the 17th to the early 18th century. One stem has a fragment of heel, unstamped but with moulded initials '?IC', probably representing James Colquhoun of Glasgow. There were three makers of this name operating in Glasgow between about 1670 and 1730. Glasgow was probably the nearest source of clay pipes at the time. There are no records of anyone working in Kilmarnock before the 19th century (Davey 1987). Colquhoun pipes are found throughout southern Scotland, especially in the W (Gallagher 1987, 48).

COINS
Nicholas Holmes

Most of the individual coins probably circulated into the 18th century. Some of the Charles II coins show extensive wear. These Scottish pieces continued in use for many years after 1707, when they were officially demonetised under terms of the Act of Union, and some possibly as late as the reign of George III, since insufficient low-denomination British coinage reached Scotland. French *doubles tournois* also circulated extensively in Scotland in the 17th and early 18th centuries. The following catalogue has been grouped by context, starting with the earliest deposit.

> 13 Scottish Charles II copper turner (1663–9), 1.84g; die axis 8.0; both sides badly off-centre; much corrosion and verdigris; fairly worn; F291.
>
> 14 Scottish Charles II copper turner (1663–9), 2.16g; die axis 12.0; green patina; very worn; F291.
>
> 15 Scottish copper turner or bodle (1642–97), 1.35g; die axis uncertain; very worn and corroded; only part of thistle distinguishable; F291.

> 16 Scottish William II copper bodle, type II (1695–7), 2.44g; die axis 6.0; dark-green patina; obverse extremely worn; reverse only moderate wear, but last two figures of date unclear; F291.
>
> 17 Scottish Charles II copper turner (1663–9), 1.69g; die axis 12.5; both sides slightly off-centre; heavy green patina; mostly worn; F277.
>
> 18 Scottish Charles II copper turner (1663–9), 1.38g; die axis uncertain; much corroded; degree of wear uncertain; F277.
>
> 19 Scottish Charles II copper bawbee (1678), 7.96g; die axis 6.0; all-over light pitting; dark-green patina; fairly worn; F277.
>
> 20 French Louis XIII (or possibly provincial) copper *double tournois* (1639), 1.78g; die axis uncertain; green patina; very worn; F264.
>
> 21 Scottish Charles II copper turner (1663–9), 1.98g; die axis 5.0; both sides off-centre; some verdigris; slight to moderate wear; F264.
>
> 22 Scottish Charles II copper turner (1663–9), 2.05g; die axis 3.0; obverse off-centre; uneven striking; grainy green patina; moderate wear; F264.
>
> 23 Irish George II copper halfpenny (1741), 7.4g; die axis 6.0; worn; F245.

Discussion

The earliest occupation evidence is from towards the end of the tower's useful life. The floor seems to have been kept clean up until this point. Deposits in shallow depressions in the floor of the vault (F294, F307 and F314) can be no earlier than the end of the 16th century due to the clay pipe stems found in them and, given the rest of the evidence, are probably a century later. The only of these lower levels with firmly datable finds (F291) could have been deposited no earlier than about 1700 due to the worn William II coin. Given that most of the copper alloy finds and at least one of the wine bottles (no 4) is 17th-century or earlier in date, these must be either redeposited or were of some age when finally dumped. The coins could all have still been in circulation in the first half of the 18th century, and this is consistent with the worn state of most of them. A few pieces of possible barrel hoop suggest the room was used at some point for storage.

The date of the rubble infilling of the tower can be inferred from the wine bottles. The latest date for bottles within the occupation layers of the vault is 1750–70. A group of bottles found during work in the castle courtyard are dated 1770–1800. This implies that the vault could not have collapsed before 1750 but probably no later than 1800, the most likely date being around 1770.

4 THE DEVELOPMENT OF THE BUILDING

Thomas Addyman

In this study the general phasing of the structure as understood from dated stones, historical documentation and cursory observation of the building was subject to a systematic assessment. Existing records, principally a series of stone-by-stone survey drawings of the structure, were systematically annotated with analytical data contained within the standing fabric to produce a detailed appraisal of the stratigraphy of the building (Illus 26).

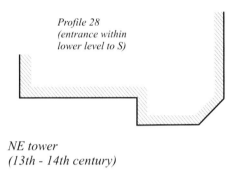

*Profile 28
(entrance within
lower level to S)*

*NE tower
(13th - 14th century)*

26 Moulding profile on entrance to NE tower (*Addyman Associates*)

This evaluation of the analytical history of Rowallan was primarily led by the identification of physical relationships – where there was unequivocal evidence of one build distinct from another. Study of moulded and decorative detail contributed significantly to this analysis, though major pitfalls in relying too heavily on such data were recognised. For instance reuse of moulded stones and even complete features was seen, as were the use of the same detail in two or more phases and the use of decorative details retrospective or outmoded in style, suggestive of an earlier date than was actually the case. It was possible, however, to chart a broad progression of the evolution of the use of individual details.

MEDIEVAL ORIGINS: THE NE TOWER

Description

Exterior of tower

The early tower (Illus 49) measures 8.25m by 9.5m (E–W) in plan and its W wall still stands to a height of 5.5m above its basal plinth course. The latter is well preserved at the base of the N wall of the tower. The plinth can also be traced along parts of the E wall and at the SE corner where is abutted by the NW corner of the E range (and is visible in profile internally). On the S wall the clawed back plinth course stones can be traced for about half the length of the wall face (eastern side) and can also be seen as truncated stones at points along the W wall; at the N end of the W wall the full profile of the returning plinth is preserved within the upper part of a later alcove.

The lower parts of the S and E walls have been clawed back to the line of the wall face above, and refaced below. Above the line of the plinth course at the SW corner can be seen eight or nine courses of original quoins – massive blocks of red sandstone. Below this level they have been replaced with less substantial blonde sandstone quoins. The plinth course, other dressings and general masonry are constructed of a hard, fine-grained, deep pinkish-red sandstone. The general masonry is formed of roughly coursed rubble of massive blocks of the stone, only roughly dressed at the face but otherwise unworked.

Interior at entrance (lower) level

The existing entrance from the courtyard to the S is a secondary insertion, discussed below. This entrance, offset to the W, leads firstly to a straight intramural stair running up immediately to the E, and then beyond into the basement level of the tower proper. The entrance into the basement appears to be original to the surrounding fabric. It had presumably only originally provided access to the stair. There is evidence that the stair itself, doubtless in its original position, has been modified, apparently widened. It is suggested that this occurred when more convenient access from the secondary courtyard entrance to the well-appointed upper levels of the tower was needed.

The lower tower chamber contains few features. The interior parts of a splayed opening are visible in the centre of the E wall – a probable window loop, although its external dressings are unfortunately missing. A recess in the centre of the W wall may originally have been a similar feature, though possibly subsequently blocked off and left as a recess.

The entrance, which faces into the chamber at the W end of the S wall, has a broad 90mm chamfer and is diagonally tooled (Illus 26). These details suggest it is an original feature and that the intramural stair is similarly early (had an original stair in this position been widened?). Apparently confirming the early relative date of the entrance is the fact that the springing stone of the vault has been crudely cut into one of the entrance jamb stones (E side).

The remains of this barrel vault can be seen springing from each longer wall to N and S. This had clearly been a secondary insertion. The crest of the vault must have risen above the level of a pre-existing offset that marked the level of the timber first-floor flooring. Part of the actual vaulting remained *in situ* at the NW corner of the chamber when first exposed by excavation; here it clearly rose above the level of the base of the fireplace. Remains of this offset can be seen at the NE and SW corners and is well-preserved to the NW.

First floor chamber

At the W end of the first floor of the tower there survive the remains of the lower parts of a substantial central fireplace. The lowest jamb stones remain on either side; these bear deeply cut quirked angle rolls. The fireplace had had a raised hearth edging.

The W part of the N wall is recessed and contains many diagonally tooled pinkish-yellow blocks of dressed sandstone. These define the lower parts of an apparent entrance (subsequently infilled with rubblework). The entrance may have led to an intramural stair running up to the E (?).

Within the N wall at about 1m above the offset that indicates the (original) floor level, as one turns the right-angle to the E there is the lower part of an entrance surround, formed of a single block – threshold and lower jambs; its dressings are detailed with a chamfer. This seems to be a secondary intervention although its stratigraphy is obscured by the recent consolidation; paving is also evident, emerging from further secondary masonry infill, to its W.

Discussion

It is unfortunate that so few diagnostic details remain from the original construction of the tower. Those that can be compared include the plinth, details of the fireplace, plan form and wall thicknesses, the presence of a straight intramural stair, and so on.

The only moulded details include the broad chamfered basement entrance and that of the fireplace jambs. Of the former all that can be said is that typologically it falls into the earlier part of the general trend of chamfers, which tend to reduce in size throughout the later Middle Ages and beyond. The hollow quirked angle rolls of the fireplace are more diagnostic. These bear a notable similarity to those of the upper hall windows of nearby Craigie Castle, including the curvature of the quirk and the chamfered basal stop. The Craigie chamber was an addition to the very early tower or hall house that forms the nucleus of that site, though the chamber itself has been attributed to the 15th century. It is suggested as a possibility that the Craigie chamber is in fact considerably earlier in date.

The presence of a plinth of this form is not necessarily an indicator of great age in its own right but may nevertheless be early. For instance, it bears a notable similarity to the plinth of the barbican at Dunure Castle, South Ayrshire (perhaps 14th-century). However, such plinths also appear on much later structures (the perimeter wall of Castle Campbell, for example, is very similar in detail).

A principal indicator of early date is the general character of its construction. In contrast to all subsequent phases at Rowallan, the wall faces of the tower are massively built of very substantial blocks of sandstone. Where these retain an unweathered surface (the lower fireplace stones and adjacent internal facing stones on its N side, and basement entrance), the tooling is of neatly cut diagonal form, again consistent with an early date.

In plan the structure is diminutive for its period and, in the almost total absence of knowledge of the surrounding complex that must surely have existed, it remains open to question how it had functioned. From the early 12th century onwards Cunninghame was firmly within the political orbit of the medieval Scottish kingdom; comparisons with early hall houses of the western seaboard may therefore be of less relevance here. If considered as a hall house, it is by far the smallest of a limited group of comparable structures in this region – Craigie and Dunure (the latter at least perhaps had more affinities with similar structures on the western seaboard, outwith the Scottish kingdom). It is perhaps possible that the early tower at Rowallan formed part of a non-permanent residence – perhaps a hunting lodge? In this respect Hallforest Castle, Aberdeenshire, which measures 9.4m by 14.5m, may provide a comparable example.

In conclusion, a secure date for the early tower is not possible; it may indeed date to as early as the late 13th century, but equally could date to the following century or later.

LATER MEDIEVAL: MASONRY FABRIC WITHIN THE S RANGE
(LATE 15TH–EARLY 16TH CENTURY?)
(?JOHN MURE: SUC 1504; D 1513)

Exterior

There are a number of indications that the lower parts of the
S range contain parts of a pre-existing structure (Illus 53).
Externally this is visible as a band of rubblework of darker
hue, principally consisting of unworked pieces of whinstone.
This survives to a height of about 1.5m, running from the
SE corner of the range for a distance of about 14.5m (at this
point stones protruding at the external wall foot also stop).
It is not wholly clear whether the three dumb-bell gun loops
at this level in the S wall and the one in the E wall are original
to this fabric, later insertions or reused from other locations
(the dressings may have been replacements for simpler
openings in the same locations). One patching at the wall
face between the second and third loops from the E suggests
some form of earlier loop at that point, although the internal
evidence here is unclear.

Caution is required in respect of these lower wall faces
as there has been extensive recent reconstruction, to
the E in particular, as the Historic Scotland photography
archive evidence demonstrates (Illus 27; Historic Scotland
photography archive: A302–3; 16 November 1976).

Evidence in room 9

The existing vault in Room 9 is clearly inserted into a pre-
existing structure. The footing of the original W wall of the
chamber can be seen; there are corresponding vertical
construction breaks on the N and S walls that demonstrate
that the interior wall faces to the E of these breaks are coeval
with this footing. This in turn confirms that the lower walling
described on the exterior in this area is of an earlier period
than the vault and upper structure.

The pend (Component 6)

The extent of the predominantly whin rubblework may
define what survives of the earlier work elsewhere. Much of
the S wall of the pend, to the W of the first vaulted chamber,
is of similar construction (Illus 48). Along the S wall a series
of entrances led into chambers within the range on that side,
three of which remain. The entrances all have sandstone
dressings with chamfered arrises. The walling steps out to
the N towards the E end of the pend; this is of secondary
construction, relating to the formation of an intramural stair
at the next phase.

The N wall of the pend appears to be wholly of this
construction; up to the short northwards return towards its
W end, its rubblework construction is wholly of whinstone.
However, this may be misleading and the N walling may in
fact relate to the construction of the vault over the pend at
the next phase (see Discussion below).

27 Conservation work in 1976 at the east end of the south range (*Historic Scotland ©Crown Copyright*)

Evidence in Components 7 and 8

It is not clear to what extent the two remaining internal vault-supporting cross walls (between Components 7 and 8, and the W wall of Component 7) are of the earlier construction, but, being of far greater thickness than the one further to the E, it is likely that they are at least in part early. A further observation is that the surviving western two vaults are of notably different character to the eastern vault; they are broader, lower pitched and considerably lower set. Indeed, the vault apexes of these two lie at 2m below the floor of the rooms at entrance level; the vault apex of Component 9 by contrast lies only about 0.8–0.9m below the floor above. Such an extraordinary depth of redundant space, in addition to the other features already discussed, strongly suggests that the Component 7 and 8 vaults belong to the earlier structure, and in turn the cross walls that support them. This conclusion implies that the western part of the cross wall between Components 8 and 9 is also of the earlier period but has been reduced in width, leaving the footing of the eastern face of the wall as a relict feature. The existing E wall must therefore be a refacing.

Stair to the W

The lower parts of the stair at the W end of the pend, Component 4, belong to the early phase of work. Here a straight flight of steps (the first five existing steps) rises to the W. Just beyond this point, where the early masonry of the N side of the pend abruptly stops at quoins, the stair must have angled up to the N in a further straight flight up to the courtyard level, now removed. The existing upper steps and turnpike stair belong to later phases, work that also involved the thickening of the S wall in this area – the original steps run below this masonry.

Discussion

After close further examination of the gun loops it was felt probable that they were in fact original to the surrounding early masonry fabric and could thus be used a dating indicator for the lower parts of the range. Dumb-bell gun loops of the form employed at Rowallan (Illus 28) are first seen in Scotland at the Threave Castle artillery house of c 1450, but it is not until the later decades of the century that they make a more general appearance. One within the gatehouse of Newark Castle, Renfrewshire, for example, is dated to c 1480. The Rowallan loops and the range to which they relate probably date to the period c 1480–early 16th century.

The range seems to have been unfinished as there is little evidence to suggest that an upper storey had been built at this phase. A context for an incomplete work may be the death of John Mure in 1513 at the catastrophic battle of Flodden Field.

The construction of the range had likely involved some modification of the topography of the site. The range was erected along the S side of the natural whinstone crag occupied by the early tower. With the existence of this tower

(and other associated buildings) the new range should clearly be viewed as an addition to an existing complex and was presumably not intended as a free-standing structure. The problems of relative levels on the S side of the early tower would therefore have had to have been addressed. The formation of access to the vaulted basement level rooms may well have required cutting into the mound to the N. It is open to interpretation whether the court above was reduced in level at this stage or the next. However it is doubted whether the creation of the existing entrance level hall had been at the expense of a relatively recently completed existing structure.

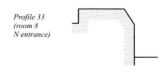

Profile 33
(room 8
N entrance)

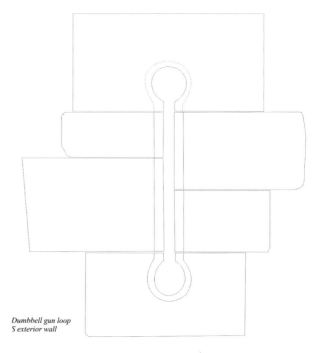

Dumbbell gun loop
S exterior wall

S range, basement level
(15th — 16th century)

28 Moulding profile and dumb-bell gun loop at basement level, S range (*Addyman Associates*)

WORK OF THE EARLY 16TH CENTURY: THE RENAISSANCE HALL RANGE (Mungo Mure: suc 1513; d 1547; m Isobel Campbell)

Introduction

Historical

This Moungon Muire [Mungo Muir, d 1547] rasit ye hall vpone four vouttis and laiche trance and compleitit the samen in his avin tyme; he decessit in battell fechtand agains Ingland in pinkie feilde: 1547.

He from the ground and completed it in his owne time

(Sir William Mure 1657, *Historie and Descent of the House of Rowallane*, 225)

Of interest within this passage is not only the authorship, and thus broad dating, of the major part of the S range, but the particular wording of the section 'rasit ye hall vpone four vouttis and laiche trance'. Grammatically this does not necessarily imply that he built the vaults and low trance [pend] (the meaning generally assumed), but that he raised the hall upon four vaults and the pend, which could therefore have been pre-existing. Perhaps this is too fine a distinction to be read into a text written over a century after the event, but at least it reinforces the notion that such texts should be treated with due caution.

There are now only three vaults. However, the evidence of the fabric demonstrates that the range had extended further W, but was subsequently reconstructed (Illus 48 and 53).

Diagnostic details

Apart from the major entrances to the courtyard, the openings throughout this range bear narrow chamfered arrises (5cm) and, where surfaces are unweathered, neat, generally perpendicular, tooling with a broad-headed chisel. The paired entrance from the courtyard on the N elevation and the entrance at the E end of the hall (Component 21) both display detailing, including roll and fillet moulding, that is more characteristic of the Renaissance period in Scotland (Illus 29). The two surviving entrance-level fireplaces are robustly detailed in a similar vein (Components 21 and 22). The wall heads of the range are surmounted by a large hollow cornice.

Basement level

The principal evidence for modification at basement level lies in two areas, the vaulted cellar to the E (Component 9) and the pend (Component 6).

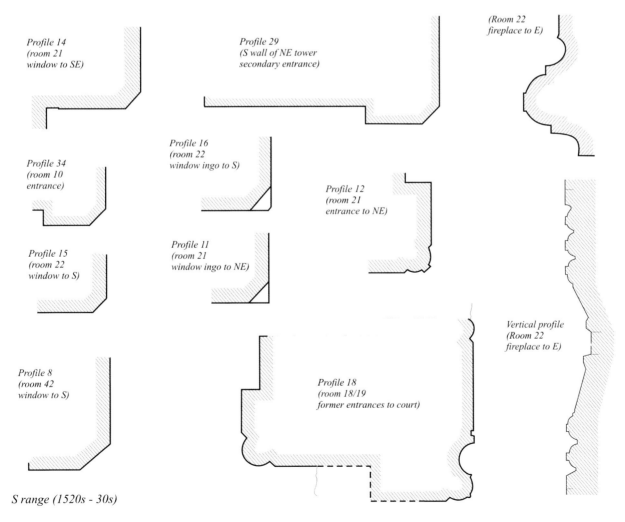

Profile 14 (room 21 window to SE)

Profile 29 (S wall of NE tower secondary entrance)

(Room 22 fireplace to E)

Profile 34 (room 10 entrance)

Profile 16 (room 22 window ingo to S)

Profile 12 (room 21 entrance to NE)

Profile 15 (room 22 window to S)

Profile 11 (room 21 window ingo to NE)

Vertical profile (Room 22 fireplace to E)

Profile 8 (room 42 window to S)

Profile 18 (room 18/19 former entrances to court)

S range (1520s - 30s)

29 Moulding profiles of the S range (*Addyman Associates*)

Component 9

The W wall of this cellar space was reduced in thickness, an operation associated with the insertion of the present vault structure, which is of different character and height to those further W. The purpose of this higher apex level seems to have been to accommodate a new straight flight of steps to the hall chamber on the floor above (Component 22). This stair, Component 10, necessitated the thickening of the pre-existing S wall of the pend (Component 6) towards its E end by about 0.4–0.45m. This thickening extends from the side of the entrance into Component 8 (where a butt joint is visible) all the way to the E exterior wall. A new entrance was formed into Component 9 within which the stair was accessed. The stair was provided to the N with a laird's lug, opening into the pend; this was formed of part of a reused dumb-bell gun loop. If reused at this stage, this may provide indirect evidence that the existing basement level loops are not inserted.

Vaulting the pend

The pend (Component 6) transe

The second area of the basement that saw modification is the pend, where there are two possible interpretations of the evidence. The first is that the pend was vaulted over using the N wall that was part of a pre-existing phase of construction. The alternative is that the N wall is of this phase and required in order to support the vault. The use of whin may have been a result of the deconstruction of parts of the whin-built pre-existing S range. Whichever is the case, it is probable that the vault itself belongs to the early 16th century and was required in order that the courtyard could be fully paved at single level. Vaulting the pend was specifically necessary in order to allow access to the courtyard frontage of the new hall range; this frontage was actually partly built over the span of the vault.

Evidence that appears to corroborate this is the absence of vaulting over the eastern part of the pend, from the point at which the pend narrows in the area of Component 9 (the narrowing also being part of the works of this phase as described). Here it was possible to bridge the narrower gap with substantial sandstone slabs.

What appears to be new walling belonging to this phase was erected in order to close off the E end of the pend. The remains of a window can be seen embedded behind the later masonry of the southern entrance tower on the E façade. This window, which is detailed with a chamfered external arris (similar in detail and tooling to the entrance surround into Component 9), was clearly intended to provide light to the pend. To the E exterior the earlier whinstone rubble walling also gives way to sandstone construction in this area.

Modification to the stair at the W end of the pend (Component 4)

The W end of the pend appears to have been modified at this stage in order to provide covered access up to courtyard level. This involved the removal of the upper parts of the presumed pre-existing stair – the straight flight rising northwards to courtyard level. In its place was erected a stone turnpike stair that rose to a courtyard-level entrance within a stair tower projecting northwards from the new hall range. The S jamb of this entrance survives; this is detailed with a chamfered arris.

The entrance level

Courtyard frontage and entrance arrangements

The N elevation facing into the courtyard (Illus 55) is now partly obscured by a stair tower to the E. Discounting this, there had been two hall windows on either side of a substantial fireplace and a massive chimney stack rising above the wall head (the latter exists but has been largely reconstructed). At the W end of the courtyard elevation there had been a double entrance – a principal entrance to the low end of the hall and, to the W, a more simply detailed ancillary entrance. Both are now blocked. The hall entrance is the better preserved, its moulding consisting of a hollow chamfer with a quirked and narrow filleted roll.

Hall and screens passage (Components 20 and 21)

Internally, between the two courtyard entrances, there survives the N side of a further entrance. This is detailed with a broad quirked angle roll. The stump of a southwards-running lintel demonstrates both that this had been an entrance connecting two compartments and that there had been a N–S masonry partition wall at this point. The entrances within this wall had doubtless given access to service chambers within the lost western bay of the range (Illus 49).

It is probable that there had been a screens passage defined to the W by the masonry cross wall and to the E by a transverse wooden screen just to the E of the eastern (principal) courtyard entrance (on the line of the W wall of the existing Component 20). That there had been such a feature is supported by the original fenestration of the N wall of the hall, which would have thus rendered the hall interior symmetrically arranged. This screen would have defined the W (low) end of the original hall. If there had been an open roof structure, there may also have been a gallery above and to the W of the screen.

In other respects the hall interior was symmetrically arranged. Windows at either end of the S exterior wall mirrored those to the N. A central window to the S lay directly opposite a substantial fireplace and projecting chimneybreast that still remains in a good state of preservation behind the later panelling. The only asymmetrical features are a possible buffet recess in the eastern part of the S wall, now hidden by modern linings

30 The fireplace in Component 22 in 1968, before repair and restoration (*Historic Scotland © Crown Copyright*)

(this appears on a number of early plans), and an entrance to a chamber to the NE. The latter is detailed with a quirked angle roll and fillet that is reminiscent of the moulding of the courtyard entrance.

Of the hall windows only that at the E end of the N wall is free of later linings. The window itself has gone (the insertion of a later stair), but its broad and deep ingo is visible, with a low segmental arched head and broad chamfered internal arrises with angled stops.

Hall roof structure

It is not apparent whether the hall roof structure had originally been open. A series of either five or six moulded stone corbels, irregularly spaced, were formerly visible at ceiling level to S and N, now largely obscured by later linings (Historic Scotland drawings – 228/254/80, 85, 232 and 246). These could either have supported ashlar posts for an open roof or principal joists for a closed structure (ie floored and with upper chambers). Two hollow-moulded dormer cornice/lintel stones have been incorporated into the wall head of the S wall, presumably dropped when the dormers were removed. Though possibly from this phase (and thus indicating an upper level), it is felt that they are more likely to be secondary.

Internal arrangements to W

Despite the loss of the western bay of the range, some suggestions can be made as to its former appearance and internal arrangement (Illus 49). The line of the earlier W wall most probably lay about 2m short of the present W wall. This follows the line of the E wall of Component 3. That the early wall could not have lain further W is demonstrated by the presence of a S-facing wide-mouthed gun loop in the short

eastwards return of the perimeter wall (this is now visible within the present entrance-level WC, Component 18); for the loop to be positioned at this point would require a clear field of fire.

In the absence of obvious remains of an early kitchen in the S range, it is suggested that the basement-level western vaulted chamber had formed this space. This would not have been an unusual arrangement in relation to the hall on the floor above at this period, although kitchens are also often seen below the chamber end. Whether the existing stair at the SW corner of the court had provided access from this to the hall or whether there had been a further internal stair cannot now be known with certainty.

At entrance level the western parts of the range – to the W of the cross wall – would typically have contained further service areas (buttery and pantry).

E end of the range

General

The junction between the early 16th-century S range and the mid 16th-century E range is one of the most complex individual areas of Rowallan Castle, not least because shortly after construction the E range itself was very substantially remodelled with the addition of a further storey (Illus 49). On account of this, the archaeological evidence for the form of the E end of the S range, and particularly the arrangements in the area of its N wall, is somewhat ambiguous.

Entrance level chamber (Component 22)

The chamber that led off the E end of the hall, presumably a withdrawing room, was a well-appointed space, the principal feature of which is a fine fireplace in the centre

31 Component 22, looking SE with fireplace to left (*photo: Simpson & Brown*)

of the E wall (Illus 30). This had formerly been reduced in width on its S side on account of a cracked lintel (Historic Scotland photograph A2408/2 and 3; drawing 228/254/26), but was reinstated to its original width, and a new lintel, dated 1986, installed. Historic Scotland archive photographs (A4509/1–3) document the process of reconstruction that had begun by 1979. A small garderobe chamber with a small exterior window was formed to the NE. Its entrance, which is unusually set at 45°, is rebated for a wooden door. At the S end of the E wall and within the S wall there are two finely detailed window recesses. These have broad ingos with low arched heads and broad chamfered arrises, and stone seats (Illus 31). The head of the SE window was reconstructed in the 1980s; early photographs indicate that wooden lintels had been inserted in this area. These windows are identical in detail to the former NE window in the hall. At the W end of the N wall exists the entrance to the cellar stair (Component 10).

There is a projecting masonry baulk at the E end of the N wall; this relates to the formation of a turnpike stair on its N side. At this period it appears that there was no direct access from the chamber to the stair. The possible significance of this projection is examined in greater detail in the next section.

Upper chamber (Component 42)

This range was two-storied for much of its length, except to the E, where there exist the remains of a full additional storey, the part of the structure now occupied by Component 42. The E wall of this chamber is largely complete. It contains a substantial fireplace towards the S end of the wall (partly infilled), and an entrance at its N end. The entrance, which is rebated for a wooden door,

32 Blocked doorway to possible garderobe (left) in E wall of Component 42 (*photo: Simpson & Brown*)

33 NE corner of Component 22, projecting masonry corresponds to former stair below Component 33 (*photo: Simpson & Brown*)

was subsequently blocked. A small blocked window on the exterior (with chamfered arris) a little to the S of the entrance within suggests that this may have been a garderobe chamber.

The S wall contains a large window recess, offset to the E, the external dressings of which appear to have seen some modification but which may incorporate original chamfered jamb stones (Illus 32). The W wall is apparently wholly of this phase. It is dominated by the massively constructed arch that spans the width of the room from N to S. In the absence of obvious evidence for its insertion such as construction breaks, etc., it must be considered possible that this feature is original to the phase – see Discussion below.

Little survives of the N wall other than a fragment at its W end and a jamb at its E end. The jamb is detailed with a chamfered arris that indicates it had been an entrance leading from a chamber (or stair?) to the N. The fragment further W is confusingly embedded within the masonry of the later stair to the second floor. A dressed corner faces into the later stairwell; this is detailed with a chamfered arris. Being close to the line of the internal face of the N wall of the range, this could not have been masonry relating to a window but rather an entrance from an intramural space into Component 42 at the W end of its N wall.

Stair tower? (*Component 33*)

The northern, courtyard frontage of the hall range continued considerably further eastwards than at present. Within the 'guard chamber' on the S side of the entrance pend (Component 33) an area of rough rubblework upon the central part of the S wall face indicates the former return of a northwards-running wall. Now clawed away, this return seems to have been integral to the early 16th-century hall range. That this had not simply been part of a perimeter wall is demonstrated by the walling at the E end of the basement pend (ie the E frontage), which contains a window within walling running northwards of the hall range proper.

At the SE corner of Component 33 the walling describes a curve that can only have related to a turnpike stair. This appears to have risen clockwise, as suggested by irregularities within the lower masonry indicating the patched former positions of stair keys. The stair corresponds to the projecting eastern part of the N wall of Component 22 (Illus 33).

34 East frontage showing the twin-towered entrance (*photo: Simpson & Brown*)

Discussion – scenario 1

It is not completely obvious whether this turnpike stair belongs to this or the next (mid 16th-century) phase. If the stair is secondary, then the evidence of the jamb at the NW corner of the first-floor chamber (Component 42) may indicate that there had been a further straight intramural stair immediately above the one from the basement to entrance level (Component 10). The jamb would therefore represent the entrance from this into Component 42. The second jamb to the E might therefore be the remains of an entrance into an upstairs chamber within a northwards-projecting jamb.

If an insertion (which itself could be no later than the next, mid 16th-century phase), then the irregularity of Component 22 might be explained – irregularities of the ceiling structure, the masonry baulk of the N wall and the angled gardrobe entrance.

Discussion – scenario 2

If the turnpike stair is integral to this phase – the presently preferred alternative – then its principal function must have been to provide access from entrance level to the first-floor chamber (Component 42). It is curious in this respect that there would have been no direct communication from the interior of the hall range to the spaces above. The jamb at the NW corner of the room would therefore probably relate to access to an upper level.

An upper level

Although the evidence is complex and widely obscured by modern recessed repointing in cement, it is possible to suggest that there had been an early stair up to a second-floor level above the E end of the S range (ie above Component 42). The evidence includes the chamfered jamb at the NW corner of Component 42 as already discussed. This is set considerably back from the lines of both the N wall of the range and from that of the N–S cross wall – the W wall of Component 42. There is enough space on each side for a stair/passage to be comfortably accommodated. The space to the W, Component 43, seems to have been the location of a straight flight up to the next level (Illus 42). The existing stair seems to be a remodelling (widening and lowering) of its predecessor. Patching on the lower E wall of Component 43 suggests the former line of the earlier stair. This evidence in turn strongly suggests that the arch on the W side of Component 42 in fact dates to this phase, and was intended to support both the stair and the wall on the E side of the stair.

Close scrutiny of the existing entrance leading from the Component 43 stair into the existing second-floor gallery (Component 49) suggests that this is an early *in situ* entrance that has been extensively retooled (at the time of the formation of the gallery). The nature of the original upper level must remain a matter of debate. Whether the stair led to a loft room or something grander cannot now be known. It is possible that, in contrast to the remainder of the S range, the E end had been conceived in the form of a tower that had had a full parapet rather than crow-stepped gables. The later battlemented enclosure wall around the NW and W parts of the castle may have been an intentional echo of other parts of the castle that were hitherto more martial in appearance.

E side of courtyard

It is possible, but uncertain in the absence of excavated evidence, that the line of the W wall of the stair tower had extended northwards to the SE corner of the early tower in order to close off the court on the E side. It is also suggested that an original principal external entrance may have been sited immediately N of the tower, thus roughly on the same line as the present entrance pend.

The courtyard and early tower

The lower parts of the early tower on its S and W sides were refaced following the dressing back of the plinth and clawing away of the masonry below. This seems to have been undertaken at this or the next phase in association with the levelling off of the area between the early tower and the new hall range, the purpose of which was to form a level courtyard surface. It was probably at this stage that a new entrance was opened into the basement level of the early tower. This entrance is detailed with a chamfered arris, of about 650mm. This is formed of a grey-cream/slightly yellowish sandstone that is different to the pinker stone of the hall range dressings which may either be reused stones or attributable to a different phase.

WORK OF THE MID 16TH CENTURY (JOHN MURE: SUC 1547, D 1581 OR 1591, M MARION CUNNINGHAME)

Introduction

Historical

There are key references for the mid 16th-century construction history of Rowallan in the *Historie and Descent of the House of Rowallane* by Sir William Mure (1657). According to this, John Mure, who succeeded in 1547:

tooke great delyte in Policie and planting. He builded the fore wark, back wark, and woman house, from the ground. He lived gratiouslie and died in peace, the yeare of his aige 66, and in the yeare of our Lord 1581
    (*Historie*, 225)

This documentation appears emphatic that John Mure was responsible for the E range – the 'fore wark' and that he built it 'from ye ground'. However, the range was constructed in two major stages.

General stratigraphy: E range

The 'fore wark' referred to must represent the E range, the principal entrance frontage to the castle (Illus 34 and 52). The stratigraphic evidence is equally emphatic that the entrance and first-floor levels of the existing E range post-date the construction of the S (hall) range of the early 16th century, but pre-date the erection of the twin-towered E entrance ensemble and second floor of the E range, the latter works bearing a date stone of 1562. It must thus be the case that the E range embodies two phases of construction attributable to John Mure and that the earlier most likely dates to the period 1547–1550s. It is of particular note that the *Historie* is specific that John Mure 'builded the fore wark from the ground', suggesting that the solid masonry of the basement level of the range is all of this period. This is an area where the physical evidence is ambiguous, the walling of the E façade of the range having been extensively repointed and subject to major reconstruction following the removal of later buttresses to the N and NE. Despite these obscuring works, there seems to be little evidence for structural complexity in the visible area to the N of the N entrance tower in particular.

The principal diagnostic detail of those parts of the E range certainly attributable to this phase is the narrow rounded arris (ie in stark contrast to the chamfer used in the previous periods). This detail is common to the other constructions of this phase, described below.

35 NW corner of the N range, showing remains of bartizan (*photo: Simpson & Brown*)

General stratigraphy: perimeter wall to N and NW

Although the direct stratigraphic evidence is less clear-cut in terms of its relationship to the S range, it is evident on stylistic comparison that the NW and W perimeter wall (which abuts the early NE tower) may have been constructed at the same time as the E range, the rounded arris employed upon external openings on both. The *Historie* seems specific that John Mure was responsible for these works, describing the 'back wark' and 'ye bak wall'.

The woman house

The *Historie* also describes the 'vomanhouse/woman house' practically in the same breath as the 'back wark'. In contradiction to the received wisdom about the so-called 'woman house' – which ascribes it to the existing upper chamber of the W end of the S range (in actuality itself a wholesale reconstruction of early 18th-century date) – this author proposes that the woman house occupied the NW corner of the Rowallan Castle complex. This part of the complex is defined to the N and W by the 'bak wall' – the existing perimeter wall. This wall is of homogenous construction; it is battlemented to the W, rising up to a bartizan at the NW corner (Illus 35). The N end of the W wall and the N wall both contain rounded-arrised windows that are very clearly not later insertions. These openings unequivocally demonstrate that there had been a two-storied range at this point running westwards from the W wall of the early tower. The existing S wall of the range and the basement vault within are of demonstrably later date and only serve to obscure the evidence for the earlier structure.

Addressing the suggestion that the woman house may have occupied the W end of the S range, a number of observations can be stated. Firstly, the lost original western bay of the S range was considerably shorter than the existing structure; accommodation in this area would therefore have been limited. There is no evidence that the SW courtyard stair tower rose above courtyard level before the early 17th century. The range to the NW far better fits the appellation 'house', being both a self-contained unit and relatively commodious.

General

If this interpretation is correct, the works to the E and W can be seen as a deliberately coordinated scheme to fully enclose the castle site (whatever the pre-existing arrangement had been) and by doing so create a formal courtyard area.

E range

Entrance level

The existing entrance archway, robustly detailed with a quirked triple roll, belongs to this phase at the latest and subsequently incorporated within the 1560s' redesign of the frontage. This opening leads to the short pend (Component 30) that also forms part of the scheme . Of the three entrances within the pend, the one to the S and the one at the W end of the N side are original. The former gave access to the pre-existing turnpike stair to the upper levels, and a probable guard chamber on its W side (Component 33). This chamber had been lit by a small window to the W, now blocked, and the stair by a narrow inserted window opening to the E.

The northern entrance off the pend now opens into a narrow chamber lit by a small window to the W (Component 31); evidence for the former appearance of the E end was lost following a slapping through to the later entrance tower (Component 32). It is not clear, however, whether the narrow chamber is the original intention or whether there had been a single interior space occupying the N half of the range at entrance level. Apparent evidence for the latter is suggested by the existing internal cross wall that clearly abuts the W wall. It is possible that this is a secondary insertion of the 1560s' phase. Whether the cross wall occupies the site of a less substantial predecessor is now difficult to determine. The existing larger chamber to the N (Component 29) has its own entrance from the court to the W, and a window in the W wall. The window, which is notable for its horizontal form, retains *in situ* two vertical wrought iron bars, each with cross prongs. Similar windows face into the courtyard at Newark Castle, Port Glasgow, though these are about a generation later in date (c 1590). A larger window exists in the E wall. This is detailed with a substantial quirked angle roll and may be original. The window has seen considerable structural distortion and the surrounding masonry extensive reconstruction. There is an aumbry at the N end of the E wall and the remains of a fireplace in the N gable wall. The N and E walls have seen extensive modern repair.

First floor

At first-floor level, which was presumably accessed at this phase by means of the turnpike stair at its S end (eastern part of Component 40), the internal arrangement of the range has been much altered. It may have contained two principal chambers as suggested by substantial fireplaces in the N gable wall and within the W wall (Components 35 and 38/41 respectively). All window openings at this level have either been obliterated (in the area of the later entrance towers to the E – the existing opening into the N tower chamber (Component 32) incorporates the remains of a window ingo) – or heavily remodelled (the E window to the N in the 1560s and the two W windows in the 1660s). There exist the remains of an intramural garderobe chamber (Component 36) in the E wall, just to the N of the N entrance tower; this was subsequently heavily modified. There is a small aumbry at the E end of the N wall(Illus 36 and 37).

Evidence for the arrangement of the interior space to the S and SW – the critical junction between the E range and the pre-existing S range – has largely been eradicated by subsequent works.

36 Component 35 looking NE (*photo: Simpson & Brown*)

37 Component 35 looking SE to Component 36, the intramural garderobe (*photo: Simpson & Brown*)

Upper wall details

The upper parts of the E range were substantially remodelled in the 1560s. The existing wall head cornice may in large part constitute reused stones from the pre-existing wall head (these are of identical form to those of the coeval NW range, N wall).

Enclosure wall to W and N, and the NW range

Wall to the W

Abutting the NW corner of the early tower is a later defensive perimeter wall that extends westwards for 8m. This angles to the S continuing for a further 16.25m before returning again to the E, a further 1.9m. To the W this wall is topped with the well-preserved lower parts of a parapet supported externally by a continuous moulded corbel course. To the N the latter steps up twice, culminating at the corbelled base of a bartizan. Along its western stretch are a series of corbels supporting inwards-projecting parapet paving slabs and a series of four round 'murder holes' – defensive apertures to the exterior within the paving of the parapet (Illus 54).

At its SW corner the perimeter clearly had had a further bartizan; the stones at the corner have been patched in a corresponding silhouette. The W wall contains two broad-mouthed gun loops. A further loop of identical character occurs at the W end of the S return, now visible within Component 18, an entrance-level WC.

Evidence for a range to the NW

To the NW the perimeter walling contains a series of windows at entrance- and first-floor levels that demonstrate there had been a range on the site of the existing ruined structure – Component 26, etc. Substantial entrance-level windows exist in the W wall and the centre of the N wall, with a further smaller window at the W end of the N wall, all blocked. These are all detailed with rounded arrises. These windows, which appear wholly coeval with the construction of the perimeter wall, must demonstrate that there had been a roofed range within this part of the castle complex.

Two further windows at first-floor level in the N wall are evident, although their dressings are badly perished – apparently fire-damaged. Part of the N wall survives to full height and retains three hollow-moulded cornice stones and other coping stones at its E end that indicate the point where a roof structure had coincided with the wall head. Externally there is no apparent indication of a construction break to demonstrate that this roof structure was secondary to the perimeter wall. A single large block of rubble rises above the level of the cornice stones; this appears to be the remains of a stack, with corresponding evidence for a large first-floor fireplace within (also serving a ground-floor fireplace – see below).

The stair tower and turnpike stair at the SE corner of the existing ruined range may be of the same phase. However, this is now difficult to demonstrate and the tower has, at the very least, been heavily remodelled externally. At ground-floor level there is an entrance at the base of the stair to the interior ground-floor space; this is detailed with rounded arrises. The stair rose through two flights; part of the first-floor entrance remains, dressings similarly detailed. The wall face of these entrances on the stairwards side may represent the line of the original S wall of the range as it extended further to the W. This wall was evidently substantially rebuilt and thickened to the S to accommodate the insertion of the existing vault, which is secondary. A short section of the S wall to the E, between the stair entrance and the E wall of the chamber, is on a notably different alignment to the remainder of the S wall further W and may be part of the pre-existing mid 16th-century structure. The existing S wall further W abuts the W perimeter wall and at this point overlies a wide-mouthed gun loop – it is thus clearly later. Just to the N of the loop there is a vertical zone of apparently patched walling that may indicate the line of the original S wall. A wall at this point would render the blocked window to the W centrally positioned in relation to the chamber within.

Internally at entrance level there exist the remains of a fireplace central to the N wall; this has rounded arrises. Curiously, this corresponds to the position of the blocked window seen externally. The blocking of the fireplace is clearly coeval with the insertion of the later vault. It is possible that the window, the upper dressings of which are missing, was partly dismantled and infilled during a redesign during the original construction. Alternatively, the formation of the fireplace may have been a localised remodelling relatively shortly after construction (but before the insertion of the vault). That the former may be the case is suggested by the absence of evidence for an alternative fireplace to heat the lower level.

The only other internal feature that appears to relate to the original construction of the NW range is a recess at the E end of the N wall at entrance level; this may have contained a small garderobe.

Lost range to W?

The possibility that a further range may have occupied the western side of the courtyard, and was subsequently demolished, was considered. It was noted that the line of the E wall of the SW courtyard stair tower lay in precise alignment with the SW corner of the stair tower of the NW range. If the SW tower wall had extended northwards, it would have precisely met the latter corner. The corner itself appears, possibly, to have seen some reconstruction – insertion of lower quoins – although ultimately this was felt to be ambiguous. Likewise it was possible to believe that the opposing corner of the SW stair tower formed part of its reconstruction in the 17th century – had an intervening wall been dismantled? Could its removal be linked to the construction of the existing frontage of the NW range?

Against these possibilities is the evidence of an archaeologically monitored services trench running along the N side of the SW stair tower. This revealed no structural remains. In addition, there is no hint that a structure had ever been supported by the W perimeter wall. It was ultimately concluded that the W side of the court had always been open.

WORK OF THE EARLY 1560s

General

Study of the E range increasingly revealed that it was internally very complex and that the mid 16th-century structure had been very substantially modified (Illus 52). The principal modifications were associated with the period of the formation of the twin-towered frontage; this conveniently bears a date of 1562. Windows within the two towers are of notably idiosyncratic form with extremely broad chamfered arrises. These windows exist throughout the second storey of the range and the internal evidence of tooling details further demonstrated that the entirety of the upper floor, a long gallery, was also a creation of this phase. Increasingly, on the lower levels of the E range, it was realised that there had been many further individual modifications.

E frontage

Historical

An inscription at the wall head above the principal entrance reads,

JON MVR	John Muir
M. CVGM	Marion Cunningham
SPVSIS	his wife
1562	1562

This inscription is integral to the construction of the twin-towered entrance ensemble that is the most characteristic feature of Rowallan Castle.

Fabric

It is clear that these towers were appended to a pre-existing frontage. This is most dramatically seen where a much later passage has been cut through the base of the southern tower into the basement level pend (Component 6). Above one's head at the junction of tower and E frontage are the remains of a pre-existing window.

Stair tower at the SE corner of the courtyard and associated access arrangements

A new stair tower was erected at the re-entrant of the E and S ranges (Component 25; Illus 38); the masonry of the tower abuts both ranges. The access to the stair was at entrance level, from the NE corner of the hall (Component 21), at which point one of the hall windows was enlarged for the purpose, its jambs dressed back, the sill dropped and new steps inserted.

Internally the stair tower contains a stone turnpike. The keys of the stair extend down counter-clockwise to just above the level of the exterior court. This arrangement would suggest that there had originally been an exterior entrance within the N wall of the tower to the court. Externally, however, despite some possible irregularity of the masonry of the N tower wall, there is no certain evidence that there had ever been an entrance at this point, and

38 Interior view of stair, Component 25, from the hall (*photo: Simpson & Brown*)

Long Gallery (Component 49)

A second-floor long gallery (Illus 40 and 51) was erected along the E side of the castle. To the S this incorporated some masonry of the pre-existing structure of the E end of the hall range; further N the roof and wall heads of the E range were dismantled and an additional storey added. The gallery later saw use as a church in the later 17th century. Two 'kirk stools' were preserved here in the early 19th century when the room was called the 'auld kirk' (Tough 1898, 319–20)

Associated works within the E range

The entrance-level space on the N side of the pend (Component 31) was subdivided into two chambers by a major E–W partition, perhaps in place of a less substantial predecessor. This cross wall seems partly to have been required for the erection of a wall on the same line on the floor above. Within the pend itself a new doorway was opened through the eastern part of the N wall and the chamber within subdivided. The subdivision, a short N–S section of walling, is now missing but appears on early plans such as that of MacGibbon and Ross (1887–92).

At first-floor level a further E–W cross wall subdivided the eastern range into two large chambers, the one to the N (Component 35) slightly smaller than that to the S (Component 38/40/41). The pre-existing garderobe closet (Component 36) at the SE corner of the northern room was reconstructed at this stage.

Apartments above the hall: S range

At its head the Component 25 stair provides access through to the first-floor apartments of the E range (door to the E), a flight up to the second-floor gallery and by a further few steps to the SW access to a first-floor chamber above the hall (Component 44; Illus 39). This chamber appears to have been created at this phase, although the evidence is now obscured behind a general lining-out undertaken in recent years. The only visible contemporary features are the dormer window to the S and a fireplace in the centre of the E wall. This is a notable design where the lintel and upper jambs break forward, the heavy bolection moulding continuing around the whole. This fireplace displayed French renaissance influences in its design; if it can be tied to the c1562 phase this happens to be the period in Scottish architecture when French influence was at its most pervasive, and at this period the Mures were particularly well-connected, moving in court circles.

It is possible both that this room may have been created at the expense of a pre-existing open hall roof structure and that there had been additional first-floor rooms further W. Possible evidence for additional rooms can be seen to the S exterior where there are two anomalous stones incorporated into the otherwise pre-existing wall head cornice. These stones are both reused window lintels and it is suggested that these had originally been lintels for dormers that formerly broke above the wall head and served the now lost upper rooms in that area. With the removal

internally there is no evidence to suggest entrance splays. The lower part of the understair area has been infilled with rubblework that appears integral to the N wall. The remainder of the lower part of the stairwell has been partitioned off with a panelled screen of early to mid 17th-century character; this contains a six-panelled door, above which is an aperture containing vertical turned spindles with small arched heads above.

The keys of the stair are correctly set throughout. The lower six remain intact; keys seven to nine had been correctly placed but were dressed back to accommodate the short straight flight of steps up from the hall. Above this level – key ten and above – the stair is again well-preserved. This evidence suggests a number of possibilities, most significantly that the stair keys are salvaged from elsewhere – an obvious possibility is the turnpike stair at the E end of the S range (N wall), which no longer exists. An alternative is that a stair tower with a courtyard entrance did exist that this point but was very heavily remodelled in the early to mid 17th century, at which point the link into the hall was made. If there had been a pre-existing stair, the former hall window would have had to have been blocked off. A possible parallel is the stair at the SW corner of the court, which itself saw a heavy early to mid 17th-century remodelling (indeed it shares window details on the N elevation).

At first-floor level the stair was broken through into the E range, the entrance surround reusing rounded arrised dressings of a predecessor.

of these rooms and the dormers, the lintels were simply dropped into their present positions, their hollow-moulded profiles being similar enough to the original wall head cornice to provide a rough match.

Gardens

Further information relating to the policies is contained in the *Historie and Descent of the House of Rowallane*, by Sir William Mure, Knt (1657):

This John Muire 3 of yat name [died 1581 or 91] delytit in policye of plaintein and brigging, he plantit ye oirchzarde and gardein, set ye vpper banck and nether bank ye birk zaird befoir ye zett,
 (Historie, 83)

The 'vpper banck' may refer to the substantial scarping into the natural slope seen to the W and NW of the castle. This encloses a level area that had perhaps been intended to encompass parterre gardens. It is possible that the yew trees that surmount the crest of the scarp were planted at this time. What the 'nether bank' refers to is less apparent.

39 Component 44, looking NE (*photo: Simpson & Brown*)

40 Interior of the long gallery (*Royal Commission on the Ancient and Historical Monuments of Scotland © Crown Copyright*)

EARLY TO C MID 17TH-CENTURY WORKS (SIR WILLIAM MURE: SUC 1616; D 1639; M ELIZABETH MONTGOMERIE (1); JEAN PORTERFIELD (2); SARAH BRISBANE (3); SIR WILLIAM MURE: SUC 1639; D 1657; M ANNA DUNDAS)

Stair tower at SW angle of court (Component 4)

Whatever the pre-existing form of the stair at the SW corner of the court (whether a free-standing tower or as part of a now lost W range) the early to mid 17th century saw a comprehensive reconstruction. The courtyard entrance to the stair may have been widened (the existing N jamb contains reused stones and others detailed with a rounded arris, as has the lintel). The NE corner of the stair tower may also be a reconstruction of this period – it is detailed with a rounded arris – although the new work merges into the pre-existing walling of the returning enclosure wall. This walling contains an inserted stair window at low level, detailed with rounded arrises. The tower was wholly reconstructed above entrance lintel level. There is a cornice that extends along the E and N elevations; on the north side the cornice terminated after an overall distance of 3.4m where there is a return into the masonry. This point marks where the NW corner of the tower had existed above the cornice; both the cornice and the walling above were subsequently extended to the W (Illus 41).

41 Exterior view of Component 4, E elevation (*photo: Simpson & Brown*)

Above the cornice the early masonry is of neatly cut blocks of creamy sandstone that terminate to the NE at strap-ended quoins with raised margin. Similar quoins had existed at the original NW corner, subsequently reset further W. Central to the N wall of this stair tower exists a narrow window (raised margin and rounded arris); a bull's-eye window above that may have had cabled ornamentation but is now badly eroded. As reconstructed in the 17th century, the stair tower measured 2.58m N–S by 3.2 E–W.

This reconstruction of the stair balances the S court elevation, the tower itself mirroring in general form and some details (the window arrangement) the other stair tower to the SE. The tower had evidently provided access to a room or rooms at first-floor level, the area now occupied by Component 46. Nothing of this earlier chamber is now visible although fragments may still survive in the present N wall of Component 46, behind the later linings. Although no evidence is visible, it is possible that the upper parts of the W end of the S range proper were modified at this stage, the reason for the reconstruction of the stair being the provision of access to the upper level.

Discussion

Hitherto the dating of this work seems solely to have been upon the basis of stylistic comparison of the strap-ended (or buckle) quoins, and their similarity to strapwork detail, including quoins, upon the celebrated Skelmorlie Aisle at Largs of c 1636–9. Other examples include Argyll's Lodging, Stirling, of c 1632, and Glasgow Tolbooth, post-1623/ mid 17th century. However, strap-ended quoins remained popular into the latter part of the 17th century (a notable example being Prestonfield House, Edinburgh, of c 1687). Admittedly the Rowallan quoins bear closest comparison with those of the 1630s. A further general observation is that the works of the 1660s at the castle repeatedly employ details that are retrospective in style and mannerist in mood, combining details that were fashionable from the later 16th century to the early 17th century.

It is possible but by no means certain that the work to the stair tower might in fact date to the 1660s' phase of extensive remodelling throughout the castle rather than being an isolated individual construction of a slightly earlier period.

WORKS OF THE 1660S (SIR WILLIAM MURE: SUC 1657; D 1686; M ELIZABETH HAMILTON)

Remodelling of the NW range c 1660

Historical

MacGibbon and Ross (1887–92) incorrectly attribute the construction of the NW range to Sir William Mure III (suc 1639; d 1657). They confused the evidence of both a monogram and heraldic panel upon the pediment over the entrance to the range which both refer to Dame Elizabeth

Hamilton, wife of Sir William Mure IV (suc 1657; d 1686), the son of the above. While this marriage is well attested in the *Historie,* further corroboration comes from the outer court entrance which bears a monogram identical in all respects and the date of 1661 (three times). It must thus be concluded that the entrance to the NW range and works associated with it date to about the period of construction of the entrance court shortly after the succession of William IV in 1657, thus c 1660.

The fabric

The pre-existing NW range was largely rebuilt in the 17th century. With the possible exception of parts of the stair tower, the S wall was dismantled and rebuilt with considerable additional width extending a little further S. The purpose of this was clearly to provide support for the barrel vault that was then inserted. The ultimate intention of these works was the creation of a ground-floor kitchen. At the W end the W window was blocked off and a broad arched fireplace and chimneybreast inserted; the stumps of the lower jambs remain, as does an adjacent slop-sink, inserted through the fabric of the N wall.

The N wall was also strengthened to support the vault by the thickening of the walling internally. The pre-existing window in the centre of the N wall had its lintel and upper jamb stones removed, although its relieving arch remained *in situ*. Internally, corresponding to the position of the window, there exists a blocked fireplace. However, it is

difficult to understand the need for a fireplace at this point, given the massive kitchen lum to the W and the feature was probably pre-existing.

The stair tower may have been wholly a construction of this phase, although its S exterior face displays some possible structural complexity. The existing entrance on its W side, curiously out of general view within the court, is surmounted by a tympanum that contains the entwined monogram initials of Sir William and those of his wife, Dame (Elizabeth) Hamilton, accompanied by the Muir and Hamilton arms. There is also, very unusually, an inscription in Hebrew, 'The Lord is the portion of mine inheritance and of my cup' (Groome 1883, 4, 371). The windows of the S wall of the range have a rounded arris and raised margin. The hollow-moulded wall head cornice may have been reused from the pre-existing structure.

Entrance court to E c 1661

General

There are substantial remains of the walls that had formed a small entrance courtyard framing the principal entrance to the castle. The court aligned itself on the principal, E-facing elevation of the castle, but was entered from the N (now leading to the drive that crosses the small bridge). The existing entrance is of elaborate form and is dated 1661 no less than three times; it also bears the monogram of Sir William Muir intertwined with that of his wife, Dame (Elizabeth) Hamilton. On either side are small pistol loops. Between the gate and the castle this walling incorporates what appears to be pre-existing masonry, apparently the lower parts of a range that had extended to the N from this line (apparent quoins are visible on the court side). The court wall abuts the NE corner of the E range of the castle. At the E end of the court wall it is clear that there had been a return to the S; the walling beyond this has now been removed. The low walled 'enclosure' abutting the S end of the E façade of the castle also forms part of the courtyard walling construction. The walling extending eastwards from the SE corner of the range clearly extended beyond the present enclosure walls, and had doubtless continued and returned to the N to close off the court. The walls of the 'enclosure' within the perimeter are coeval with it. The lower parts of an entrance exist at its NE corner, detailed with a hollow chamfered edge roll. It is probable that the 'enclosure' walls are the remains of a courtyard building such as a stable.

Earlier remains

The N side of the entrance court wall, to the W of the arched entrance, incorporates the remains of an earlier structure, apparently a S gable wall. On the S side of the wall there exists rough quoining at two points, at 2.2m and 7.7m from the E façade of the castle respectively. Between these points there is some indication of a projecting basal course on the S side. This structure had clearly extended to the N, suggesting

42 Component 43, stair to gallery level looking N (*photo: Simpson & Brown*)

that there may have been an additional court in that area – perhaps containing stabling and other ancillary functions. There is some suggestion of further buried masonry remains on the N side of the N wall, to the E of the entrance, although its nature is unclear.

General remodelling

E range

Various windows were modified at this phase in the E range; usually this involved the insertion of new external dressings within existing openings, a process that may also have involved some individual enlargements (Illus 52). Generally the moulding employed was a rounded arris and raised margin of similar detail to the rebuilding of the NW range. In the courtyard the two first-floor windows were treated in this manner, than to the N detailed with an elaborate surround and cornice over; its neighbour to the S was plainer.

New windows were cut into twin entrance towers on the E elevation at entrance level, just above the pre-existing pistol loops.

Masonry entrance stair to E

The existing masonry stair that provides access to the principal E elevation entrance abuts the façade, overlying the fabric of the entrance towers. The shallow gradient, broad treads and the botel-nosings of the risers all suggest a date no earlier than the later 17th century (it is possible that the stair may be even later).

S range

The southernmost entrance-level window on the E elevation, that of the chamber (Component 22), was enlarged and new moulded dressings inserted. A similar insertion occurred at the window at the SW corner of the hall (Component 21) (Illus 53).

WORKS OF THE 1680s

Walled garden

The garden walls that enclose a substantial area of ground to the N and W of Rowallan Castle appear to be datable to some degree of accuracy. There are two surviving date stones, one forming the lintel over an entrance within the NW wall – 1687, and one upon the apex stone of the E-facing crow-stepped gable of the small cottage just to the NE of the castle – 168[8?].

The structural archaeology of the gardens is internally coherent. The main walled garden circuit is rubble-built, of homogenous construction and consistently about 2.5– 3m in height (in some areas the early wall has been subsequently raised or built upon). The masonry of the E wall of the cottage at the SE corner of the garden is contiguous with the garden wall. The northwestern section of the wall continues

to the SW, eventually returning to the SE at the bank of the burn. In this area the eastwards return angles once again, the walls forming a rectangular terminal enclosure. At the SE corner of this enclosure there is an entrance facing E, on to the ha-ha-like retained bank that follows the course of the burn round to the bridge. The entrance, which is detailed with a rounded arris that is sunk or 'razed' on its external face only, provides direct access to the levelled top of the raised embankment, the latter apparently intended as a perimeter walk. This relationship and the fact that the revetted burn-facing side of the bank lies in precise alignment with the SW terminal wall of the garden enclosure would suggest that the bank is coeval with the walls.

There is a blocked opening within the section of walling forming the SW side of the enclosure. Externally this is detailed with a broad quirked angle roll (reused stones?); an ingo is visible internally. This feature, which is now blocked, appears to have been an entrance that provided access to the land beyond the walled circuit to the SW; although offset to the NW within its section of walling, this entrance is roughly symmetrically spaced in relation to the ground beyond. The entrance may have opened onto a burnside walk that extended for some distance to the SW (the burn angles in this direction at this point). This may in turn have led to a bridge that led to an apparently early curling pond earthwork occupying low-lying land on the other side of the burn (N Campbell pers comm).

The other entrances into the garden – the above-mentioned doorway within the NW wall, and a pair of gate piers running S from the SW corner of the cottage, are also detailed with the sunk rounded arris. The lintel of this entrance in the NW wall has been raised and two additional jamb stones inserted. It is notable that the mouldings of these stones have been lugged to meet the ends of the moulding on the lintel. It would appear that the moulding of the lintel was intended to span a wider aperture than that of the apparently *in situ* early jambs below – is it possible that one of these has been reset (the walling immediately to the SW may have been affected by the base of a large yew that perhaps had caused distortion).

The cottage

It is likely that the cottage formed the gardener's house and, if so, it must rank as one of the earliest surviving examples in Scotland. Another possible gardener's house, of very similar form though heavily remodelled, exists at Pittmedden Garden, Aberdeenshire (c 1675). The Rowallan example, an attractive compact structure, steeply pitched and crow-stepped at each gable, was entered by a doorway outwith the garden circuit towards the E end of its S wall. A further entrance in the W gable provided direct access into the garden. To the N of this entrance there is a small ground floor window; a larger loft-level window exists in the E gable wall, but is now blocked. With the exception of the S entrance, all of these openings are detailed with a simple rounded arris. A further loft-level window exists in the W gable; this has a chamfered arris (reused stones?). Two further small openings in the S wall are only roughly formed of rubble.

The S entrance, though now blocked, appears to have identical moulded detail to that of the adjacent gate piers, namely the razed rounded arris and chamfered stops. Incidentally, this perpetuates a detail seen within the arch of the courtyard entrance in front of the castle – it is dated 1661 (three times).

Internally there is a fireplace in the W gable wall, but few other features. The roof structure appears to be original – rafter couples with raised tie and collar, all lapped and affixed with hand-wrought iron nails. One individual curiosity is a rafter couple offset to the E that is of far greater scantling than its companions; the reason for this was not apparent.

The lower parts of the E gable wall now contain a broad Lorimer period window. This work also involved the infilling of a broad entrance which itself is likely to have been a secondary slapping – the original cottage may have been formed into a shed for a wheeled vehicle. There is therefore no surviving evidence for original openings in the E wall at ground-floor level – perhaps there had been a further window.

The building was provided with a simple hollow cornice along the length of its S wall; however, on its N wall the cornice only exists at each corner where it was required to support the skew-put. This appears to be a clear illustration of the relative functions of the ground on either side of the cottage; with the area to the S and E forming part of the highly visible approach to Rowallan Castle and the areas to the N and W facing into the comparatively utilitarian realm of the walled garden.

Integral to the SW corner of the cottage is one of the two gate piers – the cornice of the cottage is contiguous with that of the pier.

EARLY 18TH-CENTURY REMODELLING

Introduction

The S range was comprehensively remodelled at the beginning of the 18th century (Illus 53 and 54). The extent of the work can be traced by the incidence of fireplaces characteristic of the period – either inserted into pre-existing openings or built anew – that have restrained moulded surrounds detailed with flat arched lintels generally detailed with a quarter-ovolo external moulding and a narrow internal quirked angle roll. The lintels of these are quadrant-curved at either end (ie of flat arch form). Components 17, 21, 22 (now removed), 42 and 46. These were principally intended for panelled interiors and such panelling survives in three of the rooms (Components 17, 21 and 46). Again the form of the panelling is characteristic of the early 18th century as are the form and details of the western parts of the range generally, which were reconstructed at this phase.

Reconstruction of the W end of the S range

General

The principal development of this phase was the erection of a three-storied reconstruction of the western end of the S range (Illus 54). It appears that the main reason for this work was to improve accommodation at entrance- and first-floor levels, with the provision of two substantial, well-lit and fashionably appointed panelled chambers. The impetus may have been the instability of the pre-existing structure in this area. The western end of the surviving earlier parts of the S exterior elevation shows a substantial outwards lean and great effort was made within the new work to rectify this distortion. This is most dramatically evident in the entrance-level window in the present entrance passage (Component 20), the W side of which has been reconstructed on the new line – this necessitated resetting the lintel at its present curious and ill-fitting angle.

It is possible that it is at this stage that the first-floor rooms above the central part of the S range were dismantled – the structural instability may have necessitated a more extensive reconstruction of the western parts of the roof structure than needed for the new extension. The removal of the dormers so close to the new work may also have been seen as advantageous in terms of unifying the roofscape and line of the wall head.

It is thus clear that the pre-existing rooms at the W end of the S range, including the presumed fourth basement-level vault, were almost wholly dismantled. An exception is the N wall, which was embedded within surrounding constructions (the courtyard SW stair tower, S end of the perimeter wall, etc).

Exterior

Externally the new work was provided with regular fenestration, symmetrically placed in relation to the rooms within. Although the window surrounds were detailed with low raised margins, their arrises were chamfered – somewhat archaic at this period but perhaps intended to respect or blend with the earlier external openings elsewhere. The quoins are similarly detailed with low raised margins and it is possible that the intention had been to harl the whole of the new work.

The hipped roof structure to the W is typical of the early 18th century. The W elevation below contains some confusing internal complexity that relates to the roof form. Its profile was intentionally echoed by the provision of false quoining that forms the illusion of a NW corner balancing that to the SW. This is in spite of the fact that the elevation continued further N. In the latter area the NW corner of the range overlies the earlier perimeter wall and is detailed with the same strap-ended quoins employed on the early 17th-century stair tower in the SW corner of the courtyard (Illus 54). While superficially suggesting a common date, these quoins (which are 17th-century originals) were in fact reset in the early 18th-century reconstruction. The N side of

43 Panelling and doorcase in Component 21, looking through to the entrance hall, from MacGibbon and Ross, 1892

the stair tower had been widened (the evidence for this is clear in the N gable) to the line of the W perimeter wall so that small closets could be formed at the NW corner of the reconstructed W end of the S range (Components 18 and 47).

While the false quoining suggests more than one phase of construction, two of the quoins are tusked to the W to tie into the masonry of the closet rooms. The two must therefore be coeval. At basement level the gap between the false quoining and the SW corner of the perimeter wall was bridged by an arch, subsequently infilled and provided with a window (Component 3). When formerly open, this arch permitted access to a discreet kitchen entrance at the basement level.

Kitchen area (Components 1, 2 and 5)

The kitchen (Component 1), possibly located on the site of an early 16th-century predecessor, provided spacious new facilities that re-established the traditional relationship with the hall on the floor above by means of a new flight of stairs up to the entrance level. The lower parts of these are of masonry that to the E butts against the pre-existing walling of the earlier vaulted basement. The S side of the stair was formed by an entirely new internal cross wall. On its W side this contains the substantial kitchen fireplace and further fireplaces within the new rooms on the floors above. It is at this stage that the N wall was reduced in thickness

and refaced. To the NE this created additional space for an entrance into the kitchen at the foot of the Component 5 stair.

The understair area (Component 2) is a relict of the pre-existing structure. It contains a well that is probably of early 16th-century date; this partly underlies the new cross wall. A narrow opening was formed at the SE corner of the new kitchen to permit the drawing of water. On its S side this opening also contains a slop-sink to the exterior; on the outer face this reuses the lower part of a dumb-bell gun loop. Perhaps incidentally this gun loop is in approximately the correct position for a predecessor relating to the fourth basement vault; however, its details differ from those further E and the stone is probably reset from elsewhere.

Woman House?

Whatever the nature of the 16th-century woman house may have been, there are no remains of it within the present S range. However, it is possible that this function perpetuated and is represented by the existing upper chamber of the new work (Component 46) – it is also possible that the original woman house (the NW range) had been abandoned/ ruined by this stage. The Component 46 chamber is only accessed by the stair tower at the SW corner of the courtyard (Component 4) and contains no intercommunication with other areas of the S range – apparently a deliberately segregated area.

44 Panelling formerly in Component 22, now in Rowallan House entrance hall, from MacGibbon and Ross, 1892

Reordering of the hall level (Components 16–22)

A new entrance arrangement from the courtyard was created. The present courtyard entrance was inserted; this involved the loss of the western hall window on this side. The original paired entrances further W were blocked and a window inserted. Internally a narrow entrance vestibule was created – effectively a screens passage (Component 20). To the SW wooden stairs (Component 16) led down to a new withdrawing room or morning room with fine views over the garden areas to the S and W (Component 17). This was panelled throughout and supplied with a small closet to the NW (Component 18).

Further stairs led down to the basement level kitchen area (Component 5) as already described and a further entrance off the vestibule led to a small chamber to the NW, an apparent service area, with an unornamented fireplace in the new cross wall to the W and a window to the N as described (Component 19). This room was formed by a brick-built partition wall (now rebuilt with cement) shared with the vestibule to the E and, at its S end, was provided with a wooden press cupboard.

A new N–S partition wall formed the E side of the vestibule and the vestibule itself was flagged with stone. This provided entry to the hall by means of a magnificent doorway with a moulded, lugged architrave and cornice above. The upper part of the architrave had been lugged but has recently been reconstructed incorrectly. The elements

forming the lugs have changed sides and the lugs themselves have been removed; the entrance within is now too wide as a result. The original arrangement is depicted in various historic sources. The partition wall is now largely a modern reconstruction. Historic Scotland archive photographs of 1972 (HS photography archive A3148: 9–11) show the partition removed and a series of seatings at the edge of the wooden floor at the W side of the hall that apparently suggest the entrance had formerly been more centrally placed.

The vestibule seems to have had half or two-thirds height panelling; it is possible that some of this is represented by fragments currently held in storage by the present proprietor.

The interior of the hall (Component 21) was refurbished. The substantial 16th-century fireplace to the N was infilled and a new fireplace installed. The room was panelled throughout, a scheme that incorporated elements of earlier 17th-century panelling at the E end of the N wall. The entry from the W was furnished with a similarly elaborate lugged architrave to that on its W side. The panelling within the room is now largely a reconstruction, although original elements survive to the N. Its former appearance is recorded by MacGibbon and Ross (1887–92) and other sources (Illus 43).

While little now remains of this phase in the chamber to the E of the hall (Component 22; Illus 44 and 45), record

45 Former aumbry doors, surround and window shutters within the SE corner of Component 22, from MacGibbon and Ross, 1892

photographs demonstrate that the early fireplace in its E wall had been infilled and a smaller one inserted. This was removed when the earlier fireplace was reconstructed, c 1988 (Illus 30).

A similar fireplace was inserted in a similar manner on the E wall of the room directly above (Component 42). It is possible that the woodwork of the existing bed recess and twinned presses occupying the W side of this chamber and the existing studwork partition wall to the N were inserted at this stage (Illus 46).

In the E range the curiously constructed studwork and cob partition wall that now divides Components 38, 40 and 41 may be of 18th-century date, as suggested by the sawn timber and lath employed.

Discussion

The impetus for the extensive works of this phase may well have been the instability (or possible collapse) of the W end of the S range. By the early 18th century Rowallan was no longer a principal residence and may have seen neglect. The NW range appears to have been abandoned at a relatively early stage and the damage to the first floor windows on its N side suggest burning. The adjacent early NE tower similarly seems to have been abandoned, perhaps for the same reason. Supporting the possibility of abandonment of the NW range at this stage was the formation of a new basement level kitchen at the W end of the S range – hitherto the kitchen was located in Component 26.

It is possible that the building works were intended to upgrade Rowallan as a secondary residence by one of the female successors – Dame Jean Mure, Countess of Glasgow (suc 1700) or her daughter Lady Jean Boyle Mure (suc 1724). A sense of familial responsibility may also have provided an impetus for the works.

46 Bed recess in W wall of Component 42 (*Addyman Associates*)

47 The N-facing courtyard elevation in 1951 prior to the demolition of the brick addition (*Historic Scotland © Crown Copyright*)

LATER CONSTRUCTIONS

There is little evidence for extensive activity at Rowallan, either aristocratic occupation or continuing architectural development from the mid 18th century on. The history of this period is one of benign decline, reflected in the fabric by a series of relatively minor interventions such as the entrance cut through to the basement pend at base of S entrance tower (Component 52) and the lean-to structure erected against S range within courtyard and subsequently removed (Illus 44).

CONCLUSION

The later history of the castle during the 17th and early 18th centuries is one where repeated attempts were made to update an existing, increasingly awkwardly arranged and outdated building to meet the requirements of the time. There is little doubt that if Rowallan had not been relegated to a secondary residence and if funds had been available, that the castle would have been radically reworked in later periods. Evidence for this lies in the four schemes for its reconstruction from the mid 19th to the mid 20th century for which documentation survives. While each of these made some reference to the historic fabric, the result would have been a major reconstruction and massive loss of historic fabric. In many ways therefore Rowallan is an extraordinary survival.

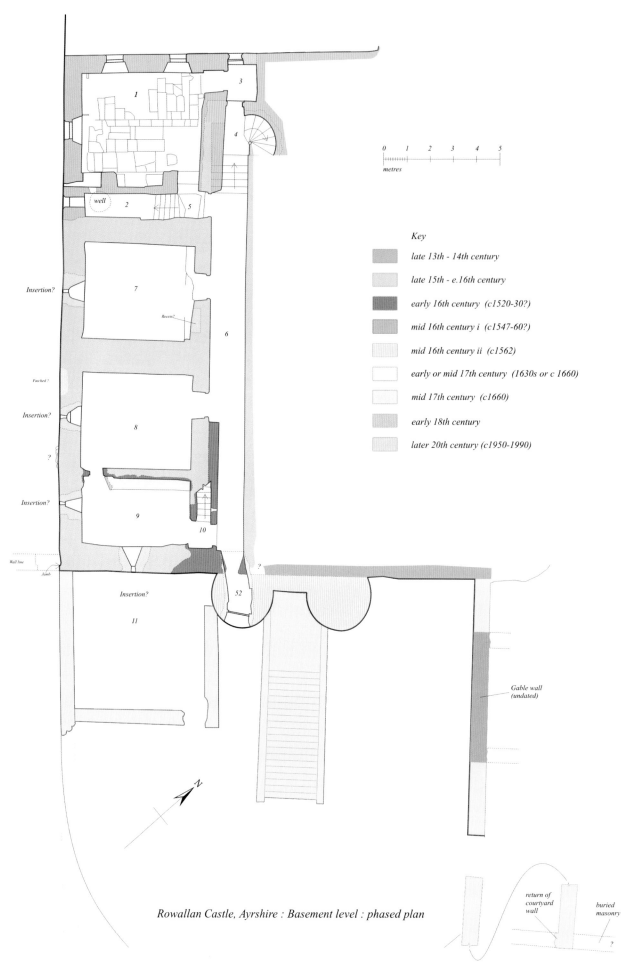

Rowallan Castle, Ayrshire : Basement level : phased plan

Key

- late 13th - 14th century
- late 15th - e.16th century
- early 16th century (c1520-30?)
- mid 16th century i (c1547-60?)
- mid 16th century ii (c1562)
- early or mid 17th century (1630s or c 1660)
- mid 17th century (c1660)
- early 18th century
- later 20th century (c1950-1990)

48 Basement level: phased plan (*Addyman Associates, 2005, based on drawings supplied by Historic Scotland, by Loy Surveys and Kirkdale Archaeology*)

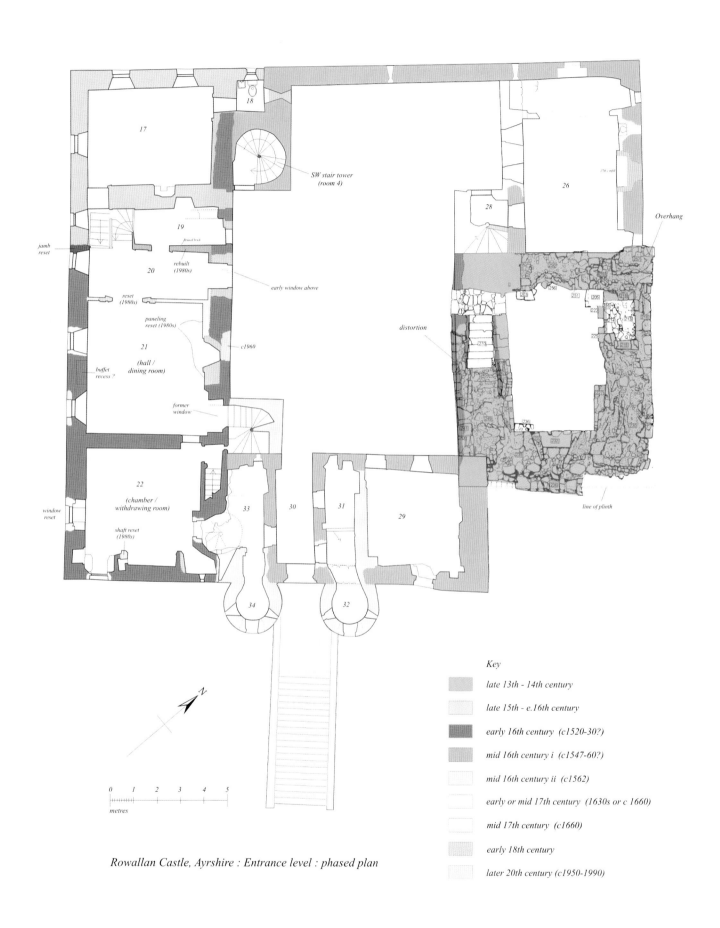

Rowallan Castle, Ayrshire : Entrance level : phased plan

Key

late 13th - 14th century

late 15th - e.16th century

early 16th century (c1520-30?)

mid 16th century i (c1547-60?)

mid 16th century ii (c1562)

early or mid 17th century (1630s or c 1660)

mid 17th century (c1660)

early 18th century

later 20th century (c1950-1990)

49 Entrance level: phased plan (*Addyman Associates, 2005, based on drawings supplied by Historic Scotland, by Loy Surveys and Kirkdale Archaeology*)

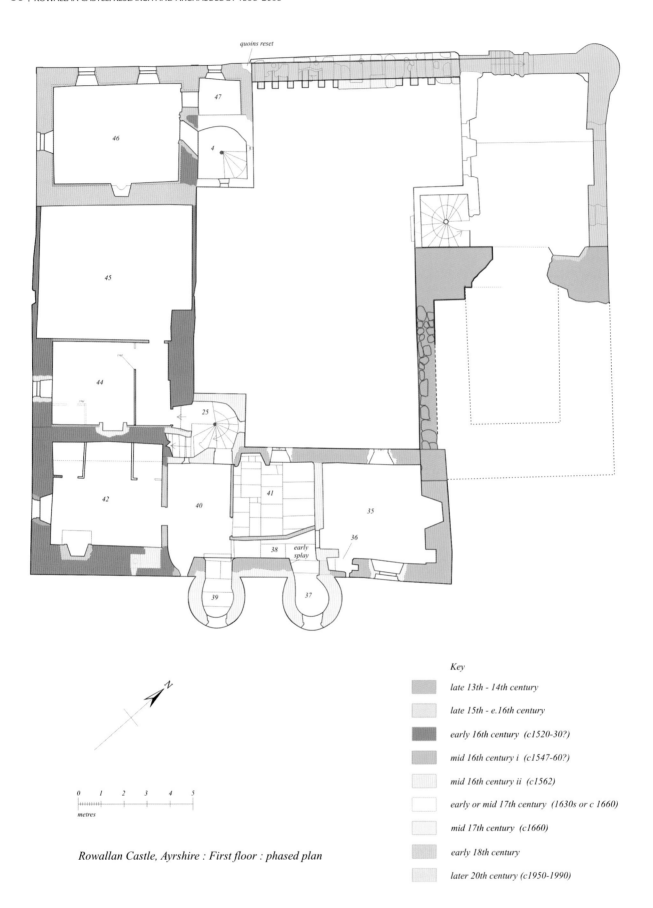

Rowallan Castle, Ayrshire : First floor : phased plan

Key

late 13th - 14th century

late 15th - e.16th century

early 16th century (c1520-30?)

mid 16th century i (c1547-60?)

mid 16th century ii (c1562)

early or mid 17th century (1630s or c 1660)

mid 17th century (c1660)

early 18th century

later 20th century (c1950-1990)

50 First floor: phased plan (*Addyman Associates, 2005, based on drawings supplied by Historic Scotland, by Loy Surveys and Kirkdale Archaeology*)

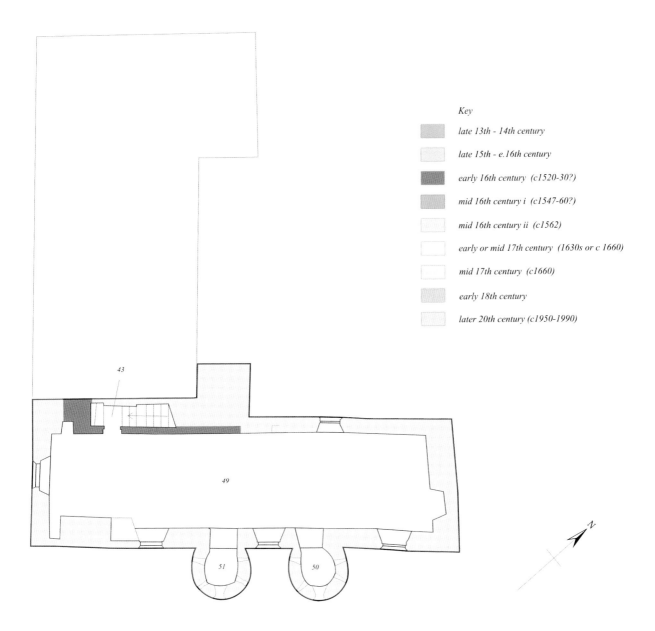

Key

late 13th - 14th century

late 15th - e.16th century

early 16th century (c1520-30?)

mid 16th century i (c1547-60?)

mid 16th century ii (c1562)

early or mid 17th century (1630s or c 1660)

mid 17th century (c1660)

early 18th century

later 20th century (c1950-1990)

Rowallan Castle, Ayrshire : Second floor : phased plan

51 Second floor: phased plan (*Addyman Associates, 2005, based on drawings supplied by Historic Scotland, by Loy Surveys and Kirkdale Archaeology*)

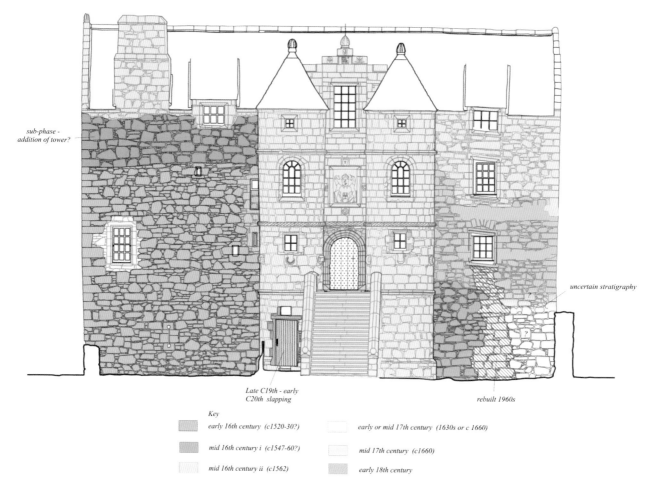

*sub-phase -
addition of tower?*

uncertain stratigraphy

*Late C19th - early
C20th slapping*

rebuilt 1960s

Key

early 16th century (c1520-30?)	early or mid 17th century (1630s or c 1660)
mid 16th century i (c1547-60?)	mid 17th century (c1660)
mid 16th century ii (c1562)	early 18th century

52 E exterior elevation showing suggested phases of development not to scale (*Addyman Associates, 2005, based on drawings supplied by Historic Scotland, by Loy Surveys and Kirkdale Archaeology*)

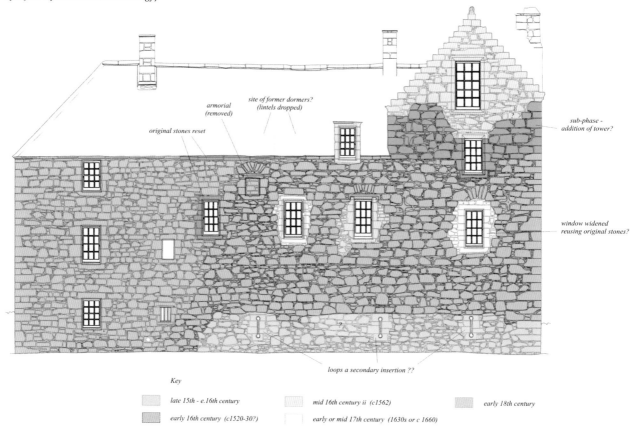

*armorial
(removed)*

*site of former dormers?
(lintels dropped)*

original stones reset

*sub-phase -
addition of tower?*

*window widened
reusing original stones?*

loops a secondary insertion ??

Key

late 15th - e.16th century	mid 16th century ii (c1562)	early 18th century
early 16th century (c1520-30?)	early or mid 17th century (1630s or c 1660)	

53 S exterior elevation showing suggested phases of development, not to scale (*Addyman Associates, 2005, based on drawings supplied by Historic Scotland, by Loy Surveys and Kirkdale Archaeology*)

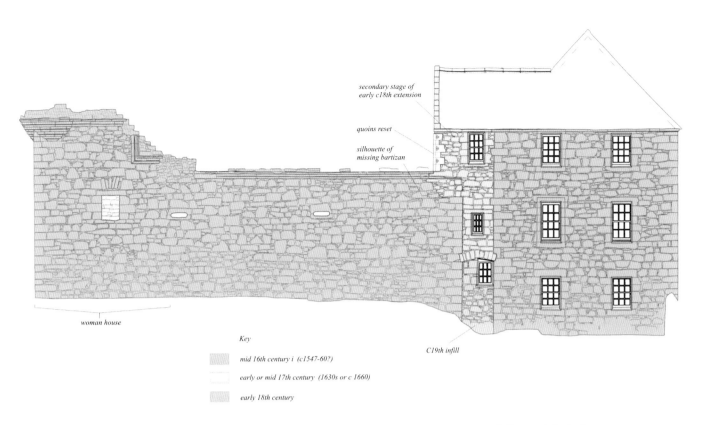

*secondary stage of
early c18th extension*

quoins reset

*silhouette of
missing bartizan*

woman house

C19th infill

Key

mid 16th century i (c1547-60?)

early or mid 17th century (1630s or c 1660)

early 18th century

54 W exterior elevation showing suggested phases of development (*Addyman Associates, 2005, based on drawings supplied by Historic Scotland,
by Loy Surveys and Kirkdale Archaeology*)

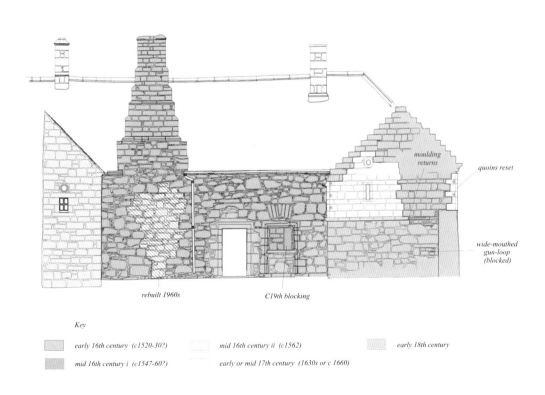

*moulding
returns*

quoins reset

*wide-mouthed
gun-loop
(blocked)*

rebuilt 1960s

C19th blocking

Key

early 16th century (c1520-30?)   mid 16th century ii (c1562)   early 18th century

mid 16th century i (c1547-60?)   early or mid 17th century (1630s or c 1660)

55 Courtyard elevation facing N showing suggested phases of development (*Addyman Associates, 2005, based on drawings supplied by Historic Scotland,
by Loy Surveys and Kirkdale Archaeology*)

56 Dundonald Castle (*Historic Scotland © Crown copyright*)

57 Auchans House (*Royal Commission on the Ancient and Historical Monuments of Scotland © Crown Copyright*)

5 DISCUSSION

Gordon Ewart and Dennis Gallagher

Excavations within the tower of Rowallan have demonstrated that the natural mound on which it was based had been the site of a Bronze Age burial and was a focus of human activity during the Iron Age and later. In the medieval period it became the centre of an estate, the tower in the landscape acting both as a stronghold and a symbol of seigneurial presence. The territorial limits of early medieval estates must have been well established by the 12th century. It was onto this early medieval geo-political framework that the baronage was imposed. The new Anglo-Norman lordships and baronies tended to respect earlier estates and territorial divisions at the level of shire, bailiary, and individual lordships. It is highly probable therefore that the 12th-century feudal estate at Rowallan respected the parameters of an earlier power base. The selection of already recognisable and well-defined estates as part of the process of territorial land holding from the 12th century is confirmed at the nearby royal Stewart Castle of Dundonald (Illus 56).

In the case of Rowallan the continuity aspect of early medieval colonisation/expansion is also evident. The confirmation of the lands of Rowallan to Gilchrist Mure by Alexander III, after their having been appropriated by a Walter Cumyn, may imply that they were not the principal 'messuage' of the family at this time. The house and lands of Polkellie may have been the earlier estate, enlarged by the acquisition of Rowallan after 1263. This may explain the rather small size of the tower and an uncertain level of investment in the site until the later 15th–early 16th century. Sir Adam Mure is the first to style himself 'of Rowallan' in the late 14th century, and it may be that the estate became the most significant of the family lands from that date. The early castle and lands may therefore be part of a series of small estates inherited from the old Kingdom of Strathclyde and passed out to new owners some time before the mid 13th century. Rowallan was likely to have been the site of a tower or hall of the Muir family since the later 13th century, although its early form and extent are unclear from the surviving structural evidence, although parts of the structure could be of an earlier date. The topography of the site and the positioning of the early tower were decisive factors constraining how the later building complex was extended and adapted by successive owners, to meet the needs of an increasingly sophisticated household.

The modest scale of the NE tower may reasonably imply a lesser status for the castle than the more massive structures seen at Craigie, Tibbers and Dundonald. It may be better compared with the small tower found at Auldhill, Portencross (Caldwell *et al* 1998), on the N Ayrshire coast and Sundrum Castle, near Coylton. Both sites date from the early medieval period and represent self-contained small enclosure castles. Seagate Castle in Irvine may also be cited as a parallel in terms of plan and scale (MacGibbon and Ross 1887–92, IV, 234–40). Structurally, the Rowallan intramural stair is echoed in the early 15th-century tower at Carrick, Argyll, which also featured a small enclosure alongside a tower, all perched on a rocky outcrop (RCAHMS 1992, 226–37). In all these instances the tower provided some defensive capacity alongside relatively limited accommodation.

The layout of the remainder of the castle before the 15th century is unknown. It may well be that the mound was extended and scarped to create some motte-like earthwork, which in turn was complemented from an early date by some outer enclosure. Unfortunately, no sign of an outer bailey can be identified today. The earliest surviving masonry within the S range (outwith the NE tower) is not easily dated.

It may be that it was John Mure, father of Mungo, who took over the estate in 1501, or his father (another John) who was responsible for beginning the present S range, with the hall completed by Mungo Mure. The S range can be seen on one hand as defining one side of the Period 2 enclosure and on the other as an adjunct to the tower, providing extra service and private accommodation. The juxtaposition of hall and tower elements has been noted elsewhere, for example at Smailholm Tower, Threave Castle and Dundonald Castle, where complex plans involving both elements were in place before the end of the 14th century. If, as seems likely, the S range is a late 15th-century work, the inspiration for it (and the numerous parallels in Ayrshire) may be the building traditions involving halls such as at Auldhill, Threave, and Craigie. Such sites may also represent an imitation of the great courtyard castles of James IV.

The evolution of Rowallan demonstrates a change in emphasis in the castle from defence to domestic accommodation, a growing demand for more private chambers for both family and guests, and an increased speciality in room usage. This move towards greater comfort and privacy, leading to an elaboration of the domestic aspects of the castle, is one that has been much discussed with reference to English great houses, particularly by

Thomson (1987) who saw it in terms of a decline, a position modified by others who, whilst agreeing with the change in emphasis, stressed the positive aspects of this development (Dixon and Lott 1993).

Extra accommodation was provided at Rowallan by the creation of a courtyard house that incorporated the early tower, an example of how the domestic aspects within a seigneurial residence gradually overrode the defensive. The mound, on which the early tower was constructed, was expanded to form a raised courtyard around which more complex domestic ranges developed. The raised courtyard, by raising the principal windows above immediate reach, provided an element of defence, as did the walls of outer courts. This development evolved into the plan of the present castle, consisting of a series of ranges around three sides of a central courtyard with a W rampart completing the circuit.

The courtyard plan was becoming increasingly popular in northern Europe in the 16th century and it befitted the occupant's status as a courtier. Its horizontal apartments provided greater space with flexibility that was not possible in the vertically stacked accommodation of the tower house. The origins of the design lie in the generic hall within a courtyard, seen as part of the desired combination of hall, tower and rampart defining the idealised castle. The work at Rowallan owes a considerable debt to the models advanced by the early 14th-century royal castles, where an integrated plan was advanced, effectively combining the elements of the ideal castle components. However, the growing popularity of courtyard plans (as opposed to the ubiquitous tower house) may owe something to the development of the court d'honneur featured at the royal castles in Stirling and Edinburgh and the palaces of Holyrood, Falkland and Linlithgow.

During the course of the 16th century Rowallan, was transformed from the house of a minor laird into one which aspired to a much grander scale. The building campaigns by Mungo Mure and, in particular, John Mure and William Mure were the work of men who were thoroughly imbued with the spirit of Renaissance Europe. William Mure was a recognised poet and author, and his skill and appreciation of music are evident from the surviving manuscript books for lute and song. The environment for this cultural life was provided in expanded accommodation on the scale that was becoming expected by the greater men of that era. This enhanced lifestyle was supported by the astute acquisition of land revenues and the cultivation of alliances with other powerful Ayrshire families. But the family connections went beyond those of the local community. The Mure family was proud of its link with the Stewart dynasty through the marriage of Robert II and Elizabeth Mure. It was, however, a more recent connection with the Stewart family, the marriage of John Mure to Margaret Boyd, former mistress of James IV, which provided Rowallan with a potential source of influence and extra income in the form of lands and annuities (MacDougall 1997, 107). Margaret Boyd's

children from her former liaison included Alexander Stewart, who was created Archbishop of St Andrews and Chancellor before his death in 1513, and Catherine Stewart, who married James Douglas, third Earl of Morton. Rowallan was built to reflect these royal connections.

While the rest of the building evolved to serve a more domestic function, the early tower remained not just as a functional fortification but also as a symbol of the antiquity of the Mure lordship, a visible reminder of the ancient connections with the royal dynasty. This nostalgia for the chivalric elements of ancestry is seen in the compilation of the Historie, especially in its more fictitious elements dealing with the supposed early history of the family. This element of structural symbolism has long been an element in castle design (Coulson 1979), as was succinctly expressed by the Earl of Ancrum in the 17th century when, during the modernisation of his house, he insisted on leaving the battlemented appearance of the tower 'for that is the grace of the house, and makes it looke lyk a castle, and henc so nobleste' (RCAHMS 1956, 485). The early tower could also have been used in the later stages of the development of the castle as a platform from which to view the ornamental grounds of the estate. This activity was one not purely of pleasure, but, in terms of the prevalent neo-stoicism of the educated contemporary Scot, was imbued with moral and intellectual virtue (Allan 1997). The appreciation of the gardens was compatible with the music and poetry and, indeed, moral writings of the Mure family.

It was John Mure (1560-91) who was principally responsible for the ornamentation of the castle as we now see it. He was said to have built the 'fore wark (fore work) backwark and woman house frome the ground' (Tough 1898, II, 255). His major contribution was to add to the architectural presence of the E front by the building of the twin towers of the frontispiece, greatly adding to the grandeur of the entrance (Illus 52). The entrance is decorated with cable moulding and has a heraldic panel containing the royal arms, surrounded by cable bosses. The gablet above is inscribed John Mure 1562 and is capped by a Moor's head. There are small gun loops under the windows, also surrounded with cable moulding. This frontispiece is in a form that is ultimately derived from the courtyard castles such as Harlech and Caerlaverock, a tradition where the urge to present the castle entrance as a symbol of power, often reinforced by a heraldic display, rivalled that of the needs of defence. This tradition continued with the gateways to the greater courtyard houses and palaces of the 16th century, their height and vertical emphasis proclaiming the seigneurial prestige that was still associated with tall towers (Barley 1986, 100). Notable examples included the early 16th-century gatehouse of Hampton Court (Thurley 2003, 18–19) and in Scotland, the royal palaces of Falkland and Holyrood, and Stirling Castle. The entrance to the inner courtyard of Rowallan is set between two wide drum towers with conical roofs and prominent string courses. The inspiration for these towers has been ascribed to the various

Scottish royal palaces, with a common source in French Renaissance architecture, such as the chateau of Bury and Azay-le-Rideau (Bentley-Cranch 1986, 87–8). Howard (1995, 62) sees them as French in style, inspired by Falkland. Hays (1984, 214) compared them to the 'foir-front' of Holyrood. The symmetrical frontage in which the towers form the centrepiece has been compared to that of Tolquhon, erected 1584–9, and Fyvie, Boyne, and Dudhope (Hays 1984, 214; MacKechnie 1995, 21). The connection between Rowallan and the royal Stewart dynasty is emphasised further by the heraldic panel over the entrance that is capped by a Moor's head, a rebus for the family name. The head wears a curious headdress that combines a turban with a crown. This same headdress is used as finials on the conical towers of the gatehouse: the whole edifice is surmounted with symbols of the family's royal connections.

The gatehouse is embellished by a string course of cable moulding and similar moulding surrounds the gun ports. The decorative use of cable moulding is a prominent feature on certain late 16th-century buildings in S Scotland. It is found applied as a horizontal string course at the castles of Blairquhan and Kenmure, the latter being, like Rowallan, a house around a courtyard (MacKechnie 1995, 17–18).

A most unusual feature at Rowallan is the stair that lead up to the gate at first-floor level. Stairs in this position would be more normal as an approach to the main apartments once within the inner courtyard, as at Linlithgow and formerly at Holyrood. A parallel may exist, however, in the original entrance to the tower of James V at Holyrood, erected in 1535–6, which was originally approached by a forestair which led to a first-floor doorway in its E wall, an arrangement which may have existed until the building of the N gallery in the 1570s (Dunbar 1999, 64). The Mure family was related through marriage to the Maxwell lairds of Newark, William Mure (d 1616) having married Janet Maxwell.

In its final stage of architectural evolution, Rowallan lacked any defences at roof level. Even the superficially martial-looking gate towers were without the usual battlemented wall head. The towers have a number of gun loops, but, whilst these would deter small-scale attacks, they would do little to deter a major assault. The gun loops on the gatetowers are emphasised with moulded surrounds. The main intention of the entrance is to present a statement of power and to emphasise to visitors the ancient ancestry and present sophistication of the family. It is essentially a place of peace, a courtier's house like those of Seton and Pinkie, although on a smaller scale.

The development of the interior space at Rowallan is an architectural expression of the widespread change in the style of domestic life during the 16th and early 17th centuries (Girouard 1978, 88). The hall was no longer a place where the whole household dined, but merely the first in a sequence of increasingly private rooms extending to the E. In these rooms the earlier multi-functionality gradually gave way to an increasingly specialised use of space, encouraged by a growing demand for privacy. The hall, however, still remained as a space for larger-scale hospitality and, like the tower, as a symbol of aristocratic tenure (King 2003, 121–2). The chamber immediately to the E of the hall (Component 22) formerly had elaborate wooden panelling decorated with pilasters and semicircular arches (Illus 44; MacGibbon and Ross 1887–92, II, 380) and is likely to have functioned as the great chamber in the late 16th and 17th centuries, being used for formal family dining. Above this was a bedchamber, probably the Best Bedchamber, which later acquired a fashionable bed alcove in the French manner.

The E range was heightened by John Mure to create a long gallery which extended the full length of the building (Illus 40). By the later 16th century a long gallery had become an expected component of the sequence of state rooms in a great house. This was a place of indoor recreation. It could also be a place of display, with portraits that again conveyed the ancestral pride of the Mure family. The view from the windows to the gardens and the designed landscape beyond was also an important factor in the location of the long gallery within the house, a reason for the increasingly popularity, in the late 16th and early 17th centuries, of galleries that occupied second-floor spaces and enlarged attics (Coope 1986, 52, 54–5). At Rowallan, large windows at the S end of the gallery, and between the two towers of the gatehouse, emphasised the social status of this room. The large S window lighting the end of the gallery has been compared with that at Auchans House (MacGibbon and Ross 1887–92, II, 176–7) (Illus 57). The S end of the early 17th-century long gallery at Pinkie House is also lit by a prominent window, there given greater emphasis by its bay form (McWilliam 1978, 336). William Mure, who married Janet Maxwell of Newark c 1575, would also have been aware of the large long gallery built at Newark Castle (Illus 58), Port Glasgow, in the late 1590s by his wife's father.

58 Newark Castle (*Historic Scotland © Crown Copyright*)

The *Historie* relates how John Mure, who died in 1591, created the 'woman house'. This was construed by the editor as that part of the building that contained the old kitchen and the rooms of the domestic servants, to the W of the old tower (*Historie*, 83). This may be correct with regard to location, but his interpretation of the term may be doubted as it is more likely to refer to separate quarters for the nursing women and children of the household. The term appears in various late 16th- and early 17th-century documents, although there is some doubt as to its exact meaning (*DOST* 12, 286). The earliest recorded reference is in a detailed inventory of the house of Caulder in 1566 where it appears as a chamber furnished with 'an auld stuile' and 'an auld kawe', possibly adjacent to the hall loft (Beveridge and Russell 1920, 101). It occurs in various records referring to royal palaces and is often also associated with children. There is a reference of 1611–12 to 'the barnes chamber called the woeman house' at Holyrood (*MW* 1, 340). In 1623–4 a door was mended in the woman house at Edinburgh Castle, along with a chair 'for the bairnes to sit in', although the two may not necessarily be connected (*MW* 2, 155). Patrick Cranstoun of Corsebie was prosecuted in 1628 for overwhelming cruelty against his wife, Marion Hume, the mother of his 'twentie bairnes or thairby'. When she returned after seeking refuge in a neighbour's house, she was again attacked by her husband who, in a charming turn of phrase, 'directit her to the woman hous whair his brood swine and grysses [suckling pigs] were' (*RPC* II, 256–8). It was common practice before c 1700 for wealthy families to employ wet-nurses who lived in the household and were treated as very superior servants, being provided with comfortable quarters and a nourishing diet (Marshall 1984, 47). It would seem from this context that the woman house was a chamber used by the wet-nurse as the nursery, situated away from the private quarters of the household but conveniently close to the kitchens, although its exact location at Rowallan is uncertain. Woman houses continued to be erected as part of large houses into the 18th century. The move away from the employment of resident wet-nurses (Marshall 1984, 47), however, and the increased separation of servants from family members, meant that the term 'woman house' was increasingly used for the accommodation of female servants.

The NW range was reconstructed by William Mure (1658–86), completing the final courtyard plan. The doorway to this range has a broken pediment framing the arms and initials of William Mure and his wife, Elizabeth Hamilton. It was probably at this period that the old NE tower was altered by the insertion of a new vaulted basement and the raising of the first-floor level in order to facilitate access with the NW range.

Those of the Mure family who expanded and embellished Rowallan would have considered the immediate surroundings of the castle to be an integral part of the whole. The castle appears on Blaeu's map of Cunningham (Illus 62), published in 1654 but based on a lost late 16th-century map by Timothy Pont, where it appears within an enclosed park approximately the same size as the present designed landscape. The approach to the castle was designed as a processional route culminating in the great hall. Heraldic displays, notably on the gatehouse, were designed to impress the visitor with the ancient lineage of the family. The outer gateway was part of this route. The gateway to the outer courtyard was completed by William Mure (1658–86). It is dated 1661 (several times) and has the intertwined initials of William Mure and Elizabeth Hamilton on the keystone of the arch. The style of the gateway is classical, with a broken pediment and obelisks finials. It replaces an earlier gateway of which the gun loops, in a different stone from the later work, survive. These are of a similar style to those in the drum towers of the castle gatehouse and may be attributed to John Mure who is said to have 'plaintit the oirchyarde and gairdein' (*Historie*, 83). The walled garden to the N of the castle, with a lintel dated 1687, is testimony to his work. It is also likely that there was a parterre or similar form of decorative garden before the gatehouse which could be appreciated from the windows of the long gallery. Great changes were made in the winter of 1745/6 when extensive planting of woodland is documented. This is shown on General Roy's *Military Survey* of 1747–55 (Illus 64) and main elements survived to be depicted on the first edition OS map of 1856 (Illus 65). The principal parts of this new landscape were the Mains Park and the Great Avenue. The Mains Park was a large square enclosure, defined by belts of trees, around Rowallan Mains, site of the present Rowallan House. An avenue led from Rowallan Mains to the northern edge of the castle garden. Another, wider, avenue leads SW from this enclosure and terminates in a large circular expanse. This designed landscape is centred on Rowallan Mains, suggesting the emphasis of the planners had changed from the castle as symbol of ancient family to the castle as the centre of a new improved landscape.

In short, the evolution of the building owes much to a manorial rather than martial style. It witnessed the domestic arrangement of space dictated by the changing demands of a hierarchical society and a statement of the long-established position of the Mure family within that society.

HISTORICAL RESEARCH

59 Charter by Walter Comyn of Rowallan (*East Ayrshire Council www.futuremuseum.co.uk*)

6 THE OWNERS OF ROWALLAN

Dennis Gallagher, John Harrison and William McQueen

Previous histories of the estate, the castle and the Mure family have relied heavily on the *Historie*, first written in the mid 17th century. However, evidence for the period prior to the 1390s suggests that the estate was more probably in the hands of the Comyns than of the Mures until quite late in the 14th century. From the 1390s to c 1500 the Mures certainly had Rowallan, but they seem almost to flicker in and out of focus and it is unlikely that there was a direct line of descent, at least down to the Sir Robert who probably succeeded c 1460.

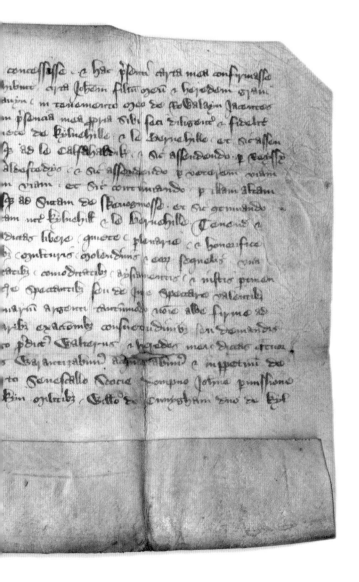

BEFORE THE MURES

The estate of Rowallan was associated with the Mures and their kin from the later 14th century until its disposition in the early 20th century. The *Historie* claims in one version that the Mures had regained their forfeited lands of Rowallan from the Comyns as a reward for their support of Alexander III at the Battle of Largs (1263) and in another that they gained it by marriage (*Historie*, 17–19, 35). The possibility of a marriage link between the Comyns and Mures cannot be discounted, but the only primary documents from before 1391 located so far link Rowallan with the Comyns.

In 1361–2 Maurice Murray was granted the ward of Walter Cuming (Comyn) 'of Rowallan' at least in relation to some lands in the vicinity of Hawick (*RMS* I, App II, doc 776). The wardship implies that this Walter is at least the second generation 'of Rowallan' and there is a strong chance that he is a descendant of the Walter Comyn, who had been granted a £7 0s 6d land in Hawick by Robert the Bruce at some time prior to 1315x1321 and which was therefore excluded from a grant to Henry de Balliol (*RMS* I, doc 24). Young (1997, 206) uses the earlier grant to support his argument that Bruce could afford to be forgiving of the lesser members of the Comyn kindred after 1306 and wonders if the Hawick Walter might be the man mentioned in Peeblesshire in the 1290s.

A new manuscript can now be added to this previously published evidence in the form of an undated charter by Walter Comyn 'dominus de Rowallane' to William Surrurges de Stanley of the four merk lands in the town of Muckle Gawyn, Rowallan (Illus 59). The manuscript was catalogued by NRAS as being dated 1490 and in bundle 31, but was actually found amongst loose items in bundle 29 and, whilst it has no date, it is clearly 14th-century (EACMAS, Cessnock Papers). It is mentioned in an Inventory of Writs for Gainleitch made in 1852 and described as:

Charter by Walter Comyn, dominus de Rowallan to William Surrurgess de Stanley in the forest of Paisley of a four merk land in the town of Muckil Gawyn in the granter's tenement of Rowallan to be held blench for payment of a silver penny at the manor place of Rowallan at Martinmas yearly.
(EACMAS, Cessnock Papers, bundle 31)

The maker of the Inventory rightly says that it has no date but is probably wrong in concluding that it does not concern

Gainleitch. Gainleitch was a one merk land and one of a series of 'Gain' sites including Gainhill and Gainford, lying W of Fenwick. A Royal Letter in favour of John Mure, son of Mungo who died at Pinkie, grants him the non-entries and other rights of (*inter alia*) the 10s land and the 20s land of Govinleitch (NLS Adv MS22.2.9 f 49r–v). The 5 merks of Muckle Gawyn would comprise all of these Gain, Govin or Gawyn lands together. Later charters for Gainleitch show it in the hands of the Halls (from 1490) Peebles and others and it was still held by vassals of Rowallan in the mid 19th century (EACMAS, Cessnock Papers, bundle 31). The continued Comyn connection is also demonstrated by a copy of a charter by Robert, steward of Scotland, dating between 1358 and 137 confirming a charter by Walter Cummyng, Lord of Rowallan, to Richard Boyl, whilst, in the same period, the steward confirmed a charter by Gilchrist Mor (probably More or Mure) in favour of Aircia, his daughter, of a part of Rowallan. Together they would be consistent with the first Mures holding the lands from the Walter Comyn (NAS CS7/3 f. 256).

But, whether in the hands of the Mures, the Comyns, or anyone else, Rowallan could have had an earlier existence within the Kingdom of Strathclyde. Evidence regarding the huge common grazing, now known as Glenouther Moor, discussed in relation to the farming and economics of the area, would support such a conclusion. Even in the 12th to the 14th century, Rowallan would have been but one of several Comyn lands in Ayrshire and a small part of the family's vast holdings extending across much of Scotland (Young 1997).

THE MURES OF ROWALLAN

Introduction and Early Records

Any review of the Mure family history must use as its base the *Historie and Descent of the House of Rowallane by Sir William Mure*, written c 1657; the edition of 1825 incorporated later material and there was a further edition edited by Tough and published in 1898. Two key problems face modern research into the family. Firstly, the male line of the Mures came to an end in the early 18th century and the estate passed, via the female line, to the Campbells of Loudoun and others and so lost its distinct identity when assimilated into their wider holdings. Any coherent collection of estate papers has been dispersed or lost. Secondly, whilst Sir William (and perhaps the 19th-century editors) had documents to hand which have now been lost, such family histories often drew on tradition and even extended into the mythic past as is amply seen in genealogies of, say, the Campbells (Boardman 2006) or of the kings of Scotland themselves.

The *Historie* claims that the Mures were displaced from Rowallan by the Comyns but were restored following their gallant support for Alexander III at the Battle of Largs in 1263 (*Historie*, 17–19) and it peoples the late 13th century and

60 King Robert Stewart and his queen, Elizabeth Mure of Rowallan, from the Forman Armorial (NLS Adv MS31.4.2, fol10r (*reproduced by permission of the Trustees of the National Library of Scotland*)

the 14th century with Sir Gilchrist and others who are not otherwise confirmed . Such documentary evidence as does exist for Rowallan prior to the later 14th century has it in the hands of the Comyns. Anderson (1863, 218) and others have identified a Gilchrist 'of the Craig' and others, signatories of the Ragman Rolls, with Rowallan, but the only Gilchrist in the Rolls is not 'of the Craig' and Reynaud de Cragg was from Lanarkshire. The suggestion that the Mures of Polkelly were the senior line was not followed by the *Historie* and is contradicted by the charter evidence and the later pattern of lordship.

It was during the 1330s that John Stewart, son of Robert the Bruce's sister Marjorie, enjoyed what has been called a 'secular marriage' with Elizabeth More or Mure, said by the *Historie* to have been a daughter of Adam 'of Rowallan'. In 1346, as the prospects of his eventually succeeding to the crown became clearer, Stewart (later to become Robert II) moved to have the children legitimised. This royal connection was a source of great pride to the Mure family. The royal pair are depicted in the Forman Armorial, a work of c 1562 compiled for presentation to Queen Mary (Illus 60). An Adam Mure is recorded as a Steward in the royal household in 1328 though he is not specified to be 'of Rowallan' at this time and the 14th-century records of Comyns of Rowallan pose a problem for that view.

The early origins of the Mures of Rowallan cannot be confirmed. Six men called More witnessed the Ragman Rolls, two from Lanarkshire (including the one 'of Cragg'), one from Dumbartonshire, and four, including a Gilchrist, from Ayrshire. But only one of these four is given a topographical designation (de Thaugarfton); on that evidence, the others might or might not be 'of Rowallan'.

More positively, Agnes More, wife of Walter of Tullach, is described as a cousin of Robert III and she was a daughter of Reginald More, the Chamberlain, and a sister of William More of Abercorn, according to a charter in favour of herself and her husband issued in 1348. The editor of the Exchequer Rolls cautiously 'draws the inference that Reginald More was not distantly related to the mother of Robert III'(*ER* III, lxxiii n.). Such links with East Lothian must further undermine the family's own unsupported claims of ancient connection with Rowallan as related in the *Historie*. The Mures or Mores of Abercorn were active at court by the later 14th century.

Another key pointer is a series of records of Andrew More. He was ambassador to France in 1380 when he also received a gift of £3 6s 8d from the king (*ER* III, 652, 653). He was paid a salary of £6 13s 4d from the Exchequer in 1380 (*ER* III, 53) and was paid two terms salary in 1384 (*ER* III, 117). He is presumably the same Andrew More who received a pension of £20 per annum from 1388 to 1398 and who, in 1391 and later, is described as 'uncle of the king' (*ER* III, 276, 280, 430, 457). Clearly, if Agnes, the king's cousin, was of the Abercorn Mures, so was Andrew, the king's uncle, and so was Elizabeth, wife of Robert II and mother of Robert III. Of course, the Abercorn family could have had interests in Ayrshire or been rewarded with lands there. The first contemporary record of a Mure associated with Rowallan is a copy of a charter by Robert, steward of Scotland, confirming a charter by Gilchrist More of a part of Rowallan in the period 1358-1370 (CS7/3/ f. 256). But records become much more frequent in the 1390s. Robert II had died in 1390 and it was Robert III who, on 11 November 1391, issued the first charter to Adam Mure, the king's 'consanquineus' or kinsman and it is from this point onward that we can speak with confidence of Mures of Rowallan as fully historical people.

Sir Adam Mure of Rowallan (1)

The key document is a charter under the Great Seal dated 11 November 1391 (*RMS* I, 329, doc 835). Since Adam resigned the lands into the king's hands in the first instance, it is clear that he already had some form of right to them, though there is no reference to previous charters. The grant is said to be for 'services done and to be done' and there was no payment or reddendo demanded, just three suits of court yearly at Irvine. The lands are not described beyond being 'all the lands of Rowallan' within the usual bounds and to be erected into a free barony. The charter was issued at Irvine, close to the Stewart heartlands, and those present included the king's brother and two other kinsmen, Archibald Douglas of Galloway and Thomas Lord Erskine, so it was quite a family affair.

The following year there was another grant, this time to Adam Mure of Rowallan and [blank] Danielstoun his spouse of the lands of Polnekill, Grey, Dumblay, Clunche, Clony Herber, Darlache and Balgram in Cunningham and of Lyntslare [Linflare, in Lanarkshire], the latter on the resignation of Janet Danielston (*RMS* I, APP II 1669). This second grant seems to be duplicated the following year when a charter dated at Dumbarton gave Robert Mure and his spouse the lands of Polnekel, Grey, Drumbuy, Cliniche (Clundie), Clonyherbire, Darclath and Bagraw in Cunningham and of Lenflare, sheriffdom on Lanark, all to be united into the free barony of Polnekel. The 1393 grant does not survive but is mentioned in a confirmation of 1440 (*RMS* 1424–1513, 58, entry 253).

Some months previous to this grant, the king had also given a charter to John of Crawford for land of 'Ardache' (Ardoch) within the lordship of Rowallan (*RMS* 1306–1424, 330, doc 836). The relationship between the lordship of Rowallan and the barony of Rowallan is presently unclear, but it might be that the lordship was an older and larger unit. The two grants were issued at Irvine and Dundonald respectively, important power centres within the Stewartry. Adam Mure was a witness to a charter granted by the king at Ardnel, in Cunningham, on 26 November 1391 (NAS GD1/19/1). Suddenly, it seems, in 1391, the Mures became prominent local people, rewarded with lands and access to the king, their kinsman. Given the charter evidence of Walter Comyn 'of Rowallan' at least as late as 1361–2 and perhaps later (see above), we have to wonder if they were not quite new arrivals on the local scene.

According to the family history, this Sir Adam died in 1399 and was succeeded by his eldest son in Rowallan, the younger son taking the lands of Polkelly 'together with the lands of Limflare and Lowdoune hill'; as just noted, this suggests that the Polkelly line were the cadets. The lands themselves will be discussed elsewhere in this report, but it should be appreciated that the Polnekel or Polkelly lands lay to the N of Rowallan; it marched on its northern edge with Glenouther or Macharnock Moor, which largely lay in Stewarton and was an important asset of the Rowallan estate; control of Polkelly confirmed access from the Rowallan lands to the S up to this distant pasture ground.

Adam Mure of Rowallan (2)

Adam Mure 'of Rowalane' was witness to a charter in favour of Sir Gilbert Kennedy and his wife for the lands of Cassillis and others in Carrick on 2 November 1404 and dated at Dundonald (NAS GD25/1/27; for a confirmation of this charter in 1450 see *RMS* 1424–1513, 87, entry 378).This charter evidence illustrates the role of the Mures at this stage. Robert III, throughout the later years of his reign, spent much time in the Stewartry and Clyde area, using it as a base to bolster his power in relation to his brother, Albany, and his visit of 1404, in particular, was associated with a brief, final flourishing of his authority (Boardman 1996). It is reasonable to presume Sir Adam, as a kinsman who had directly benefited from Robert III's patronage, would be seen as a reliable backer. Though they held royal charters, they were required only to give suit at the head court of Cunningham, at Irvine. So, Sir Adam attended Robert III's court at various sites within the Stewartry, but, significantly, not further afield. The family were to remain essentially local gentry rather than national players – albeit occasionally their star would shine more brightly for a time.

Shadows and glimpses c 1409–c 1440

A Robert Mure of Rowallan (along with several other men, mainly from the SW) was granted a remission by the Regent Albany on 24 October 1409 for his part in the slaughter of Maurice Nielson of Dalrymple and others, burning their houses and other damage (NAS GD8/1). His placing within the family tree is uncertain. In 1417, half the price of the ward of the heir of Robert of Rowallan was remitted, indicating that by that time he was dead, but the heir is not named in the record (*ER* IV 1406–36, 286, 288).

There then follow several decades of uncertainty. Sir Archibald, said to have married Euphemia Kennedy of Dunnuir, is known only from the pages of the *Historie* which gives their son and successor as Robert. A Robert of Rowallan appears as a witness to a charter in January 1430 (Clark 1900, 2, 338); he would, thus, be Robert (2), but his relationship to earlier and later generations is not confirmed. The explanation may lie in a charter issued in 1440 (*RMS* II, 58, doc 253). It is a confirmation of the original charters of Robert III in favour of Adam Mure and Janet Danielstoun, but, whereas the former had provided for succession to the heirs male of their bodies, the confirmation provides also for descent to the heirs whosoever. That suggests a break in the line of direct male heirs– a break which the *Historie*, with its emphasis on the antiquity and continuity of the line, might have overlooked or glossed over.

Sir Robert Mure (3?) fl 1460–c 1500

A sasine granted to Robert Mure of Rowallan for his crown titles in 1460 probably marks the period of his accession (*ER* IX, 667). Sir Robert Mure of Rowallan lent 200 merks to Stephen Scott of Muirhouse secured on the lands of Dridane, Colmanside and Over Hardwood in the barony of Hawick in 1462 , The debt generated a great deal of dispute and only in 1508 did the Lords of Council find that it had been discharged and John Mure of Rowallan, 'oo and air' [grandson and heir] of the former Robert, then granted an exoneration (Fraser 1878, I, 28; II, 59, 75, 115, 121; NAS GD GD224/903/35). This Sir Robert cannot have been the 1430 Sir Robert as the later one can be shown to survive till c 1500 (below). He probably corresponds to the Robert 'not well regarded of his house', who wasted the estate and frequented the court in the minority of James IV. The *Historie* says that his wife was Marjory Newton, a daughter of the laird of Michaelhill in the Merse, 'ane druncken woman' (*Historie*, 72). However, in 1506, an agreement was registered between Mariot Neilson, widow of the late Robert

of Rowallan on the one side and John Mure and his spouse Margaret Boyd on the other (Bain and Rogers 1875, II, 138–9). If she did, indeed, come from the Merse, that might explain Sir Robert's interest in the Hawick lands, the most distant property in which the Mures seem to have had any interest.

Disputes about land, rents, teinds, and so on were certainly inescapable in the late 15th century, given the complexities of land ownership and the overlapping interests which people had in land. But Sir Robert does seem to have been involved in more than his fair share between 1476 and 1500. Most were clearly local and he had repeatedly to find caution not to harm people or was ordered to pay compensation to people whose goods he had wrongly taken, several times protesting that he had not been properly cited to the original hearing and so had not been properly represented. Another recurring charge was that he had wilfully or negligently failed to act properly when serving on assizes to serve heirs and other civil matters though others were also involved in these cases (*ADCC* 1 1839, 260, 285, 300; *ADCC* 2, 310, 377; *ADCC* 3, 112, 142; *ALA* 47, 88, 126, 174).

In 1496, James IV confirmed a charter by John Spark, to which Robert Mure of Rowallan had been one of the original witnesses at Kilbarchan on 17 September 1496 (*RMS* 1425–1513, 495, entry 2330). In the 1480s and up to 1499, Robert and his son John were jointly involved in several legal actions (*Acts of the Lords* 1839, 126; *Acts of the Lords* 1918, 174). This son and heir is presumably the John Mure of Rowallan who granted a feu charter of Lochrig in 1483 (Ayrshire Archives ATD41/2). According to the *Historie*, he married Elizabeth, daughter to the first Lord Evandale (*Historie*, 72–3). However, in an action in 1499 the heir apparent, also called John, was Robert's grandson (*Acts of the Lords* 1918, 310) and whilst there is some confusion about the date, it seems that the elder John died before his father who survived till c 1504.

An Adam Mure of Rowallan appears as procurator for Marion Mure (undes) in 1493 (*Acts of the Lords* 1839, 316). It is notable that, by the later 15th century, there were Mures of Polkelly and of Linflair and several other places, mainly in the SW, and they were related by marriage to other local families. That could lead to tensions, as with the Cunninghams of Cunninghamhead, but it did provide a dense network of kin, likely to be useful in feuds and political struggles, whilst an extensive cousinage could provide a useful source of marriage partners (see, for example, *RMS* 1424–1513, entries 963n, 979, 1077, 1579, 1670, 1671, 3484, 3487, 3713).

John Mure suc c 1500, d 1513

As just explained, this John had been his grandfather's heir since the later 1490s and was already a mature man at the time of his succession. He had first appeared in legal disputes in the 1580s and in 1502, for example, Robert, John and John's wife Margaret Boyd were all pursued for damages by

William Campbell (*ADCC* 3, 112).

John's wife was the Mures' second family connection with Scots royalty. Her father, Archibald Boyd of Nariston, was a brother-in-law of Angus, who had been making a determined effort to return to political favour in the early 1490s. On a visit to Ayrshire in 1492 James IV made a grant in favour of Boyd and his wife (who was in fact called Christian Mure) and it was probably at this time that the king began his liaison with the daughter (Macdougall 1989, 98; *RMS* II, 2111). By the winter of 1494–5, however, she had been supplanted by the next mistress and one of James IV's first acts as he emerged from his minority to full majority was to arrange for her to be married to this John Mure of Rowallan, providing her with a generous annuity and with lands in Ayrshire (Macdougall 1989, 107). She had already born two of James IV's children: Alexander Stewart, who was created Archbishop of St Andrews in 1504–5 and who was Chancellor from 1510 until his death at Flodden in 1513, and Catherine Stewart, who married James Douglas, third Earl of Morton. [The first history of the Mures was probably written at the instigation of this Alexander Stewart.] Her background and her significance for the Douglas family is more fully given by Macdougall (1989, 98 and 100) and there can be no doubt that the marriage would bring considerable benefits to Mure too and was of major significance in the regional politics. In 1506, John Mure formally agreed to fulfil all the conditions of the marriage contract and the couple entered into various other legal agreements around that period (Bain and Rogers 1875, 271, 321, 350, 359).

Four sons of this marriage are named in the *Historie* (74): Mungo, Alexander, Patrick, and Adam, and also three daughters, meaning that Marion had a total of nine children, with those fathered by the king. Patrick Mure was appointed parish clerk of Kirkkennar in Wigtownshire on 29 April 1544 (*RSS* II, 110, doc 729).

John, 'ane very worthie man', died at the Battle of Flodden in 1513 (*Historie*, 79; NLS Ch 2042). His wife, Margaret Boyd, was still alive in 1526 when she was mentioned in a precept and charter for the 5 merk land of Blacklaw and others (*RSS* I, 519, doc 3431; NAS GD3/1/10/11).

Mungo Mure of Rowallan suc 1513, d 1547

John Mure was succeeded by his son, Mungo. A royal letter was written to compel those of his tenants not killed in the Battle of Flodden to pay him duties (NLS Ch 2042). Perhaps more valuably, the ward of the son and heir was given to Margaret Boyd herself, the mother of 'seven fatherless bairns, sons and daughters of tender age' so obviating the risks inherent in wardship by strangers (NLS Adv MS22.2.9 f 47 r–v; see also NLS MS3416, 3–5 and MS6138 (iii)). Further favour followed in 1517 with a confirmation by the governor, valid till the king reached his 'perfect age', in favour of Margaret Boyd, Lady Rowallan, of lands in Stewarton gifted to her by James IV (NLS Adv MS22.2.9 f 48r; see also NLS MS3416, 7–9 and Ch 6138 (iv).

In c 1525, Mungo married Isobel Campbell of Loudoun, whose family were hereditary sheriffs of Ayrshire. They had four sons (John, Archibald, Hugh, and Robert) and five daughters: 'the Lady Enterkine [wife of Cunningham of Enterkine], Lady Carnall, Lady Mochrum, Lady Baruchane and Lady Dreghorne' (*Historie*, 79–80).

The Arnot family had held the lands of Lochrig from the Mures since the mid 15th century (AA ATD41) In January 1524/5, Andrew Arnot of Lochrig protested before Mungo Mure, baron of Rowallan and Patrick Maxwell, the bailie, about the retention of certain documents with regard to the Arnot property of Ross Fenwick (AA ATD41/3). In 1533 Robert Arnot, son of Andrew, was granted sasine of the £5 lands of Lochrig in the lordship of Stewarton and Rowallan (AA ATD 41).

On 12 July 1526, Mungo was granted further lands by James V (NAS GD3/1/10/11). On 16 July 1526, a respite was issued to Cuthbert Cunningham, third Earl of Glencairn, (and many others including Mungo Mure of Rowallan) 'for thair tresonable art and part of the assegeing of the castell of Striveling in cumpany with Johne duke of Albany' (*RSS* I, 520-1, doc 3440).

In 1511, the lands of Polkelly and their associated rights in Macharnock Moor, the huge common grazings to the N of the original parish of Kilmarnock, passed to the lairds of Cunninghamhead by marriage. This precipitated a series of disputes with Rowallan which first surfaced in 1534 and which will be considered elsewhere in this report.

At Stirling, on 6 April 1536, Mungo was granted the wardship of the lands and annual rents of the deceased James Wallace of Crago (*RSS* II, 292, doc 1996). Mungo also held the lands of Kirkwood in ward. It was alleged, however, that he was negligent in serving the lawful heirs and his moveable goods were briefly escheat, being restored in 1540 (*RSS* II, 593, doc 3918). On 15 May 1545/46, a letter was made confirming his rights to 'the tour, fortalice, maner place, mylnis, multuris, annexis, connexis, partis, pendicles, tennentis' of Rowallan as were due to his father, John Mure (*RSS* III, 248, doc 1557). Like his father, Mungo died in battle, at Pinkie in 1547 (*Historie*, 81; Fergusson 1963, 40).

John Mure (1) suc 1547, d 1591

Like his father, John thus inherited the estate in troubled times and similarly benefited from royal favour to the families of the dead when royal letters gave him the right to the non-entries and some other duties from lands of some local survivors including Crawfordland (NLS Adv MS22.2.9 f 49r–v; see also NLS MS 3416,14–16; Adv MS4.1.7 (29)). He may already have been married to Marion Cunningham, daughter of William Cunningham of Cunninghamhead, whose mother was a daughter of William, Earl of Glencairn (*RSS* III, 467, doc 2947). They had three sons: William, John of Cassencarrie, and Mungo; and possibly four daughters, Margaret, who married William Crichton of Libry, Elizabeth, who married David Blair of Adamton, and Jean, who married Adam Cunningham of Colynane and then John Wallace of

Dundonald; and finally a daughter who married the laird of Newark and secondly the laird of Lochnaw (Tough 1898, II, 317; Young 1993, 512).

On 28 February 1552–3, John Mure of Rowallan received a royal grant of the lands of Andrew Allanson, tailor in Hillhouse, who had forfeited them as a criminal and fugitive (*RSS* IV, 310, doc 1914). In 1582, William, the heir, entered into a contract with Alexander Mure of Ormisheuch to purchase from him the 5 merk lands of Ormisheuch with the manor of Ormisheuch. William's brother Mungo was a party to the deal as one of Ormisheuch's curators, a situation which gave him great authority (*RMS* 1580–93, 130, entry 423). As with his father, John too received the rents from lands which he held in ward. For example, on 7 February 1548–9, he was granted the 'ward and nonentres of the 7 merk land of auld extent of Glenmuke and Glaikcorne in the earldome of Carrick . . . since the deceis of Gilbert Kennedy of Balneclannochane' (*RSS* IV, 16–17, doc 105).

In 1551, the Earl of Arran, as Regent, signed a letter in his favour (NLS MS3813). In 1558, a letter from de Guise asked him to prepare himself and his supporters to defend Scotland from possible invasion and to be at Duns on 2 June with 20 days' victual (NLS MS22.2.9 f 52r; see also MS3416, 27–8 and Adv MS54.1.7(1)). He was a strong advocate of the Protestant cause and he and his wife had strong family connections with those in Ayrshire who supported reform (Sanderson 2003, 30). He was among the lords of Congregation chosen by John Willock to witness his debate with abbot Quintin Kennedy of Crossraguel at Ayr in 1559 (Sanderson 1997, 94). In March 1559, a letter directed to 'our loving brother in the Lord' had enjoined him to support efforts to expel the French and set up 'the true worship of God and his religion' so as to show that he was 'well minded to our native country' (NLS MS22.2.9; see also MS3416, 29–30; Adv MS54.1.7(3); this was characteristic of the rhetoric of the reformers at this time, presenting the issue in patriotic and nationalist as well as in religious terms (Ritchie 2002).

Mure was present at the Reformation Parliament in 1560 and, in 1562, signed the bond made in Ayr in support of the reformed Church (Young 1993, 511). However, John was an adherent to the Marian cause and signed the bond for the defence of the queen (the Bond of Mary's Adherents) in 1565 along with other neighbouring N Ayrshire lairds such as Boghall, Kilbirnie and Ladyland and three other Mures (*CSP Scot* II, 403, doc 650). He and his wife's kinsman Cunningham of Cunninghamhead were at Langside to support Mary though Glencairn, head of the Ayrshire Cunninghams, who supported Moray and Boyd, with whom Mure was at feud, was on the Marian side (Donaldson 1983, 103). Donaldson recognises that this fairly solid support of Ayrshire protestants for the queen cut across both long-standing kin loyalties and more recent religious lines though it is not clear why this was so.

Like many of his neighbours, Mure supported Mary against Moray during the Chaseabout Raid of August and September 1565 (Donaldson 1983, 71–5). A letter from

Lennox, dated 2 October 1565, asked 'our traist friend' the laird of Rowallan to be at Lanark to support Mary and Darnley, though it is not clear if he responded (NLS MS22.2.9, f 52v; see also MS3416, 31 and Adv MS54.1.7(5)) and there are several similar letters, assuming that he can turn out a military force with supplies, equipment, tents and so on; that is the context in which he was listed in an English report of 1563–6 as amongst the Ayrshire lairds able to raise 'men fote and horse at a sudden or to bring at arme Royall'(Armstrong 1884, 25).

Like many other Protestants, Mure supported the murder of Riccio as a religious act (Donaldson 1983, 79). And, following her escape from Lochleven in May 1568, Mary wrote regularly to Mure. The letters, fascinating though they are for Mary's use of persuasion and threat and her skilful use of a rhetoric of loyalty to her cause, throw very little light on the motives or detailed thinking of the recipient; they show that he was known to be able to put men in the field to fight for the cause, but little else about his house or household. The first dated 6 May 1568 from Hamilton, directed to her 'traist friend' assumes he already knows of her escape from 'the maist straitest prisoun' and asks him to join her on the 8th; he was amongst those who did, indeed, support her at the subsequent Battle of Langside (NLS MS22.2.9 f 53r; Donaldson 1983, 103). After Mary's flight to England, there follows a series of letters, doubtless similar to others written to other supporters, exhorting him to loyalty and encouraging support, promising favour when she is finally victorious. On 18 May 1569, after promising further news soon in the form of a personal message via Lord Boyd, she tells him that Elizabeth has already written to Moray warning him against persecuting those faithful to Mary. She asks for his continued obedience regardless of the bragging of her enemies. She assures him that his constancy will redound to his credit. But, she warns him that if he fails, he risks being 'left in pain of baith the sides' (NLS MS22.2.9 f 56r). Shortly after this he may have begun to waver and the last of Mary's letters, dated 13 March 1570, assures him that he is one of those she trusts and asks him to support Grange, the captain of Edinburgh Castle (NLS MS22.2.9 f 57r). In July that year, Lennox wrote, reminding him of the costs of the lack of an effective government and of the danger to the 'innocent life' of the king from those who were still in arms against him (NLS MS22.2.9 f 56v–57r). These were two powerful persuasives, rhetorical flourishes to be compared with the flag-waving of 1559. By 1571 Mar as Regent was trying to mediate between Mure and lord Boyd in a local dispute and in September 1572 was disappointed that Mure had not attended a meeting for pacification (NLS MS22.2.9 f 57r–v). The later letters in this series are essentially about local or family matters and make no further reference to Mure's support for the parties either of queen or king; by default, he had accepted the new *status quo*, though it is, surely, significant, that this series of letters were kept amongst the family papers when so much else seems to have been discarded (NLS MS 22.2.9 f 58v-59r).

John Mure was embroiled in the feuds which were prevalent throughout Ayrshire in the 16th and early 17th centuries. On 6 May 1572, the Privy Council considered the allegations that John Mure and Lord Boyd had broken assurances given to the council as regards their feud (*RPC* II, 133–4). On 2 September 1580, John Mure of Rowallan was witness in Glasgow to a charter by James, Archbishop of Glasgow, in favour of Robert, Lord Boyd and his spouse (*RMS* 1580–93, 155, entry 509). Andrew Arnot of Lochrig was served heir of Robert his father in various lands including use of the 'common muir of Rowallan' in 1574 (*Retours*, Special Services, Ayrshire, 3, entry 713).

He made a testament on 7 April 1591 and died on the 13th of that month at Rowallan. His wife survived him. The document mentions William as his heir and a younger son, Mungo, still a minor at his father's death, the mother having his income until his majority. The testament shows that he had considerable agricultural wealth, but provides no useful information about the house or contents beyond a conventional valuation of insight, plenishing, domiciles, etc, of £100 (NAS CC8/8/23/210 ff). According to the *Historie* 'he leuit graciouslie and deit in peice anno: 1581: of age 66' (*Historie*, 83; Tough 1898, II, 255).

William Mure (1) suc 1591; d? 1616

According to the Family History, this William married Janet Maxwell of Newark, in c 1575. They had five children, two sons: William and John of Blacklaw 'who was slaine at a Combat at beith' and three daughters: Margaret, 'the lady Caldwell'; Marion, who married Nigel Montgomery younger of Langshaw (NAS GD25/1/1024); and Isobel, 'the lady Skeldone Campbell' (*Historie*, 85–6; Tough 1898, II, 256, 318).

William Mure of Rowallan had been chancellor of an assize 25 April 1593 regarding lands in Kyle-Stewart now granted to George Ross on non-entry for 52 years (*RMS* 1580–93, 812, entry 2341n).

In 1605, William senior entered a marriage bond with Lady Elizabeth McGill, lady of Culzean. According to the terms of the contract which was dated 4 April and 15 May 1605, Lady Culzean was granted a life-rent from the estate of Rowallan (*RMS* VII, 529, doc 1456). This marriage did take place, the charter was confirmed on 20 June 1616 (*RMS* VII, entry 1456) and Elizabeth McGill is described as Lady Rowallan senior, spouse of William senior, on 9 October that year, when her rights in Dalmusternock and Tannahill were still reserved (*RMS* VII, 554, entry 1534). William junior was already heir apparent in 1605 and by 1616 there were at least three generations alive, William senior, his son William junior and his son William, heir apparent, who was already married to Anna Dundas – indeed, the next William may have gladdened his great-grandfather's dying days. In 1605, William senior and Elizabeth McGill were to have Dalmasternock with the mansion, but in 1616 this went to William, heir apparent and his wife; probably, even by 1605, the main mansion, the fortalice of Rowallan, was occupied by William junior and his wife.

On 16 July 1607, James VI confirmed a charter of Nigel Montgomery younger of Langshaw in favour of his wife Marion Mure in accordance with the terms of their marriage contract which was dated at Rowallan on 29 May and 27 June 1607. In accordance with the terms of the contract, he gave to William Mure of Rowallan, her (Marion's) heir and assignee: the 5 merk land of Over and Nether Pacokbankis, 10 merk land of Fulwodis, Gabrochillis and Over and Nether Auchintiberis, the 20s land of Quhyteleyis, the 24s land of Boirdland et Strthur and of the mill of Pacokbank (*RMS* V, 708, doc 1948).

A month before the marriage contract, and evidently as a precursor to it, William Mure of Rowallan was served as heir of Robert of Rowallan, his 'attavi'; the word means 'great, great, great grandfather but can also be used simply to mean 'ancestor'. As the last recorded Robert was a century before there may even have been some uncertainty at the time (*Retours*, General Services, entry 309, 16 June 1607). This was not the first time William had been served heir; in 1591 he had been served heir to John, his father and also to the late Robert, of Rowallan, 'proano avi sui' who died vested and seized in the lands and barony of Rowallan with tower, fortalice, houses, buildings, garden, mills, multures, fishings, tenements, tenandries and others lying in the bailliery of Cunningham, the lands of Jagresoun and half Spittelhauch with pertinents, in the regality of Dalkeith and the lands of Commonsyde, Dridane and Onerharwode, with the pertinents, in the barony of Hawick, though those Dalkeith and Hawick lands had reverted to the Scotts a century or more before (GD224/903/35; Fraser 1878, I, 28; II, 59, 75, 115, 121).

Like his father, William was involved in the Ayrshire feuds. In 1589, the Privy Council registered a bond of caution in which William stood as surety against any harm to William Cunninghame of Caprintoun (*RPC* IV, 444). In 1592, William Sinclair, burgess of Edinburgh and Marion Cunningham, Lady Rowallan, now his spouse, borrowed £2600 from their 'friend' Alexander Hunter, burgess of Edinburgh, the contract signed at Dykehead of Cunningham on 16 November (RD1/43 f 183r). However, by the following year, Marion Cunningham, Lady Rowallan had remarried, this time to Alexander Hunter and the marriage precipitated a major dispute with the Rowallan family. In September 1593, James VI himself wrote to William Mure of Rowallan, noting the many complaints made to him about Mure's 'extraordinary and unnatural behaviour towards the Lady Rowallan your mother and [our] servitor William Hunter her husband who not only you violently stay and trouble in the peaceable shearing and intromission with the corns and duties belonging her living and conjunct fee and in the disposition and using thereof but stay their tenants, payment of rents etc'. This, said the king, was in spite of previous admonitions and was astonishing in a baron of the country, contrary to natural justice; he should amend or 'we shall provide sic remeid as sall not stand with your contentment' (NLS MSS f 60r James VI to William Mure of Rowallan, dated Stirling

12 September 1593). Mure had to find security of 2000 merks not to harm his mother and her new spouse (*RPC* V, 601) and over a year later, in January 1594, the king instructed Lord Boyd to 'do diligence' against the laird of Rowallan for molesting William Hunter, the king's servant (NAS GD8/288, royal letter to Lord Boyd, 9 January 1594).

This dispute was probably related to ongoing disagreements with Cunningham of Craigans or Craigends, tutor of Cunninghamhead, about use of Macharnock or Glenouther Moor (*RPC* V, 631 and Chapter 5). William is recorded in the *Historie* as having died in 1616, aged 69 (Tough 1898, II, 256).

Sir William Mure (2) (usually known as younger) suc 1616; d 1641

William Mure, the younger, was married three times. His first marriage was to Elizabeth Montgomery, daughter of the laird of Hazelhead, Aberdeen. His wife's mother was a daughter of Lord Sempill.

On 24 January 1593/4, James VI confirmed a charter by William Mure of Rowallan regarding the fulfilment of the contract of marriage between his son and heir William Mure on the one part and Hugh Montgomery of Hazelhead and Elizabeth Montgomery his daughter on the other. The marriage contract had been agreed at Hazelhead on 23 September 1592. According to the terms of the contract, Elizabeth was to receive a life-rent from various parts of the barony of Rowallan. (*RMS* V, 16, doc 48).

His second marriage, in c 1605, was to Jean Porterfield, daughter of William of Dochall and widow of Alexander Cunninghame of Waterstoun (Tough 1898, II, 318). They had a son; Alexander of Little Sessnock. Jean Porterfield died in June or July 1612 and her testaments provide some useful information about furniture and fabrics at Rowallan at that time which is discussed elsewhere (NAS CC9/7/8, 497–8; NAS CC9/7/8, 520–3).

He was served heir of William, his father, in the lands of Grange, Tounhead of Kilmarnock, Monkland, Skireland, and others, with an annual rent from Fynnickhill in May 1620 and he was served heir in general to Kentigern [ie Mungo], his 'proavi', to Robert 'attavi patris' and John, 'avi' in 1630 (*Retours*, I, Ayrshire, entry 192; *Retours*, General Services, entries 1685, 1686, 1687, 3 June 1630). Sasine for Grange, Tounhead, Monkland and Skireland was given in terms of the service on 17 October 1620 and the signing of the precept on 16 October by Sir William's son Alexander (MacLeod 1895, 260–70).

In c 1622, he was married a third time, to Sarah Brisbane of Bishopton (*RMS* VIII, 480 doc 1419) who survived him (NAS CC9/7/28/798). Of their many children only three daughters lived to marry: Margaret, Lady Burruchan, Marie, who married Lord Blantyre, and secondly the laird of Melgume in Angus, and Jean, who married Sir John Shaw of Greenock. The three had been served his heirs portioners in 1644 (*Retours*, General Services, entries 2987, 2988, 2989).

He had made his testament in Glasgow on 21 February 1637, emphasising that he was in good health at the time. He nominated his spouse, Dame Sarah Brisbane, as sole executor to Marie and Jean Mure, their daughters, but, if she were to die or to remarry before her tutory of them ended, he nominated John Brisbane of Bishopton and Mathew Brisbane as tutors testamentary to the children (NAS CC9/7/28/798–804). The implication is that he had already made settlements on his other children.

William also was drawn into the ongoing local feuds. In the Register of the Privy Council the following surety is found:

> *Caution in £1000 by Robert Montgomerie of Skelmorlie, as principal, and Robert Lindsay of Balhall (Balhalur), as surety for him, that he will not harm Williame Mure, younger of Rowallane, his tenants or servants*
> (*RPC* IV, 447).

According to the *Historie*, Sir William delighted much in hawking and hunting. His will and testament recorded his death as February 1641 and confirms that he had several horses, some markedly expensive and one described as a hunter (NAS CC9/7/28 f 395v–398v). At the time of his decease he was creditor to £4757 10s.

Sir William Mure (3) suc 1641; d 1657

Sir William married Anna Dundas, daughter to the John Dundas of Newliston in 1615 (*RMS* VII, 554, doc 1534; Tough 1898, II, 318) and they established their home at Dalmusternock (NS 4556 4168), 2.5km E of Rowallan. The arms of Sir William and his wife are above the doorway there, along with the date of the marriage, 1615, and the now eroded initials A D (Tough 1898, xii). The significance of Dalmusternock for a family with three adult generations alive is considered elsewhere in this report. The fulfilment of the terms of the marriage contract was a key issue of the letter will of Sir William in 1616 (NAS CC9/7/14, 207). Sir William and his wife had the following sons: William, Captain Alexander, who died fighting in Ireland, Major Robert, John of Finnickhill, and Patrick. They also had six daughters, of whom only one, Elizabeth, survived; she married Walter Knox of Ranferly. Robert Mure, second son of Sir William, recorded as beneficiary of an assignation of appraised lands in 1653 is presumably the Major Robert just mentioned (*RMS* X, 94).

Sir William's second marriage was to Jean, daughter of Archibald Hamilton of Duntreath (Young 1993, 512). Jean Hamilton died in October 1665, leaving a legacy to one of her Duntreath relatives and 200 merks to Mathew Ramsay, minister of Kilpatrick ' for the love and respect I bear to him as pastor and minister' and appointing Hew, Janet and Marion Mure, her children by Sir William, as her executors. Her death occurred in Kilpatrick parish where she seems to have been resident for some time, rather than with her stepson at Rowallan, and though she was drawing some income from the estate rentals, she also seems to have had income from her own family lands (NAS CC9/7/35/65 ff).

William was very active in public life. He was a Justice of the Peace for Cunningham in 1634, a Commissioner to the Convention of Estates 1643–4, a Commissioner for the Loan and Tax in 1643 and on the Committee for War 1643–9 (Young 1993, 512). He was created a Colonel of Horse in 1643 and was with the Scottish army in England in 1644 and saw action at Newcastle (*Historie*, 94; Paterson 1852; Young 1993, 512). He was wounded at the battle of Marston Moor on 2 July 1644, where he received 'a sore blow at battle upon my back with the butt of a musket' (Tough 1898, xvii). In 1649, he was a Commissioner for visiting Glasgow University and for the valuation of Ayrshire.

William was also active in the arts. He had a considerable reputation as a poet and contributed to *The Muses' Welcome*, a volume addressed to the king on his visit to Scotland in 1617. He wrote *Dido and Aeneas*; a translation (1628) of Boyd of Trochrig's Latin *Hecatombe Christiana*; *The True Crucifixe for True Catholikes* (1629), besides much miscellaneous verse and many sonnets. Other works included a metrical version of the psalms. In later years he lamented that in his youth 'Love's false delight and beautees blazing beame/ Too long benighted haue my dazzled eyes' and his poems became more concerned with the spiritual including 'The Cry of Blood and of a Broken Covenant' of 1650 (Tough 1898, xiii). William also excelled in music. He was the author of several songs and compiled anthologies of music for performance at the castle. These are the earliest surviving Scottish collections of music for both song and lute, notably the famous 'Rowallan Lute Book' of c 1620 preserved in Edinburgh University (MS Laing III, 487). He was said to have 'lived Religiouslie' and that he 'died Christianlie' in 1657 at the age of 63 years (*Historie*, 90).

Sir William Mure (4) suc 1658; c 1616–86

William Mure was born c 1616. Sir William was served heir of his father, Sir William, in 1658 in the lands and barony of Rowallan, extending to a 100 merk land of old extent or 400 merks of new extent, in parts of Grange, Tounhead, of Kilmarnock, Monkland and Skireland of 19 merks old extent and £76 of new extent (*Retours* I, Ayrshire Special Services, entry 500). He married Elizabeth Hamilton, daughter of James Hamilton of Aikenhead, Provost of Glasgow. They had three children: William, Jean, who married James Campbell of Treesbank, and John.

It is interesting that his siblings defined themselves by their relationship to him. Patrick Mure, 'brother to the laird of Rowallan', witnessed the testament of the dying John Lyning, servant to the laird, at Rowallan on 26 October 1661 and the testament names several other of the domestic and garden servants as witnesses and beneficiaries (NAS CC9/7/32/505 ff). Patrick Mure, 'brother german to the laird of Rowallan', collected a debt for his 'loving cousin' William of Rowallan in January 1662 (NAS GD406/1/9694). Hew Mure, merchant, burgess of Edinburgh and 'brother german of the laird of Rowallan', appears regularly in the Register of Deeds until his death in 1677 (NAS CC8/8/75/698–700).

This Sir William was strong in his support of his Presbyterian beliefs. He was appointed to enforce the Parliamentary Act *Against Profaneness* of 1672 (Howie 1870, 320–35; NLS Laing MS). He was a strong supporter of William Guthrie, who believed in an uncompromising form of Presbyterianism and who became the first minister of the newly formed parish of Fenwick in 1644 (*Fasti* III, 93). Sir William was imprisoned in Stirling Castle in 1655, but, following a petition, was released in the following year. In 1683, he was arrested again, together with his eldest son, whilst in London, and taken to Edinburgh where they were imprisoned in the Tolbooth. Both were released in April 1684 (Paterson 1852, 2, 193).

Sir William Mure (5) suc 1686; d 1700

Sir William was served heir to his father on 2 March 1686. He married Mary Scott, heiress of Collarny in Fife, around 1667 (RD2/49, 476).They had three daughters: Anna, born July 1671, Margaret, born July 1672, and Jean, born April 1678. He must be the William Mure of Rowallan admitted burgess and guildbrother of Edinburgh, gratis on 16 March 1692 (Watson 1929, 366). He was a Commissioner to Parliament 1690–8 (Young 1993, 512). William died c 1700.

Dame Jean Mure of Rowallan c 1656–1724

Jean was the only surviving heir of Sir William Mure. She married firstly William Fairlie of Bruntsfield, and, secondly, David Boyle of Kelburn, first Earl of Glasgow. They had three daughters: Lady Bettie, who died in infancy, Lady Jean, and Lady Anne, who died unmarried. Jean Mure, Countess of Glasgow, died 3 September 1724 and Jean, her eldest daughter of the second marriage, succeeded by special dispensation to the family property (M'Naught 1912, 378).

Lady Jean Boyle Mure of Rowallan 1703–30

Jean Mure succeeded to the family estates of Rowallan. She married Sir James Campbell of Lawyers, Perthshire, the third son of James, second Earl of Loudoun, at Canongate Kirk, Edinburgh, on 17 February 1720. He was killed at the Battle of Fontenoy, 30 April 1745. They had a daughter, Margaret, and a son James.

James Mure Campbell d 1786

James Mure Campbell was born 11 February 1726. He assumed the name of Mure on succeeding to the estate of Rowallan. He was elected a Member for Parliament for the county of Ayr in 1754. He married Flora, eldest daughter of John MacLeod, of Raasay on 30 April 1777. Flora MacLeod had met Samuel Johnston on his visit to Raasay in 1773 and the latter described her in a letter of that year as 'the beauty of this part of the world, and has been polished in Edinburgh' (Houghton Library Harvard, MS Hyde 1/93). Flora died in 1780 whilst giving birth to her daughter, who was also named Flora. James Mure Campbell succeeded his cousin John, fourth Earl of Loudoun, on 27 April 1782. He died in 1786 (M'Naught 1912, 378).

Flora Mure Campbell 1780–1840

Flora Mure Campbell, Countess of Loudoun, Baroness Mauchline, Lady Hastings was born in August 1780 (Illus 61). She succeeded to her father's estate at the age of six years and was raised by the Earl and Countess of Dumfries, with whom she lived until 1803 (Paul 1904, V, 511–12). On 12 July 1804, she married Francis Rawdon-Hastings, Earl of Moira (and subsequently Marquis of Hastings). Rawdon-Hastings had a distinguished career both in the army and in administration, eventually becoming Governor-General of India 1813–23. They had five children: Lady Flora Elizabeth (1806–39), George Augustus Francis, Lady Sophia Frederica Christina, Lady Selina Constantia, Adelaide Augusta Lavinia. He died at Malta on 28 November 1826, leaving a request that his right hand should be cut off and preserved until the death of his wife and then be interred in her coffin. Flora Mure Campbell died on 8 January 1840.

For much of the 19th century Rowallan Castle lay underused and deteriorating since the family lived primarily at Loudoun Castle. The estate remained in the possession of the earls of Loudoun until it was sold to the Corbett family in the 20th century.

61 Portrait of Lady Flora Hastings (*East Ayrshire Council www.futuremuseum.co.uk*)

THE CORBETTS OF ROWALLAN

Archibald Cameron Corbett 1856–1933

Archibald Cameron Corbett was born in 1856 in Glasgow. He worked for a time as a doctor in the Gorbals, Glasgow, but much of his wealth came from property development, especially in Ilford, Eltham and Lewisham. In 1887, he married Mary, daughter of John Polson, a highly successful cornflour manufacturer. Corbett remained a Glaswegian at heart, was Member of Parliament for Tradeston, Glasgow 1885–1911, and benefited the city by his philanthropic works. He is particularly remembered for his donation of the extensive Rouken Glen Park to the City of Glasgow in 1906. In 1901, he bought the castle and estate of Rowallan from Lord Donnington of Loudoun (Rowallan 1976, xi, 26). On acquiring the estate, he commissioned Robert Lorimer to design a new mansion close to the old castle. Cameron Corbett was created Baron Rowallan in 1911, following his retirement from the House of Commons.

Thomas Godfrey Polson Corbett 1895–1977

Thomas Godfrey Polson Corbett, second Baron Rowallan, was born in 1895 and, in 1918, married Gwen Mervyn Grimond, sister of Jo Grimond, later leader of the Liberal party. Prominent in the Scout movement, he was appointed Chief Scout of the Commonwealth and Empire in 1945. He was Governor of Tasmania from 1959 to 1963.

Arthur Cameron Corbett 1919–93

Born 17 December 1919, he succeeded his father in 1977 to become the third Baron Rowallan. On his death in 1993 he was succeeded by his son John Polson Cameron Corbett who is currently the fourth Baron.

Rowallan estate was sold in 1989.

7 THE HOUSE AND LANDSCAPE OF ROWALLAN

John Harrison

Documentary evidence for the 'House' of Rowallan

The earliest structures at Rowallan are thought to be 15th-century but a Comyn charter of uncertain 14th-century date required the vassal to pay his silver penny 'at the manor place of Rowallan' yearly (EACMAS, Cessnock Papers, bundle 29). No other documentary evidence for structure prior to the 15th century has been found except the unsupported claim in the *Historie* that Gilchrist Mure 'biggit ye auld tour of Rowallane, and put his armes yair' (*Historie*, 35). Gilchrist, if he existed, lived in the late 13th century; even if he did not, there is no reason to question that some ancient structure did exist at the time this account was written which had the family arms upon it.

A record which might hint at a foundation date is a charter granted by John Mure of Rowallan to his 'cousin' (*consanquiniis*) Edward Arnot and his spouse for the lands of Ross Finnick [Fenwick] in 1453 for a pair of white gloves to be rendered at the chapel of St Laurence at Rowallan at Whitsun (AA ATD41/2). It might reasonably be expected that the chapel was amongst the earliest parts of the building and to have been erected at a period when dedications to St Laurence were in fashion.

Records become more complete (and the *Historie* presumably becomes more reliable) from the 16th century onwards. Mungo Mure (suc 1513; d 1541) is said to 'bigged the hall from the ground and compleated it in his owne time' (Tough 1898, II, 255). Similarly, the family tree of 1597 commented that 'this moungv muire raisit the hall upone four vouttis [vaults] and laiche trance and compleitit the samen in his avin tyme' (Tough 1898, II, 317). Following Mungo's death, the gift of the non-entries refers to the tower, fortalice, manor place, mills, multures, etc (NLS Adv MS22.2.9 ff 50v–51r; see also *ER* XVIII, 433 for tower, fortalice, mills, etc, in 1549). In 1553, the estate of Rowallan was described as including 'touris, fortalices, maner places, mylnis, multuris, fischingis, woddis, parkis' (*RSS* IV, 443, doc 2583).

In 1568, the (King's) Privy Council tried to move against supporters of the queen who 'resort with their houses', ordering them to 'divest themselves of their servants within their houses' within six hours of being charged. The properties are variously described from 'the castle, tower and fortalice of Kilmarnock' to 'the house of Ladyland'. Rowallan is described as 'tower and fortalice' as are ten of the twenty properties and since those described as 'castles'

include such strengths as Doune as well as Kilmarnock, it seems that the list is making real distinctions (*RPC* I, 625–6). In 1592, the baillie of Cunningham was to answer for the sasine due for the tower, fortalice, houses, buildings, gardens ... woods etc of Rowallan (*ER* XII, 463).

This first use of the words 'houses, buildings and gardens' increasingly suggests that real changes on the ground are reflected in these formal documents since the *Historie* relates that during the later 16th century John Mure had built the forework (fore work) backwark and woman house 'frome the ground' (Tough 1898, II, 255) as well as expanding the designed landscape since he 'plaintit the oirchyarde and gardein, sett the uppir banck and nethir bank the birk yaird befoir the yett [gate]' (*Historie*, 83; Tough 1898, II, 318). In this case the *Historie's* claims are supported by the presence of the initials of John Mure and his wife, Marion Cunninghame on a tablet on the fore work reading JON. MVR. M. CVGM. SPVSIS. 1562. That said, a charter of 1616 refers only to the 'fortalice' (without mention of the manor, houses, etc), the fortalice to be the principal messuage of the barony (*RMS* VII, 554, entry 1534).

Two building phases have been identified as 17th-century. Sir William who inherited in 1616 'builded the new wark in the north syde of the close, & the batlement of the back wall, & reformed the whole house exceedingly' (Tough 1898, II, 256). His son (also William), who inherited in 1658, undertook the last known phase of major construction work and the gateway leading to the outer courtyard to the NE of the castle is dated 1661. It is probably not coincidence that these two phases correspond to the introduction of liming of the Rowallan farms and consequent higher productivity as discussed below; there may be a connection, too, with urban expansion and increased markets for cheese, one of the main local products. Confirmation of such a connection would require work on rents, markets and other economic factors, ideally linked to wider studies of the economy of Cunningham and the building programmes of other comparable lairds. The only later work identified is the 'screens passage' with fluted pilasters with Ionic capitals and a doorway with lugged architraves, which may be ascribed to the late 17th or early 18th century.

The change in the wording of the formal legal documents noted above may well be at the prompting of fashion-conscious proprietors since they are not reflected in liability for increased payments. McKean, particularly, sees Rowallan as exemplifying a widespread elaboration of both buildings and grounds of the mid 16th century (McKean 2004, 168). MacKechnie (2005, 307–9) notes that this architectural and horticultural flourishing had a basis in comparative peace and prosperity. In the context of Rowallan, this can be related to the known intellectual and other interests of the proprietors, whether commissioning a family tree, writing a *Historie* of their own house, writing poetry, composing music, and so on. Architecturally, that is seen in such features as the long gallery (Illus 40) in the E range, a place of recreation and a vantage point overlooking the gardens, the extensive park and landscape. Its position, occupying the whole upper part of a wing of the house, is typical of that found in great mansions of the late 16th and 17th century (Howard 1987, 116).

Rowallan had never, of course, been primarily a military or even a defensive building and the instructions of the Privy Council that if the laird had fled the country then the forces in the W should be garrisoned there in April 1678 does not change that, reflecting persecution of a prominent Presbyterian dissident rather than any truly military use (*RPC* III, 1676–8, 416).

The Hearth Tax return (NAS E69/2/3) gives an ambiguous snapshot of the situation in the early 1690s. 'Rowallan's House' in Kilmarnock parish had 22 hearths, but the laird of Rowallan was also liable for a further eight hearths at Dalmusternock House and office houses in Fenwick parish. Hearth Tax entries are notoriously variable in form and the 22 hearths at 'Rowallan' could include kilns, hearths in associated buildings, etc, as well as domestic hearths in the main house, or even hearths in subsidiary buildings associated with the main house.

The house continued to be occupied, at least intermittently and partially, by the family until the later 18th century, but it was often a second home for the Campbells and Mure Campbells whose major residences were elsewhere.

Rooms and Contents to c 1700

All testaments which could be located have been examined, though most give only general and agricultural information. Jean Porterfield, spouse of Sir William, died in 1612 and the beneficiary was to be Alexander, her and Sir William's son. The first testament (NAS CC9/7/8, 497–8) estimated the utensils, household items and clothes at only £133 6s 8d. However, there is a later and more detailed listing of her goods in a testament of 7 April 1614:

> *Two silk gowns one plain silk and the other figured taffeta together £100*
>
> *A velvet cloak, furred with 'plashe' and the laps lined with satin £80*
>
> *A velvet doublet with a skirt £40*
>
> *An old doublet and skirk £4*
>
> *A cloak of burrel [coarse (perhaps red)] cloth £8*

> *A riding cloak of 'velvet hewit' cloth £10*
>
> *A doublet and skirt of black Spanish taffeta £3*
>
> *An old brown gown and two old gowns of bombasie £10*
>
> *Two Scots scarlet wyliecoats [petticoats] £14*
>
> *Five quarters of taffeta £6*
>
> *Two hoods with their 'crappis' £8*
>
> *Two old taffetas £8*
>
> *Two pair of old plaids £10*
>
> *A riding skirt of violet hewit cloth £3*
>
> *Two old furnished women's saddles £10*
>
> *Five ells of Scots scarlet cloth £10*
>
> *Six ells of mixed hewit cloth £9*
>
> *Four ells and a half of gray cloth £4*
>
> *Eight ells of [damaged] litting cloth £8 [litting is dyeing].*
>
> *Four feather beds and four bolsters £33 6s 8d*
>
> *Nine cods [pillows] £3*
>
> *Five pair small linen sheets £13 6s 8d*
>
> *13 pairs of round sheets £20 [round here is 'made from thick thread, coarse in texture' so these were not 'circular' sheets!]*
>
> *Two pairs of 'waltit' blankets £5 [Walt and welt are strips of reinforcement or decoration applied to a garment or fabric and walting is the associated action (DSL)*
>
> *Three pair of plaiding blankets £4*
>
> *41 ells of plaiding to be blankets £13 6s 8d*
>
> *An old Ireland mat 30s*
>
> *Four sewn coverings unlined £13 6s 8d*
>
> *Five coverings of wool and five coverings of hair £9*
>
> *Nine small and eight round codwares [coarse pillowslips].*
>
> *Three pairs of old curtains £4*
>
> *12 ells of Scots red scarlet to be coverings £8*
>
> *Five pendicles 50s [probably a hanging ornament of some sort]*
>
> *Two linen board cloths £6 [in effect tablecloths]*
>
> *Five round board cloths £5 [see 'round' above]*
>
> *12 small linen serviettes and eleven round £5*
>
> *10 hardin serviettes 20s [hardin is a coarse linen]*
>
> *Two dozen round serviettes 48s*
>
> *Two bread cloths 20s*
>
> *Four round hardin towels 20s*
>
> *8 ells of round hardin 26s 8d*
>
> *9 sewn cushions £4*
>
> *Five 'spyndill' [of] hardin yarn £5 [a quantity of coarse linen yarn]*
>
> *19 hesps of bed yarn £3 [more loose yarn]*
>
> *Two hesps of 'trym' harn 6s*
>
> *Four brazen chandlarrs £4 [candle holders]*

20 plates and 23 trenchers 'by the heirship' estimated to 48lb weight at 6s 8d is £16 ['by the heirship' –in addition to the heirship goods, the best items which automatically went to the heir]

Five silver spoons £15

An iron pot 30s

Three pans £3

A long spit 6s 8d

A hanging cruik [for cooking pots] 20s

Two boits [containers] for ale 26s 8d

11 hogsheads and barrels £5

Seven kists £13

A salt burd 20s

Three chairs 30s

A gold ring set with a diamond £30

A ring set with a ruby £10

A neck chain of gold with a tablet of [?] £60

A 'chaddow' or orient pearl £10

Next entry damaged xxxx £4

Three kists £6

A 'burd' with two forms [a table and benches] £3

Two feather beds with two bolsters £12

Two coverings £6 13s 4d

30 sheep £50

A pot and a crook [cooking equipment] 40s

A mare and a filly £20

Linen sheets £8

Two stone of wool £10

Five hides £10

Two pair of [?] sheets £4

Two pair of blankets £3

Four linen board cloths and 18 codwares £6 [tablecloths and pillowslips].

Summa Inventar £828 14s

(NAS CC9/7/9/520 ff)

The quality of the clothes is evident and underscored by the jewellery and other luxury items. There are also, for example, a riding cloak and two furnished women's saddles and many other items of clothing. There are quantities of bedding – sheets, blankets, pillowcases – as is usual for such households and curtains, perhaps bed curtains rather than window curtains. There are 'board cloths' of fine and of coarse linen, serviettes and other tableware. There are cushions, 'four brazen chandlarrs' £4 [candle holders]. The 20 plates and trenchers were evidently of pewter as they are said to weigh 48lb and to be worth £16; there were evidently some better quality plates and trenchers, not listed as they were part of the heirship goods, the 'best of everything'

which went automatically to the heir. There were five silver spoons, an iron pot, some pans and other cooking utensils, three chairs, some kists, a trestle table and benches, two feather beds with coverings. There was also a considerable quantity of unmade cloth of various sorts, indicating that sewing and making up was an ongoing process within the household The diversity of qualities, of course, reflects the social range of the occupants of the house, from master and mistress down to the humblest servants, as well as goods for display and for utility.

When Sir William Mure died in 1641, his household goods and clothes apart from the heirship goods were valued at only £620 (NAS CC9/7/28/798 ff) – but the heirship was 'the best of everything' and it is likely, in any case, that much had already been assigned to his son and heir (a man then approaching 50 years of age); it is not even certain whether he was living at Rowallan or at Dalmusternock. A curiosity of this testament is that he owed 'fees' (ie wages) to a total of 19 'servants', of whom six were female, a huge number compared with the single figures more usually expected and this might reflect the political and religious tensions of the time. The men included Mr John Crawford, owed £66 13s 4d 'for the said year', and John Brisbane, owed £33 6s 8d, half as much but still a substantial sum assuming that they also had their 'bed and board'. These were all people who would require accommodation of some sort.

The importance of space for servants is again underlined by the testament of John Lyning, 'servitor to the laird of Rowallan', who died in October 1661 evidently after an illness. Apart from his clothes, his own goods included:

an iron pot, a fir kist, a meikle wainscot kist, 3 pair of sheets, a brass pan, two coverings, a pair of blankets, a crook, a tongs, a chandler, a bible, a chaff bed, a washing line, an ax, some plaiding and various small items including some papers in a codware (pillow slip), with some other small things and papers in a codwair, total £20.
(NAS CC9/7/32/505 ff)

He left the 'fir kist' to Jonet Gentle 'presently waiting on him', ie his nurse; the gardener and his family are also mentioned and another servant witnessed his letter will; his legacies will be mentioned again in relation to the religious ethos of the household. He was owed £143 on two bonds and was evidently a servant of some standing.

Gardens, Mains or Home Farm, Mill and Related Issues to c 1700

The designed landscape of Rowallan extends today over 205 acres (83 ha), including c 24 acres of parkland and 60 acres of woodland (*Land Use Consultants* 1988, 359). The layout is recognisable on Roy's map of 1747–55. The oldest known historic planting appears to be limited to the Bank Plantation, E of the present house, with specimens of lime and oak, some 300 years old. However, remains of the earlier gardens and parkland survive alongside later planting. The

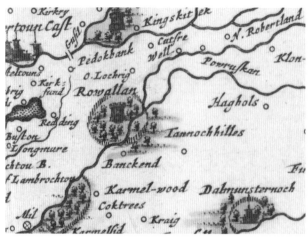

62 Detail from Blaeu's map of Cunninghame, published 1654 (*reproduced by permission of the Trustees of the National Library of Scotland*)

boundaries of earlier garden surround the castle itself, there are strong indications of the canalisation of the Carmel Water remain, and belts of woodland cut by later avenues may reflect the parkland shown in simplified form on Blaeu's map of 1654 (Illus 62). This suggests that the present layout is largely based on an extensive and complex plan dating at least from the 17th century.

As already noted, the 'garden ... woods', etc, are first mentioned in 1592 (*ER* XII, 463) and Sir John (d 1591) is said to have planted the 'orchyarde and gardein, sett the uppir banck and nethir bank the birk yaird befoir the yett [gate]' (*Historie*, 83; Tough 1898, II, 318). His testament (NAS CC8/8/23/210) makes no direct mention of the grounds, but it is significant that he had grains in the 'barn and barnyard' of Rowallan and had stock on several of the farms in the immediate vicinity such as Redding and Newhall which were probably farmed on his direct account, rather than rented to tenants. Similarly, in 1594, half the 5 merk land of Darsalloch with the meadow, the dominical lands of Newhall with the manor place, the 23s 4d land called Broomhill and the 5s land called The Kill, with the merk land on the E of the Ridding, were amongst the lands allocated to Elizabeth Montgomery, wife of William the younger; these lands all lie close about the castle and the 'dominical' lands would usually be in the direct control of the lord; they must correspond closely to the later Mains Farm (*RMS* VI, 16, entry 48). Jean Porterfield, who died in 1612, also had sown grains and farm stock, though their location is not specified (NAS CC9/7/8, 497–8). But Sir William, who died in 1616 (NAS CC9/7/14/199 ff), had 'four workhorses' on the Mains as well as grains in the 'barn and barnyard'. That he also had several coursers and other expensive riding horses implies suitable stabling and stables were often treated as fashionable landscape features. And though the charters, etc, had previously mentioned generic 'mills', Sir William's testament mentions specifically Rowallan Mill, potentially another landscape feature indicative of prosperity; mill leads, too, could be channeled to create 'water features' and even in very early times were often considerable civil engineering projects.

John Lyning, 'servitor to the laird of Rowallan', died in October 1661, leaving an iron pot, a brass pan and an andiron to Isobel Cochrane, spouse to James Stewart, gardener (NAS CC9/7/32/505 ff). But other data about the policies, planting, gardens, etc, is as sparse as for building work at this period, just one request for some seeds to be sent from Hamilton in the 1660s (NAS GD406/1/9694).

The House from c 1700

When James Mure Campbell was given sasine of the 100 merk land of the estate of Rowallan in 1733, it included the manor place, houses and buildings, gardens, mosses, moors, meadows, mills, multures and all the parts and pertinents, etc; very significantly, the tower and fortalice which formerly headed the list have now vanished, presumably as they were now ruinous or at least irrelevant (NAS RS3/144, 219–26), some 80 years after construction of the 'new' house. This James was killed at the Battle of Fontenoy in 1745; work then underway on the grounds is considered in another section. There was also some work being done on the house. This included £8 5s Scots for 140 feet of wainscot deals bought from Mr Craig in Irvine for mending the sarking of the house of Rowallan, 300 skalie (ie blue slates) which cost £5 2s. Two hundred and forty bolls of lime (this might be about 16 tonnes) were purchased and John Tamlison, 'sclater', was paid £72 for pointing the whole roofs and walls of the house of Rowallan, roughcasting outside and plastering inside and whitewashing the ceilings and walls of the low rooms (NAS GD237/98/1/37). There was some further carpenter and glazing work, a new timber and thatch roof was put on the girnel or grain store (presumably at the Mains) and the thatch of the stables was repaired, involving 13 days' work. The wording seems to imply fairly extensive work ('the whole house' and so on), but the sums involved are fairly modest as all are in pounds Scots, but the account runs only from 1744 to 1746 and work might have been begun earlier and continued later.

Between 1753 and 1759, Robert Ainslie appears in the Window Tax return with ten windows at Rowallan in Kilmarnock Parish (NAS E326/1/11). The return to Martinmas 1760 shows Mr Ainslie at Rowallan, still with ten windows, but Colonel Mure Campbell of Rowallan with 31 windows, dashing the assumption that Ainslie occupied the main house. Ainslie was assigned nine windows in 1762 and 1764 and in 1765 'the house that was Mr Ainslies' is assigned 11 windows, but appears to have been empty; it then vanishes from the record (NAS E325/1/12; NAS E325/1/13). Robert Ainslie had been factor or chamberlain on the estate since c 1745, made his testament at Rowallan on 18 July 1754 and died there in 1763, nominating his widow as his executor, but his testament provides no directly useful evidence about the house (NAS GD237/98/1/1 accounts of Rowallan estate 1744–7; NAS CC9/7/66, 5–7). Ainslie's house, though smaller than Rowallan Castle, was still substantial; its location is unclear, but it is tempting to assume that it was at the Mains of Rowallan.

Timperley (1976) indicates that though the Valuation Roll for Ayrshire is dated 1759, the revisions indicate a date nearer to 1780 and that it is incomplete. James Muir Campbell for Rowallan and Glenlieth Hall is the biggest proprietor in Kilmarnock parish (Timperley 1976, 55–6) with a total of £3174, but the two properties (Glenlieth and Rowallan) are not distinguishable and Glenlieth has not been located.

Colonel Mure Campbell of Rowallan continued to enjoy 31 windows until the Window Tax return up to 5 April 1782 (by which time he had become General Mure Campbell) and by the following year he had become the Earl of Loudoun, still with 31 windows. But from 1783 to 1786 the earl had only 13 windows at Rowallan (NAS E326/1/14; NAS E326/1/15). The earl died at Loudoun Castle on 28 April 1786 (Paul 1904, V, 511) and from 1787 to 1791 15 windows are attributed to the Countess of Loudoun at Rowallan (who was, in fact, a child).

From 1792 to 1795, Captain Cunningham had 18 windows at Rowallan and there are then two years with no return. But, in 1798, Captain Cunningham's name appears in the 'occupant' column with the figure 15 beside it and a letter W, but the house is recorded as not liable for tax and W probably stands for 'waste' (NAS E326/1/16). 1798 is the year of the last Window Tax return.

The Inhabited Houses Tax Records for Ayrshire are extant from 1778 to 1798. They show the promotion of the Colonel to General and to Earl, etc, the arrival of Captain Cunningham and, in 1797–8 the letter N and a blank in the 'liability' column (NAS E326/3/4).

The most likely explanation of the data is that the main house had been more or less unused for a time in the 1750s, James Mure Campbell having lost his mother when he was only four-years-old and his father (in 1745) when he was aged 19. Mure Campbell retired as MP for Ayrshire in 1761, was created Colonel and then moved to occupy the ancestral home at Rowallan, at least sometimes; his cousin, the then Earl of Loudoun, was still alive at that time with his main residence at Loudoun Castle. On 7 March 1777, John Balfour, bookseller, Edinburgh, wrote to James Ross that a marriage was expected between Colonel Muir Campbell and Miss MacLeod of Raasay on what he clearly thought were the slender grounds that he had danced with her at the Capillaire Ball (NAS GD44/42/176/14). His scepticism was doubtless bolstered by the fact that the gentleman was 51 and previously single. But the two were, indeed, married on 30 April 1777. The colonel might have reasoned that, as the heir of entail to the earldom of Loudoun, presently held by the fourth earl, a bachelor aged 72, his duty lay in marriage and producing a legitimate heir. The countess died at Hope Park, Edinburgh, following the birth of their only child, a daughter, in 1780. Following his cousin's death in 1782, the general inherited the title and Loudoun Castle would have become their main home. The earl died at Loudoun in 1786 and was succeeded by his daughter (Paul 1904, V, 511).

Presumably the reduction of the numbers of 'occupied' windows from 31 to 15 from 1784 follows the move to Loudoun; an obvious strategy in that situation would be to abandon a whole wing or floor. Later fluctuations up to 18 windows would correspond to parts of the house being 'shut up' or opened as demand increased or decreased. The inventory of 1787 was made following the earl's death and is discussed below. Although some rooms were furnished, there was no bedding or silver, for example; there was a cow for the nurse and mention of James Dunn's room amongst the total of 12 named rooms, several of which were actually servants' quarters, such as the butler's room. Of course, such houses could be reawakened when required and it is significant that there was still fruit and other garden produce worth selling in 1787. Probably Captain Cunningham rented it for a few years or perhaps had some administrative role on behalf of the family. But, from about 1798, it is very unlikely that the Mure Campbells or their successors occupied Rowallan Castle except very briefly and occasionally.

The only evidence for occupation of the house after 1797–8 is in the form of passing comments. Monteath, the King's Forester, in a survey of the Rowallan woodland in 1829, commented that it was 'most likely the present castle may never be repaired' (Monteath 1829, section vi). George Robertson commented in 1820 that 'it has not been inhabited for some time, and though still entire, is getting into decay' (Robertson 1820, 334). This sentiment was repeated in 1839 by the writer of the *New Statistical Account* (*NSA* V, 541), who related how the 'venerable mansion . . . is, under the unsparing hand of time, falling into decay'. Paterson, writing in 1852, referred to the castle as 'this mansion, deserted and in decay, save one or two apartments occupied by the baron baillie' (Paterson 1852, 169). Similarly, the *Ordnance Survey Name Book* records of Rowallan Castle in c 1856:

> This Castle is situated on the north bank of the Carmel Water about 3 miles north of Kilmarnock. It was the residence of the Barons of Rowallan but is now going fast to decay. And only a few apartments are occupied by the woodman, Robert Dale. It appears from a tablet over the door that it was erected about the year 1562, adjoining are the remains of a more ancient edifice, supposed to be the birthplace of Elizabeth Mure, first spouse of King Robert 2nd of Scotland.
> (NAS RH4/23/54)

Dale, the woodman, is given as a source of information about a number of other local sites which are noted in relation to the landscape setting. Anderson (1875) relates how 'the late Countess of Loudoun was greatly attached to Rowallan. She often visited the castle, carefully inspected the rooms, and expended considerable sums on repairs to prevent the old place from falling to pieces'. Despite this, the castle appears to have been neglected and in a state of decay for much of the 19th century. This image of picturesque decay appealed to 19th-century artists and early photographers. Two photographs of the castle appeared in 1855 at an exhibition

63 Photograph of Rowallan Castle by Thomas Annan (active 1855–87). (© *Glasgow City Libraries. Licensor www.scran.ac.uk*)

mounted for the meeting there of the British Association for the Advancement of Science (www.peib.org.uk/itemexhibition). It was photographed by George Washington Wilson in 1880 (RCAHMS, archive AY2394) and Thomas Annan of Glasgow (Illus 63). A detail of the courtyard was sketched by Charles Rennie Mackintosh in 1887 (Hunterian Art Gallery).

The furniture and interior fittings of the house also attracted the attention of antiquarians in the later 19th century. In 1875, an armchair with the date 1617 was described (Adamson 1875, 139). In 1882, John Pollock published two plates of engravings by J W Small of an oak press in the dining room at Rowallan (Pollock 1882, 84–6). The press was said to be 3 feet 11 inches across the front, 7 feet 3 inches in height and 1 foot 5 inches across the end and the illustrations 'drawn very carefully from measurements and full-sized drawings'. Pollock continues:

> *Amongst the other objects of wood worthy of notice are two Ambrys [sic], with characteristic moulded and decorated doors; remains of wall panelling, showing plainly that tapestry has at one time filled in the panels; a massive extending dining-table, constructed exactly on the same principle as one in Holyrood Palace; an old arm-chair with the initials S.W.M. and date 1612, carved on the back; and a remarkably effective outside door, enriched with bold carvings, especially in the upper panels. The mouldings used throughout are very fine and many of them are richly carved.*
> (Pollock 1882, 6)

Two letters (EACMAS, Cessnock Papers, bundle 35a), the first undated, the second clearly a response to it and dated December 1890 refer to Tough's enquiries for his forthcoming publication for the Scottish Text Society. Tough had written to 'Mr Blair' the previous December stating that he had been told by the housekeeper at Rowallan that a large box, supposed to contain papers, was removed to Loudoun about 50 years ago. At Marquess Henry's death in 1869, Mr Padwick (he was an executor of the marquess) seized and realised every answerable article he possibly could attach. But the respondent (a J G Yorston, writing from Bridge of Allan) had no further information to add. The marquess had estates in both England and Scotland and one would expect the probate document to be 'resealed' in Scotland and to be recorded, but search has so far been to no avail.

The Inventory of 1787

The Inventory of the Estate and Effects of Flora Mure Campbell, 1787 (EACMAS, Cessnock Papers, bundle 35b), was perhaps the most important single document found with regard to the building. The aspects relating to the garden and grounds have been noted already. It is clear that there were local staff still present, but not clear if the removal of silver and linen to Loudoun was recent and connected with the legal processes of confirmation or reflects lack of regular, recent use by the family.

This includes fruit and other articles from the garden [of Rowallan] £20; a four-wheeled chaise sold to the Hon Mr Patrick Boyle £35; and corn, wood, etc, a horse, and sheep. It continues with room by room contents of Loudoun Castle and includes Loudoun silver plate and Lawers silver plate. Pages 31–7 copies of the household inventory; the Rowallan silver was at Loudoun but not distinguishable in the list; as there is no table-linen or bed -linen, it is likely that was also included in the Loudoun list.

The following are at Rowallan:

In my lord's room.
A press with a writing desk below.
A large oak press
A chest and drawers that divides into two.
Some iron bars for a grate, fender and fire irons.

Dining Room
A large oak table
Another folding ditto
A picture with a gilt frame
Four ditto with black frames
A Carron grate, white iron fender, poker, shovel, tongs and hearth brush.

Vestibule
A Bell

White Room
A large mahogany press
A square table with a drawer
An armed garden-chair
Six small ditto with stuffed bottoms and a check cover
A small pier glass
Thirteen prints framed and glazed
A Chimney [ie fire grate] white iron fender, poker, tongs, shovel and hearth brush.
A basin stand, stone basin and bottle, a carpet and a small hand-bell.

Closet off this room
A close box and pewter pan
Two pair bedroom candlesticks

Butler's Pantry
A case with a dozen silver-hafted knives and forks
A silver sugar caster
A mustard ditto
A spoon and pepper ditto
A pair clam-shell silver salts and spoons
A pair oval ditto and spoons.
A white stone bowl
Three cups and eight saucers red and white china for breakfast and small bowl same kind
Three saucers and six cups same colour for afternoon
A brown china teapot
Two blue and white stone bowls
A large red and white milk pot
A blue and white small one
One fine blue and white china teapot with a flat sugar box, cover of the same, milk pot, slab bowl [sic, maybe slop bowl was not genteel enough?] five saucers and six cups and bread flat all of the same kind.
An old blue and white china teapot and cream pot, both wanting handles.
A japanned knife remover and silver dividing spoon.
Fourteen small ditto, two broke
Six tortoiseshell breakfast knives tipt with silver
Six green ditto tipt with ditto
An old tea kettle and stand
One pair brass candlesticks
A copper tea kettle – old
Two wooden-handled knives
A carving knife and fork with a green haft
Two dozen and five knives, different coloured hafts
Two dozen and nine forks of the same mixed kind
Old ribs or fixed grate

Green Room
Two family pictures

Kitchen
Fixed table with drawers
Fixed ribs for the fireplace

In the hall
Fixed bars or ribs for the fire
A timber sweigh [a swee or swey]
A dresser with a drawer
Two forms

In the dining room cupboard
A silver bowl

Four beer glasses with Rowallan coat of arms – one of the soles broke

Seven claret glasses – plain

Six small wine glasses

Five stalked bell glasses

Two wine decanters

A mutchkin ditto

A blue and white stone bowl and punch spoon.

Four silver wine tickets, funnel and flat

Three dozen and three plain stone plates

Ten soup ditto

In the New Room
A fixed bedstead with a blue curtain.

A charter chest

An old grate and fender.

In James Dunn's Room
A bedstead

An old iron arm chair

A square fir table and a corner cupboard – fixed.

NB the Silver Plate and China in this Branch are at Loudoun Castle.

Rowallan farm stock:
one cart horse

one milk cow for the use of the nurse.

(EACMAS, Cessnock Papers, bundle 35b)

How the rooms mentioned can be correlated with other listings or identified today is unclear, but one assumes that the White Room, with its garden furniture, was on the ground floor; the dining room, at least, is mentioned in some of the other documents above. It needs to be borne in mind that the furniture and items listed were movables (fixtures such as panelling were part of the heritable property and not included) and that there might have been other rooms with nothing in them of consequence or value.

Whilst several items are described as old or broken, the Carron grate and the mahogany press at least must have been fairly modern. Most fires seem to be set to burn coal (grate, tongs, poker, etc) though the 'fire irons' in 'my lord's room' might be for wood. Although there is equipment for coal fires, there is no coal scuttle. The Carron grate might have involved other modifications of the hearth, still visible. The lack of kitchen equipment (pans, spits, griddles, and so on) does not encourage the idea that much cooking was going on. There are only two beds, neither sounding very impressive. There is no harpsichord or card table and no books. Much depends on the interpretation of such 'negative' evidence, but the overall impression is of an elaborate picnic site, a place for a day out, where the hampers from 'home' could be unpacked, the garden furniture set out on the lawn, the neighbours roll round in their carriages – but the gentry go home again as the shadows lengthen, leaving the servants to clear up till next time.

The 1790s, with highwar-time prices and rentals, were a time of extensive building by landowners in Scotland rather than of abandonment. In the case of Rowallan, however, the heiress was a child, there was another very substantial house at Loudoun and, by her marriage, she acquired further establishments in more fashionable locations.

The Designed Landscape after c 1700

When sasine was granted to James Mure Campbell in 1733, the witnesses, present at Rowallan, were Alexander Brisbane, gardener at Lawers and John Ronald, gardener at Rowallan (NAS RS3/144, 219–26). This James had inherited Rowallan from his mother, whilst Lawers (this one was between Crieff and Comrie, rather than on N Lochtayside) was another of the family's estates and the two witnesses emphasise the links and the active importance of gardens at both sites.

Following the death of James Campbell in 1745, the estate seems to have been in the hands of trustees; probably since one of those was Mr Patrick Boyle (of Kelburn) some of the documents have survived amongst the Earl of Glasgow's papers. By a fortunate coincidence, John Kennedy (the gardener) and an unspecified number of labourers were involved in landscaping work from at least 1743, the work continuing after the general's death (NAS GD237/98/1). The most striking record is a payment of £760 Scots for trees from William Boucher, an Edinburgh nurseryman. They are specified as:

1100 five year old beech trees	*£27 10s*
1000 ditto double size	*£5*
2000 hornbeam, two and three feet high	*£7 10s*
200 ditto larger	*£1*
400 grafted ditto English	*£6 13s 4d*
200 ungrafted	*£2 10s*
400 Dutch elm	*£4*
26 Larix [larch] trees	*£1 5s*
10000 five year old thorns	*£5*
400 four year old firs	*10s*
Two mats for package	*4s*
Two carts hire to Rowallan	*£2 15s*

(NAS GD243/98/1/42)

There are also payments of £34 6s to John Finlay for 'thorns and crabs' and another payment of £4 16s for a boll of haws (hawthorn seeds); so, like many estates at this time, Rowallan would require a nursery to grow these hawthorns on till ready to plant out, an expedient necessary as commercial suppliers could not keep up with demand. Crab-apples and hawthorns were amongst the favoured hedging

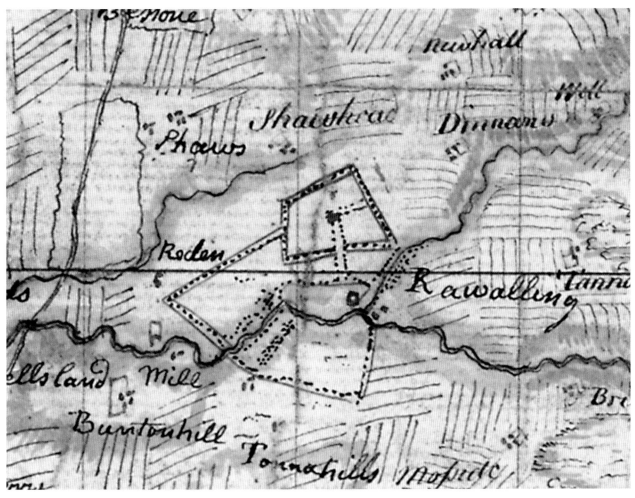

64 Rowallan Castle as depicted on the Military Survey of Scotland by William Roy, 1747–55 (© *The British Library. Licensor www.scran.ac.uk*)

species of the early phase of the 'improvement' period and hedging was certainly taking place on the Rowallan farms at this time, as indicated by a payment for a hedge and dyke at Craighall Farm as part of more general improvements there. But some of the hedging was within the ornamental grounds as indicated by two vouchers for James Grieve, hedger, from Kilmaurs:

Account James Grieve, hedger in Kilmaurs for laying the young hedges at Rowallan in Winter 1745/6

To 201 falls in the Mains park at 2.5d per fall

£2 18s 8d

To 232 falls in the Great Avenue at 2.5 p per fall

£2 6s 4d

Sterling £5 7s

Scots £64 4s

(NAS GD234/98/1/42)

Discharge by James Grieve, hedger for Bankend Park and Avenew dyke (sic);

Dated 29 Dec 1744 from Ainslie, for £36 4s Scots for 'making a dead hedge on the New Park, Bankend Land and the Avenew Dyke' [Avenue Dyke] being 241 falls.

(NAS GD234/98/1/44)

A 'fall' was around 6m in length. The 'dead hedge' would be a temporary structure of dead twigs, stakes, etc, set to protect the young growing live or 'quick' hedge from grazing stock (Harrison 2004). The precise identity of the Mains Park and Bankend Park must remain uncertain, but it is tempting to identify the latter with the Upper Bank and Nether Bank, mentioned in relation to Sir John Mure's expansion of the designed landscape in the late 16th century; there can be little question about the Great Avenue being the feature shown on Roy's map of 1747–55 and still prominent (Illus 64). That it is not orientated to the castle but to Rowallan Mains must at least suggest that a new house there was projected at some time. 'Grass Parks' of a more or less regular pattern, disposed around the mansion house, enclosed by hedges and hedgerow trees and combining the utility of improved grassland and timber production with the modern aesthetic of an ordered, enclosed landscape, were commonly the first phase of agricultural 'improvement' of the wider landscape and, whilst the striking central avenue at Rowallan is not typical, the overall layout is very suggestive of just such a process. Typically, grass parks were kept in grass either for hay or pasture and, when pastured by the tenants, the types of stock might be specified in the lease to ensure a suitably pastoral scene (Harrison 2003, 217–20; Harrison 2004, 50–1). John Kennedy, the gardener, had 'kitchen money' for half the year and 'a cow grassed in the park' for the other half in the three years to Martinmas 1744 (NAS GD237/98/31 voucher by John Kennedy, gardener). Roy's map of 1747–55 (Illus 64) suggests that these Grass Parks extend E of the Carmel Burn and the Ordnance Survey might imply that there were grass parks either side of the Avenue. The *Scotsman* (12 March 1836, 3) reported that the Rowallan Grass Parks were amongst those recently let for higher prices than in previous years and attributed this to continued high demand for fattening stock for the London markets.

Fruit and other items from the garden worth £20 were sold in 1789 (EACMAS, Cessnock Papers, bundle 35b). A survey of the woodland, carried out in 1829, noted that the trees in the Home Park were dead or dying and that the Long Avenue was in decay. There were 'a few venerable old trees about the castle' (Monteath 1829). In 1845, some work was still being carried out on the grounds with some grass cutting and drainage work paid for (EACMAS, Cessnock Papers, bundle 84; Workmen's Accounts 1845). The *Ordnance Survey Name Book* says that woodman Robert

Dale was living in the castle itself, implying some continued forestry work (though this might have been to ensure timber supplies for farms or cover for game). There are also *Ordnance Survey Name Book* entries for:

Bank Plantation, information from David Dale, Bank End and from Robert Dale, Rowallan, woodman; This is a mixed plantation situated on the western side of Balgray mill burn and near Rowallan Castle.

Janet's Kirn is a spot in the Balgray Mill Burn at the bend in the stream not far from Rowallan Castle. The derivation is not known. Near to this is the Marriage Tree, on the Fenwick side of the stream, a large sycamore under the shade of which Jean Muir, daughter and heiress of the last Sir Wm Mure of Rowallan, was married to Wm Fairlie of Bruntsfield after whose demise married 2ndly David, First Earl of Glasgow. [citing Muir's History of Rowallan].
Holmepark Plantation; a mixed plantation on both sides of the Carmel Water near Rowallan Castle.

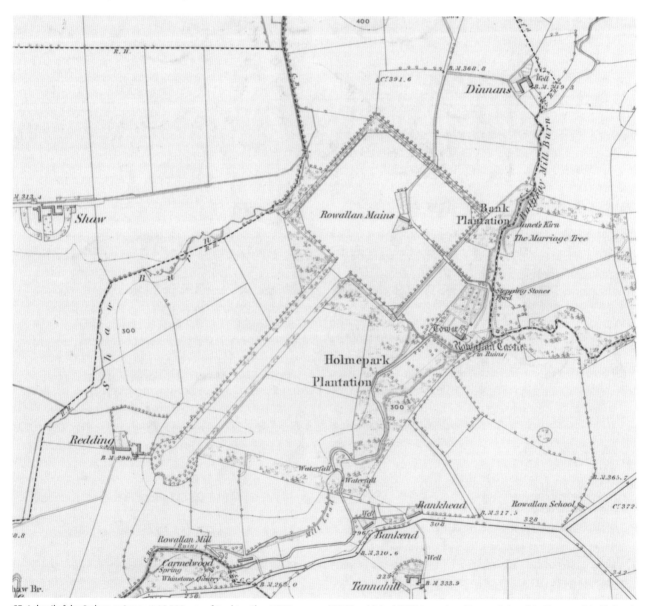

65 A detail of the Ordnance Survey 1:10,560 map of Ayrshire, Sheet XVIII, surveyed 1856, published 1860 (*reproduced by permission of the Trustees of the National Library of Scotland*)

Rowallan Mains; this was formerly the farm yard and offices belonging to Rowallan Castle. Nothing remains but an old building in one part of which the gamekeeper resides. (NAS RH4/23/54)

The gamekeeper in country like this was probably mainly raising pheasants and controlling 'vermin' and the Ordnance Survey map of 1856 shows the vicinity is scattered with circular clumps of woodland, characteristic of pheasant shoots (Illus 65).

Plans for additions were drawn up by Nicholas Joyce in 1869 and a survey of Rowallan Castle 'as at present existing' was carried out in 1896, but there is no evidence of work being carried out (Illus 68–9). The importance of the castle as an historical monument was brought to the attention of the public by its appearance in MacGibbon and Ross (1887–92, II, 375–89), although in some ways this furthered the destruction of the monument. Some panelling was removed in the later years of the 19th century (Weaver

66 Oak door from Rowallan Castle, National Museums of Scotland Acc No A.1923.364 (© National Museums of Scotland. Licensor www.scran.ac.uk)

1913, 425) and the doorway to the hall (MacGibbon and Ross 1887–92, II, 386–7) was also taken about this time; the doorway was purchased by the National Museum of Scotland in Edinburgh (Illus 66).

In 1897, when it was anticipated that sale of the estate and castle might proceed separately, it was suggested that the castle and some 20 acres around it, suitable for a garden, farm and policies, should be marked out (EACMAS, Cessnock Papers, bundle 2, November 1897, Note from James C Davidson). A report of 1898 described the estate of Rowallan as:

farms 5547 acres

Woodlands 110 acres

Policies 5 acres

Shootings set to Earl of Eglinton for £140 and there are feu duties payable by three vassals totaling £253 11s 2d.

The woods, including the nursery and grounds around Rowallan are assessed at £40.

General report on the estate which is in fairly good condition; the southern part is near Kilmarnock the northern more moorland part produces goods for Glasgow; overall is dairy and there are dairies on the farms.

The woods, except those near Rowallan, are not of money value except for shelter and sport. In accordance with instructions they have selected 20 acres round the old castle of Rowallan which they think most suitable for garden ground and policies for the castle.

This was all marked on a 25" OS map and the 20 acres included land taken from the Quarry Park and Meikle Moss-side Farm, valued at £13 5s per annum, so reducing their rental value. Sadly, the map was not found. The report continued that the 'old castle' was in the centre of this land:

It is an interesting building but must be regarded in its present condition as a ruin. The enclosure marked on the map as 'nursery' is surrounded by a good stone and lime wall in a fair state of preservation and would be suitable for a garden. The reporters estimate the whole value of the subject including the ruin and growing timber on the lands as £1500.

The estate was offered for sale in May 1900:

AYRSHIRE

FOR SALE

The ESTATE of ROWALLAN, in the Parishes of Kilmarnock and Fenwick, and County of Ayr.

The Estate extends to about 6080 Acres of thereby, of which 4196 Acres are Arable and Pasture Land, Steadings, &c, 1433, and 106 Acres Woodland.

The Property is divided into about 37 Farms, besides Grass Parks, &c. The Farms are mostly held as Dairy Farms.

The Gross Rental of the Estate is £6349. 18s. 3d., and the Public and Parochial burdens amount to £454. 4s. 11d. The

67 Rowallan House

rents are paid with great punctuality.

The old CASTLE of ROWALLAN is beautifully situated on the Banks of the Carmel Water, and is about three miles from the Town of Kilmarnock.

The Castle is a fine specimen of the Scottish Mansion of the Sixteenth and Seventeenth Centuries, although some portions are of an earlier date. It has for some time been occupied only by a Forester of the Estate, but Plans and Estimates were recently obtained for its restoration, which, if carried out, would make a most attractive Residence.

The TIMBER round the Castle is the most valuable on the Estate, and adds greatly to the amnity of the Grounds, as there are many old Trees of great size and beauty.

(The *Scotsman*, 3 May 1900)

It will be seen that the old castle was still occupied by the forester and that there were already proposals for 'restoration'. Like so many of the antiquarian descriptions, much emphasis was placed on the timber and setting, clearly seen as attractions to potential buyers. However, this was clearly unsuccessful since the estate was soon advertised again, this time with more emphasis on good communications, sporting facilities and royal historic associations, and also that the building was described in the *Castellated and Domestic Architecture of Scotland* (The *Scotsman*, 31 August 1901, 2). The 6000-acre estate was then purchased for £140,000 from Lord Donnington of Loudoun in 1901 by Mrs Polson, mother of Alice Corbett who married Cameron Corbett of the mercantile Corbett family (price reported in The *Scotsman*, 13 January 1904, 7). Cameron Corbett had become Liberal MP for the Tradeston Division of Glasgow after a prosperous career as a land developer, having originally taken on his uncle's business and developed his interests in the London area. The Rowallan estate was purchased after a search for a country house not

too far distant from Glasgow. The situation of the old castle was deemed damp and the views restricted, so the family decided to construct a new house on the hill with wide views to the coast, to Ailsa Craig and Arran (Savage 1980, 56). Corbett commissioned Robert Lorimer who designed and oversaw the building of Rowallan House (Illus 67) between November 1901 and 1906 (*The Architectural Review*, June 1911). It was Lorimer's first commission for a mansion house in Scotland and was designed at least six times as large as any of Lorimer's previous new Scots houses, planned around three separate courts. The forecourt of the new house was constructed upon the site of the farm buildings of Rowallan Mains. Alice Corbett died during the design and construction of the new house and although construction continued, it was on a much-reduced scale. Tenders for the reduced plan of the mansion house were submitted in 1902 (Savage 1980, 56). Lorimer designed a simple memorial for Alice Corbett that was located above the Rowallan estate on the windy moor (Savage 1980, 59).

A limited amount of repairs, to the value of £56 10s, was carried out on the old castle during the building of the new house at Rowallan (NLS, Acc no 6688).

The Inland Revenue Survey of the 1910s (NAS IRS55/341) described the mansion, policies and associated planting extending to 82 acres; there were various ancillary buildings such as the coachman's house, electric light plant, lodge, and gardener's house within that area. Outside the policies, at the junction of the Kilmaurs/Kilmarnock/Fenwick road were the butler's, gamekeeper's and under gardener's houses (reducing the need for servants' accommodation in and close to the mansion); there was some planting outside the policies, though of very little value. Most importantly, whilst the total value of the mansion and other buildings within the policies was estimated at £20,000 and the gardener's house at £358, Rowallan Castle itself was 'say £100'.

8 UNREALISED SCHEMES FOR THE CASTLE

John Sanders and Jen Austin

INTRODUCTION

Of importance to this study are the architects' plans for a series of three major alteration schemes (with some restoration and reconstruction) commissioned by successive proprietors from the mid 19th century to the mid 20th century, drawings that are held in the RCAHMS library, Edinburgh. While it is fortunate for the earlier fabric of the castle that the first two of these schemes were not realised, the associated plans included as records of the existing building provide important evidence of the former appearance of the structure.

FIRST SCHEME – 1869 ADDITIONS

The first proposed scheme that has been located for the refurbishment of the neglected Rowallan Castle for domestic use was drawn in 1869. Drawings for the proposed scheme itself were undertaken by architect N Joyce, ARIBA, of Stafford (Illus 68 and 69). The proposal drawings involve substantial alteration to the building, particularly to the important interior spaces.

The main components of this scheme include the addition of a two-storey corridor along the northern wall of the S range within the courtyard, the installation of a stair hall within the SE corner (Components 22 and 42) and the

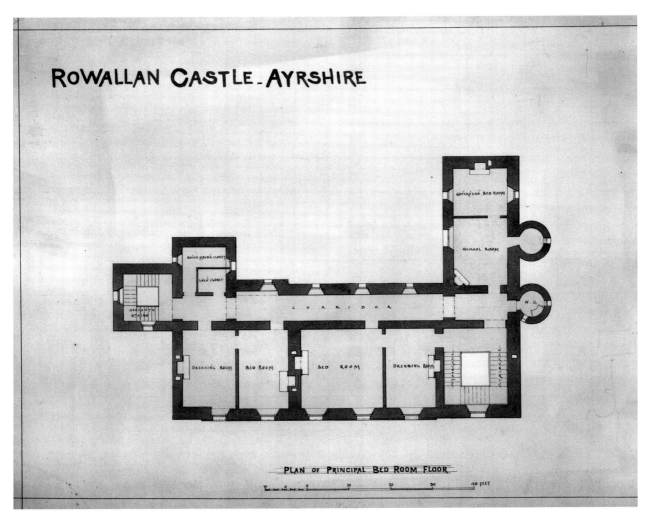

68 Proposals for alterations and additions by N Joyce in 1869: First-floor plan (*Royal Commission on the Ancient and Historical Monuments of Scotland © Crown Copyright*)

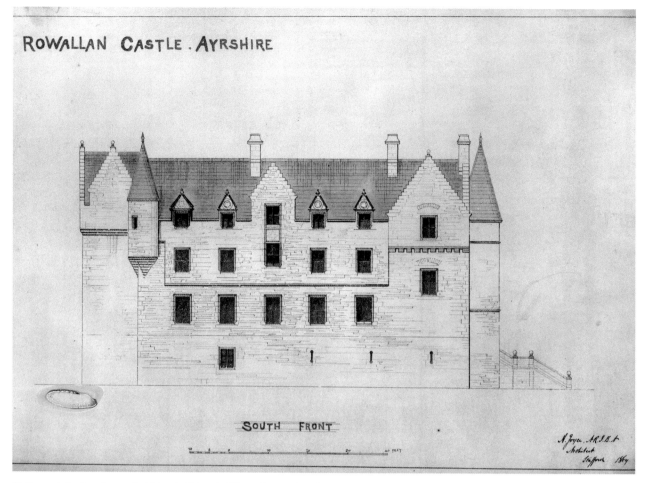

ROWALLAN CASTLE . AYRSHIRE

SOUTH FRONT

69 Proposals for alterations and additions by N Joyce in 1869, S elevation (*Royal Commission on the Ancient and Historical Monuments of Scotland © Crown Copyright*)

reconfiguration of the SW corner of the complex to provide a new servant's stair and another room at the western end of the corridor. This scheme also included the upwards extension of the entire building to provide a further storey of bedrooms.

The ground floor/courtyard level would have included the retention of the front façade, with the exception of the blocking up of the southern window and alteration of other window openings. The tower roofs would have been reconstructed at a much steeper pitch. There appears to have been no proposal for the northern, ruined range of the castle complex as part of this scheme. It was proposed that the ground floor/courtyard level would contain a 'gentlemen's room' in the room N of the entrance pend, stair hall on the S side, and drawing room and dining room in the S range. A WC was to be located in the S drum tower at this level. The front entrance stair was to be replaced with a more elaborate stair.

The E range of the first floor was to be converted to a school room and governess's bedroom, with a WC in the S tower as on the ground floor. The S range was to contain the two primary bedrooms, each having a dressing room and accessed off the new corridor to the N. Adjacent to the servant's stair at the western end was to be a housemaid's and linen closet.

The plans also indicate that it was proposed to effectively rebuild the gallery level and create bedrooms along the E and S ranges and construct a bartizan at the SW corner of the uppermost level.

No evidence was found for what, if anything, was proposed for the basement level within this scheme.

SECOND SCHEME – JULY 1896

A second scheme for the conversion of Rowallan Castle into a substantial country house was prepared in 1896 by architects Leadbetter and Fairley of Edinburgh (Illus 70–71), this following a survey of the existing building undertaken by James and Robert S Ingram, architects, Kilmarnock. This scheme, titled *Proposed Addition to Old Scots Mansion*, involved very extensive alterations and additions to the original building.

Ingram's initial survey shows the basement level and gallery generally as they still remain. The survey of the courtyard level shows a small, single-storey addition against the N wall of the S range, and a partition separating the S range entrance hall from the dining room. The survey also

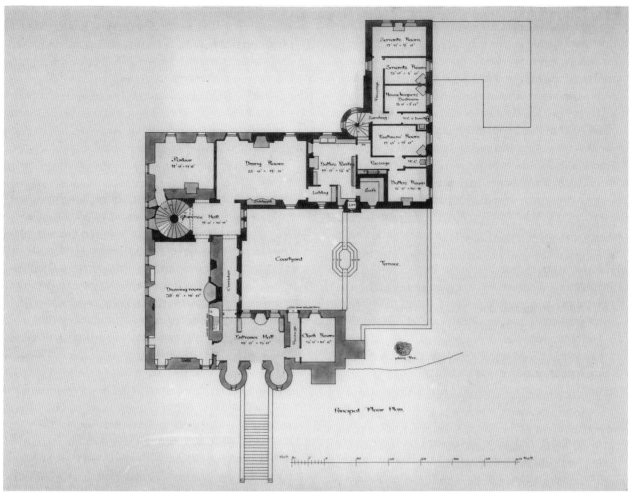

70 Alterations and additions proposed by Leadbetter and Fairley, Architects, 1896: Ground-floor plan (*Royal Commission on the Ancient and Historical Monuments of Scotland © Crown Copyright*)

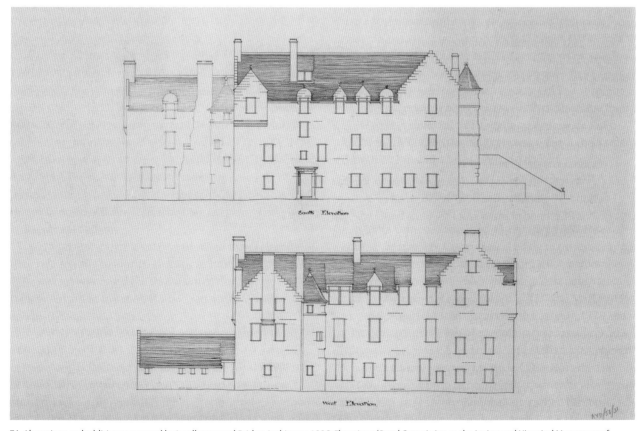

71 Alterations and additions proposed by Leadbetter and Fairley, Architects, 1896: Elevations (*Royal Commission on the Ancient and Historical Monuments of Scotland © Crown Copyright*)

represents the buttress supporting the northern part of the E range exterior wall and the location of a room within the current attic space.

The basement level proposal in 1896 would have seen extensive excavation and rebuilding, particularly along the W side of the castle complex. The basement-level S range would have been subject to the removal of the internal vault/cellar walls, and the installation of a new billiard room in the SE corner, a new and very substantial turnpike stair that accessed all levels, a WC, and a gun room in the SW corner. A proposed W range was to contain the service wing, this comprising housekeeper's rooms, a servant's hall, kitchen, servant's stair, pantry, dish room, boot and lamp room and a cook's room. The S and W ranges would have been connected by a northwards-running extension of the existing E–W aligned pend.

At ground-floor/courtyard level, a new access corridor was proposed along the N side of the S range, this in a similar manner to the previous scheme by Joyce. The W end of the entrance pend was to be blocked with a fireplace and opened up to form an entrance hall, with a cloakroom installed in the northern end of the E range. The S range was to be opened up to form a large drawing room at the E side, with a parlour at the W end. The new W range would have contained a large dining room, butler's pantry and the rest of the service wing in the dogleg wing extending out to the W at the N end of the W range. The courtyard was to be extended to the N, the ruined early tower removed and a large terrace formed upon its site.

The first floor of the E range was to contain Lady Loudoun's suite of rooms, work that was to involve some modification to the existing internal layout. The central part of the S range would have contained the stair and bathroom, whereas the W range would have contained Lord Loudoun's suite of rooms. The dogleg section extending W from the northern end of the W range would have contained more service areas and bedrooms for female servants.

The upper level would have seen the gallery in the E range divided to form storage rooms and the S range attic space was to contain a suite of rooms for the male servants.

Although it proposed considerable alteration to the interior and to the N and W elevations, the 1896 scheme was designed with considerably more respect for the aesthetic qualities of the original fabric than displayed by the Joyce scheme, which had proposed a radical change in appearance and wholesale alteration to the windows and doors. In contrast, Leadbetter and Fairley's design appears to have been motivated by an attempt to leave the E elevation unchanged, even to the point of leaving the buttress in place. The suggested alterations to the S elevation drew their inspiration from other Scots precedents – the distinct implication of this proposal was that the S elevation was not considered to be sufficiently 'baronial'. The means of providing the additional accommodation required for the creation of a commodious country house was to extend to the W and NW so that the wholly new building works could not be seen in the context of the E elevation, particularly when viewed from the approach across the Carmel Water. This seems to clearly reflect a greater antiquarian concern for, and consideration of, historic buildings that had developed over the last quarter of the 19th century.

THIRD SCHEME – 1943–48

In 1943, an investigation was undertaken at Rowallan Castle by the Inspector of Ancient Monuments (NAS MW/1/1383); this led to the recommendation that the authority assume guardianship responsibility. Between August and October 1943, a Ministry of Works condition survey of the building was undertaken by architect John Houston, whose detailed notebook entries and plans remain in the possession of Historic Scotland; the Inspector, James Richardson, seems to have been involved in the process. Guardianship was not finally agreed until 1950, before which time, in 1948, proposals to reinstate residential use had been undertaken for Lord Rowallan – the feasibility of the two options was clearly being judged in parallel. It was suggested that only the financial situation of the family at the time prevented these works from going ahead.

The 1948 proposals were prepared by Ian G Lindsay and George Hay, then of Orphoot, Whiting and Lindsay. Lindsay was Scotland's leading historic buildings architect of the time. He laid the foundation for the listing and historic buildings grant programme as the first Chief Investigator to the Historic Buildings Council, a predecessor to that of the present Historic Scotland Chief Inspector. His firm became Ian G Lindsay & Partners. George Hay later left the partnership to become Principal Architect in the Ancient Monuments Division of Works, now part of Historic Scotland. The 1948 scheme entailed only minimal interventions within the building. This was perhaps a consequence of the limited resources available to Lord Rowallan at the time, but it also doubtless reflects the more scholarly inclinations of Lindsay and Hay and the early development of modern attitudes to conservation in the post-war years.

At basement level, the interior was to remain as it exists today, retaining the kitchen at the W end of the S range and positioning the larder, store and a wine cellar within the vaulted cellar spaces.

At courtyard level, the layout of the interior was also to be kept largely as it exists today, but including the reroofing of the ruined NW corner of the complex and inserting partitions to form a servants' wing. The SW corner room (Component 17) was to become a dining room, the chamber (Component 22) was to become the library and the hall to remain at the centre of the S range with the entrance hallway remaining partitioned off. It was proposed to retain the small single storey addition off the northern side of the S range in the courtyard. There would have been a cloakroom off the library (Component 22) and a WC installed in the S tower at this level. The ruined tower in the NE corner was to become a terraced area off the central courtyard.

The first-floor level was to remain the bedroom level, with the installation of bedrooms in the attic space of the S range and in the E range, the retention of internal partitions, including the cob and timber stud walls (Component 41 – within which it was proposed to insert a bathroom). The first floor of the NE corner of the complex would serve as the bedrooms for the servants' wing. The second-floor/ gallery level would have been divided into bedrooms, with a bathroom inserted within and adjacent to the southern tower.

Unlike the previous schemes, the proposals demonstrate sensitivity to the existing building. Alterations to the fabric were to be kept to a minimum and would have been reversible. There seems to have been a general presumption against alterations, even at the expense of the convenience of the occupants.

72   Detail from *A New Map of Ayrshire* by Andrew Armstrong, 1775 (*reproduced by permission of the Trustees of the National Library of Scotland*)

9 SOME OTHER MURE HOUSES AND PROPERTIES

John Harrison

This chapter presents information on some Mure properties with a direct relationship to Rowallan (Illus 72).

THE MURES OF POLKELLY

Anderson (1863, 208) follows Nisbet in suggesting that the Mures of Polkelly were 'the stem' of the Mures of the Rowallan. The point is of some importance for the present study since Polkelly Castle (NS 4568 4524) was the other power centre within the Rowallan barony in the medieval period. The remains were removed to form a road in the 1850s and it survived as a mound measuring 23m by 16m (RCAHMS NS44NE 1).

According to the family history, Sir Adam (1) died in 1399 and was succeeded by his eldest son in Rowallan, the younger son taking the lands of Polkelly. According to the confirmation charter of 1440, a charter of 1395 had granted the lands of 'Polnekel' including, Grey, Drumbuy, Cliniche (Clundie), Clonyherbire, Darclath and of Bagraw in the barony of Cunningham, sheriffdom of Ayr as also the lands of Lenflare, sheriffdom of Lanark to Adam Mure and his spouse, Jonet of Danyestone, all to be united into the free barony of Polnekel (RMS II, 58, 25), though this seems to be in addition to and distinct from their grant of Rowallan. There are several later references to the Mures of Polkelly and one appears as a royal administrator during the later 15th century, collecting royal rents in east central Scotland (RMS II, 200, entry 963n; RMS II 1670, 1671; ER X, 697).

Robert Mure of Polkelly was dead by 1511 when his daughter and heir, Margaret Mure married to Robert Cunningham of Cunninghamhead, resigned her interest in the reversion of the lands at Inverkip, Renfrewshire (RMS II, 3651). In March 1512, Margaret Mure, Lady Polkelly and Robert Cunningham of Cunninghamhead, her husband, were confirmed in their lands of Wester Linflair and of Polkelly, now enumerated as: Polkelley alias Ponekell, Darclavoch, Clonherb, Clunch, with the mill of the same, le Gre, Drumboy, lands of Balgray, with the tower, fortalice, manor and mill of the same with the common of Mauchirnoch pertaining to the lands which were all now incorporated into the free barony of Polkelly, but the principal messuage was to be the tower and manor at Balgray, rather than Polkelly (RMS II, 3713). Polkelly Castle should, therefore, have been in use from the late 14th or early 15th century until c 1512.

This transfer of Polkelly to the Cunninghams precipitated a series of disputes which continued through much of the 16th century about the extent of their respective rights on the Moor of Machirnock, the huge common grazing to the N of Polkelly. A royal letter of 1534 said that the Cunninghams had not been infeft in the moor though they had claimed to be so (NLS Adv MS22.2.9 ff, 47–60 f 49r). In 1540, it was found that the moor pertained heritably to Rowallan but allocated the souming proportionately between Rowallan and Polkelly, 200 soums to the 26 merk land of Polkelly and 700 to the 100 merks of Rowallan (Acts of the Lords, 484 and 486). This was recalled in 1594 when William Mure of Rowallan claimed that despite this judgement, there were encroachments by the Polkelly stock both by extra cattle and by geese and other livestock that had continued in spite of their finding caution of lawburrows to desist on 20 May 1593 (NAS GD148/246).

Whilst direct evidence is lacking, it is very probable that the medieval moor was the common grazing for the whole northern part of Kilmarnock [with Fenwick] parish and of parts of Stewarton, too, and was the property of Rowallan. The Historie provides a simple and credible explanation; assignation of Polkelly to a younger son on marriage would allocate a proportionate use of the moor, but the heritable rights would remain those of Rowallan and serious tensions arise only when the property interests were divided between the Mures and the Cunninghams.

DALMUSTERNOCK (NS 4556 4168)

In January 1594, James VI confirmed a charter by William Mure of Rowallan in favour of Janet Maxwell, his wife, of a life-rent from lands including the 5 merk land of Dalmusternock, with the place and manor, in the barony of Rowallan (RMS VI, 16, entry 49). And, in 1605, when he remarried, the contract gave a similar annual rent to his new wife, Lady Elizabeth McGill (RMS VII, 529, doc 1456). However, William junior was already heir apparent in 1605, (recently) married to Anna Dundas, whose rights to the annual rent and the mansion at Dalmusternock were confirmed in 1616 (RMS VII, doc 1534) and it is their initials and the date 1615 which appeared over the doorway of the mansion. But these charters reserved the life-rent rights of the lands to Sir William senior and when he died in 1616, he was owed rent and other dues from the several tenants in Dalmusternock (NAS CC9/7/14/199 ff).

The documents imply that there was already a high-status house at Dalmusternock in 1592 and the date stone confirms that a new one was built later. This need for additional house space was the result of there being three generations of adult male Mures flourishing at this time. How the house was used subsequently is presently unclear, but the 'mansion' at Dalmusternock makes it clear that Rowallan was not the only Mure house, even in the immediate locality.

WIDOWS, DOWER HOUSES AND OTHER RESIDENCES

Anna Dundas predeceased her husband who then married Dame Jean Hamilton who survived him (1657). She herself died in 1665 in the parish of Wester Kilpatrick where it is clear she had been living for some time (NAS CC9/7/35/65 testament of Dame Jean Hamilton). This may reflect the fact that she was not the mother of the heir and present proprietor of Rowallan – though the terms of her testament suggest that she shared his radical religious views. Where other Mure widows lived is uncertain, but it would not be usual for them to continue to live in the main house. The situation is further complicated by the transfer of major interests in Rowallan to the heirs even whilst the older generation was still alive (as in the case of Dalmusternock, just considered).

Charters and contracts indicate that the Mures regularly visited Irvine, Glasgow and Edinburgh; the possibility of their having houses in one or other of those centres cannot be discounted. They also had relatives in those towns who might have provided space for visits.

10 AGRICULTURE AND ECONOMY OF THE MURE LANDS

John Harrison

The basis of the Mures' wealth was the Barony of Rowallan which comprised the entire northern part of the medieval parish of Kilmarnock (from which the parish of Fenwick was carved in 1642) and some additional lands in Stewarton parish. The valuation of the barony (a purely notional figure) was found to be £100 by the Lords of Council in 1540 in the dispute about the pasturage of the Muir of Rowallan (below) and that remained the same into the 18th century (NAS GD26/7/393; NAS GD90/2/47 c 1610; *Retours*, Ayrshire, entry 500, 1658; NAS, RS3/144, 219–26, sasine 8 November 1733). The Mures' interest in property rarely extended beyond Cunningham. Sir Robert's transient interest in lands near Hawick in the later 15th century was exceptional. Before discussing the major source of income, the rents of the agricultural lands leased to tenants, some other sources will be considered.

Wards and non-entries were potentially a two-edged sword as families could lose out if a minor inherited, but gain from the grants of other estates. The Mures seem to have done particularly well from wards and non-entries in the 16th century and as the deaths of Mures at both Flodden and Pinkie was followed by the regrant of the wards and non-entries to the widows and heirs, they did not lose as others did.

The Mures also benefited from royal grants of new lands. There is no positive evidence of how they gained Rowallan itself and though royal favour for support at the Battle of Largs and in connection with Marion Mure's relationship with Robert II have both been suggested, the first documents appear 130 years after the first and 60 years after the second. But they certainly did do well from direct royal favour in the late 15th and early 16th centuries. James IV granted lands to his former mistress Margaret or Marion Boyd, most importantly Warnokland, Glassiter, Gaynleith, Gaynhill and Wellis; though partly already in the southern part of the barony, they had been forfeit from Lord Boyd and so were in royal hands at this time (*RMS* II, 526, doc 2472). Later James V granted Kentigern Mure the 5 merk land of Blacklaw, the 5 merk land of Hairschaw, the 6 merk land of Corshillis, the 6 merk land of Clerkland, the 40s land of Cuttiswray and the 5 merk land of Ormisheuch to be held of the king. These lands, except Ormisheuch, were in the northern part of Stewarton parish and flanked the important and contentious Machirnock Moor so they were strategically important; the total grant extended to a £20

land, adding some 20 per cent to the notional value of the overall holding, a convenient addition to anyone's income (NAS GD3/1/10/1/11). In 1560, John Mure resigned his remaining interest in Blacklaw and Cuttiswray by selling an annual rent right in the lands to Cuthbert Cunningham (NAS GD39/5/47; NAS RD1/1, f 453r–454v). This, of course, would have raised money at the time of major building work at Rowallan itself and is in the tradition of sacrificing recently acquired lands whilst retaining the core or ancestral ones. Ormisheuch, on the other hand, which was in Irvine parish, seems to have been assigned to a younger son of the Mures and became an independent, small estate (*RMS* V, 130, entry 423; NAS RD1/33, f 264r–268v); having spare land of this sort protected the core lands as such sons had to be 'set up' from some source.

Parts, even of the barony, might be assigned to family members, widows, younger sons, and so on and could, particularly in the latter case, pass from direct control if the heir was a daughter, as happened in the case of Polkelly. Some of the land within the barony was always in the hands of vassals. The charter by William Comyn granting 'Meikle Gawyn' to a vassal has already been noted and Gainleitch, at least, was in the hands of vassals probably till it was bought back in the 19th century. The Arnots held Lochrig in *blench ferm* from at least the mid 15th century and there were other examples. Of major importance until the 'improvement' period were the huge common grazings of the Moor of Machirnock, to the N of the area; they will be discussed below. Of the remainder, the great bulk was rented to tenants, but some seems always to have been farmed directly for the Mures, and the emergence of a Mains Farm from the dominical lands is discussed in relation to the landscape development.

Whether held in property by the landlord, let to tenants, or feued to vassals, the land was probably farmed in much the same ways. There has been no study of the agricultural economy of Cunningham (and this brief essay is not such a study), but in the 16th century the coastal strip was most developed for arable, with dairy more prominent inland (Sanderson 1997, 3); in the 17th century the importance of seaweed for manuring arable along the shore was noted (Whyte 1979, 70). The slight evidence for Rowallan in the late 16th century is that farming was mixed but that dairy was clearly important. Of particular importance was the Macharnock Moor (now Glenouther Moor), an extensive area of common grazing 6km and more from Rowallan itself and largely in Stewarton parish but with the alternative name of the Moor of Rowallan and found to pertain to Rowallan, albeit the Mures of Polkelly had had rights in it. Part of its boundary was the common parish and shire boundary.

In the early 16th century the moor was judged able to support 1000 soums though actual usage was to be limited to 900 soums (*RMS* II, 3713; NLS Adv MS22.2.9, f 49r; *Acts of the Lords*, etc, 484, 486; NAS GD148/246; NAS GD148/259; a soum varied from area to area and time to time but might be the pasture of a cow or four sheep (Ross 2006). The rights in the moor were clearly ancient; the Arnots of Lochrig, who had held their feu in Stewarton parish from the Mures since at least the mid 15th century, had right to use it (*Retours*, Ayrshire, entry 713), but the boundary anomalies and the coincidence of the parts of the boundaries with those of the parishes and county suggest that its origins probably lie at least as far back as the origins of Rowallan as a unit, perhaps at the period of parish formation – or even earlier, during the British period of Strathclyde. The moor, its location and boundaries, might well be relevant to the possibility of a 'lordship of Rowallan', older and larger than the barony of the 1390s, noted in considering the career of the original Sir Adam. Such a large pasture, so far from many of the associated farms, must have been used for summer pasture for dairy production.

By the early 17th century, liming was being used to enhance fertility in parts of inland Ayrshire. This early liming is usually associated with an expansion of arable and had an 'immediate and spectacular' impact on rents (Whyte 1979, 207) Pont comments that in parts of Stewarton and Dunlop parishes liming was in use and the pasture had become 'much more luxuriant than before', yielding a great deal of excellent butter (Strawhorn 1975, 49). The advance in arable seen in other areas slackened during the wars of the 1640s, but was resumed with the Restoration. Sir William, who died in 1616, had applied lime to land in his own hands at Balgray (NAS CC9/7/14/199 ff). Sir William had an astonishing 83 cows in milk, 41 dry cows with their followers, and no fewer than 83 quoys and stirks of from one to three years old. With the three bulls, these cattle accounted for £2090; in addition, he was owed for 517 stones of cheese at £1 each. A 'stone' at this time would vary regionally and according to the commodity, but 517 stones would fall in the range of 4136lb to 12408lb, a minimum of 1.88 tonnes of cheese paid as rent – and there must have been a great deal more which

the tenants retained to market themselves. More general liming is confirmed by tacks from the 1630s for Stewarton and adjacent areas (eg NAS RH11/19/6, 127–9 and *passim*); by the 1650s and early 1660s the Mures were issuing tacks and having them recorded though time has not permitted checks to see how many insisted on liming (eg NAS RD2/6, 259, 260, 306; NAS RD2/17, *passim*; NAS RD2/55, 95). The issuing of tacks is itself a sign of change and indicates more substantial tenants demanding a greater degree of security in return for higher rents. A feature of several of these tacks, however, is that the landlord supplied specified numbers of 'tidy kye', ie cows in milk, to the tenant at the beginning of the tack, the tenant to pay an excess on the rent to cover them and to return equivalent cattle at the end. This suggests that Sir William's vast herds of 1616 were the pool from which such cows could be drawn and the whole system recognises that the landlord has capital where the tenants do not. The testament of the later Sir William, who died in 1641, shows a similar system, though in this case the emphasis is on the grains supplied rather than cattle (NAS CC9/7/28, 798–804).

Many of Rowallan's tenants were warned from their holdings in July 1679 (NAS SC6/59/2 medium bundle) and many new tacks on the estate were registered in 1682 (NAS RD3/54 *passim*) and it seems that some sort of major reorganisation was underway at that time, perhaps a switch towards more emphasis on arable production, though again based on the use of lime, implicit in early 18th-century rentals where 'improvement' was clearly part of a regular programme and with particular emphasis on arable (NAS GD237/98/6/19; NAS GD237/98/6/20; NAS GD237/98/6/22; NAS GD237/98/6/23). Again, such a switch would reflect wider changes in the Scottish economy and an emphasis on arable which would persist till the mid 19th century, albeit Cunningham continued to have an important dairy component. The slight evidence so far seen suggests that there was a corresponding decline in the value of the Moor of Macharnock (NAS GD237/98/1/1, charge of £30 Scots for Moor of Rowallan set to William Wallace); astonishingly, a moor which had precipitated major disputes throughout the 16th century, such that there were proposals for a formal Division of Commonty in the 1590s (NAS GD148/259) 150 years before such divisions become commonplace, was not in fact divided until 1904 (Adams, 1971 43; NAS RHP1200; NASRHP25000).

REFERENCES

PRINTED WORKS

Adams, I H 1971 *Directory of Former Scottish Commonties*. Scottish Record Society, new series **2**, Edinburgh.

Adamson, A R 1875 *Rambles Round Kilmarnock*. T Stevenson, Kilmarnock.

Allan, D 1997 '"A Commendation of the Private Countrey Life": Philosophy and the Garden in 17th Century Scotland', *Garden History* **25**.1, 59–80.

Anderson, W 1863 *The Scottish Nation: Or, The Surnames, Families, Literature, Honours and Biographical History of the People of Scotland*. Fullarton & Co, Edinburgh.

Armstrong, R B (ed) 1884 'Military Report on the Districts of Carrick, Kyle and Cunninghame . . . between the years 1563 and 1566', *Archaeological and Historical Collections of Ayr and Wigton* **4**, 17–25.

Baillie, M G L and Pilcher J R 1983 'Some observations on the high precision calibration of routine dates', in Ottaway, B S (ed) *Archaeology, Dendrochronology and the Radiocarbon Calibration Curve* (= University of Edinburgh, Department of Archaeology Occasional Paper **9**), 51–63.

Bain, J and Rogers, R (eds) 1875 *Diocesan Registers of Glasgow*, London, Grampian Club **8**.

Barley, M 1986 *Houses and History*. Faber and Faber, London.

Bass, W M 1987 'Human osteology a laboratory and field manual', *Missouri Archaeological Society Special Publications, Columbia*.

Beek, G C van 1983 *Dental Morphology: an illustrated guide*. Wright, Bristol.

Bentley-Cranch, D 1986 'An Early French Architectural Source for the Palace of Falkland', *Review of Scottish Culture* **2**, 85–95.

Beveridge, J and Russell, J 1920 *Protocol Books of Dominus Thomas Johnsoun 1528–78*, Scottish Record Society, Edinburgh.

Boardman, S, 2000 *The Campbells 1250–1513*. John Donald, Edinburgh.

Breathnach, A S 1965 *Frazer's Anatomy of the Human Skeleton* (sixth edition). J & A Churchill Ltd, London.

Brothwell, D R 1981 *Digging up Bones*. Oxford University Press, Oxford.

Caldwell, D H, Ewart, G and Triscott, J 1998 'Auldhill Portencross', *Archaeological Journal* **155**, 22–81.

Clark, J T (ed) 1900 *MacFarlane's Genealogical Collections*. Scottish History Society **33** and **34**, Edinburgh.

Coope, R 1986 'The "Long Gallery": Its origins development, use and decoration', *Architectural History* **29**, 43–78.

Coulsen, C 1979 'Structural Symbolism in Medieval Castle Design', *Journal British Archaeological Association* **132**, 73–90.

Courty, M A, Goldberg, P and Macphail, R 1989 *Soil and Micromophology in Archaeology*. Cambridge University Press, Cambridge.

Crummy, N 1988 *The Post-Roman Small Finds from Excavations in Colchester 1971–85*, Colchester, Colchester Archaeological Report **5**.

Dickson, C and J 2000 *Plants and People in Ancient Scotland*. Tempus Publishing Ltd, Stroud.

Dixon, P and Lott, B 1993 'The courtyard and the tower: contexts and symbols in the development of late medieval great houses', *Journal British Archaeological Association* **146**, 93–101.

Donaldson, G, 1983 *All the Queen's Men: power and politics in Mary Stewart's Scotland*. Batsford, London.

DOST: Dareau, G et al (eds) 2002 *A Dictionary of the Older Scottish Tongue*. Oxford University Press, Oxford.

Dunbar, J G 1999 *Scottish Royal Palaces. The Architecture of the Royal Residences during the Late Medieval and Early Renaissance Periods*. Tuckwell Press, East Linton.

Ewart G 1985 *Cruggleton Castle, Report of Excavations 1978–81*. Dumfries and Galloway Natural History and Archaeology Society Monograph (1985).

Ewart G 1992 'Dundonald Castle: Recent Work', *Chateau Gaillard* **16** (1992), 167–78.

Ewart G 1996 Unpublished report of Excavations at Culzean Castle (Report for NTS).

Ewart G and Murray H 1978–80 'Two early medieval timber buildings from Castle Hill, Peebles', *Proc Soc Antiq Scot* **110**, 519–28.

Fasti = Scott, H 1915 – *Fasti Ecclesiae Scoticanae: the succession of ministers in the Church of Scotland from the Reformation*, 11 vols, Edinburgh.

Fergusson, J 1963 *The White Hind*. Faber, London.

Franklin, J 1998 'Finds', in Ewart, G and Baker, F 'Carrick Castle: symbol and source of Campbell power in south Argyll from the 14th to the 17th century', *Proc Soc Antiq Scot* **128** (1998), 955–84.

Fraser, J 1878 *The Scotts of Buccleuch,* 2 vols.

Gallagher, D B 1987 'Tobacco Pipemaking in Glasgow, 1667–1967' in Davey, P (ed) 1987 *The Archaeology of the Clay Tobacco Pipe: Vol X. Scotland*, Oxford, BAR British Series **178**, 35–109.

Girouard, M 1978 *Life in the English Country House*. Yale University Press, Yale.

Goodall, A R 1983 'Non-Ferrous Metal Objects' *in* Mayes, P and Butler, L A S *Sandal Castle Excavations 1964–1973*. Wakefield Historical Publications, Leeds.

Groome, F H 1883 *Ordnance Gazetteer of Scotland*. Jack, Edinburgh.

Harrison, J. G., 2003 *Ben Lawers*. A Report for The Royal Commission on the Ancient And Historical Monuments of Scotland.

Harrison, J G 2004 *Hedges in Scotland, Particularly in East Lothian.* A Report for the Royal Commission on the Ancient and Historical Monuments of Scotland.

Hays, G 1984 'Scottish Renaissance Architecture' in Breeze, D (ed) *Studies in Scottish Antiquity presented to Stewart Cruden*. 196–231, John Donald, Edinburgh.

Historie: *The Historie and Descent of the House of Rowallane by Sir William Mure, Knight, of Rowallan*. Written in, or prior to 1657. Glasgow, 1825.

Howard, D, 1995 *The Architectural History of Scotland. Scottish Architecture from the Reformation to the Restoration, 1560–1660*. Edinburgh University Press, Edinburgh.

Howard, M 1987 *The Early Tudor Country House. Architecture and Politics 1490–1550*. George Philip, London.

Hume, I N 1961 'The Glass Wine Bottle in Colonial Virginia', *Journal Glass Studies* **3**, 91–117.

Jennings, S 1981 *Eighteen Centuries of Pottery from Norwich,* Norwich, East Anglian Archaeological Reports **13**.

Kinnes, I, Gibson, A, Ambers, J, Bowman, S, Leese, M and Boast, K 1991 'Radiocarbon dating and British beakers: the British Museum programme', *Scottish Archaeological Review* **8**, 95–109.

King, C 2003 'The organisation of social space in late medieval manor houses: an East Anglian Study', *Archaeological Journal* **160**, 104–24.

Kinnes, I, Gibson, A, Ambers, J, Bowman, S, Leese, M and Boast, K 1991 'Radiocarbon dating and British beakers: the British Museum programme', *Scottish Archaeological Review* **8** (1991), 95–109.

Land Use Consultants 1988 *An Inventory of Gardens and Designed Landscapes in Scotland*. Edinburgh, Historic Scotland.

Leeds, E T 1941 '17th and 18th Century Wine-Bottles of Oxford Taverns', *Oxoniensia* **6**, 44–55.

Macdougall, N 1989 *James IV*. Tuckwell Press, East Linton.

MacGibbon D and Ross, T 1887–92 *The Castellated and Domestic Architecture of Scotland from the 12th to the 18th Century*. D Douglas, Edinburgh.

MacKechnie, A 1995 'Design Approaches in Early Post Reformation Houses', in Gow, I and Rowan, A (eds) *Scottish Country Houses 1600–1914*, 15–33. Edinburgh University Press, Edinburgh.

MacKechnie, A 2005, 'Court and Courtier Architecture, 1424–1660' in Oram, R and Stell, G (eds) *Lordship and Architecture in Medieval and Renaissance Scotland*, 293–326. John Donald, Edinburgh.

MacLeod, W 1895 'Protocol book of Robert Broun', *Archaeological and Historical Collections relating to the Counties of Ayr and Wigton* **9**. Edinburgh.

McKean, C 2004 *The Scottish Chateau: the country house of renaissance Scotland*, Sutton, Stroud.

McKinley, J I 1993 'Bone fragment size and weights of bone from modern British cremations and the implications for the interpretation of archaeological cremations', *International Journal of Osteoarchaeology* 3 (1993), 283–87.

McWilliam, C 1978 Lothian except Edinburgh (= Buildings of Scotland series), Pevsner, London.

M'Naught, D 1912 *Kilmaurs Parish and Burgh*. Gardner, Paisley.

Marshall, R K 1984 'Wet-Nursing in Scotland: 1500–1800, *Review Scottish Culture* **1**, 43–51.

Mays, S 1998 *The Archaeology of Human Bones*. Routledge, London and New York.

Monteath, R 1829 *Survey and Report on the Rowallan Estate in Ayrshire*. Glasgow.

Moorhouse, S 1971 'Finds from Basing House, Hampshire (c.1540–1645): Part Two', *Post-Medieval Archaeology* **5**, 35–76.

Morrison, A 1971 'Cist burials and food vessels – some recent discoveries and rediscoveries in Western Scotland', *Glasgow Archaeological Journal*, **2**, 8–36.

Morrison, A 1978 *The Bronze Age in Ayrshire* (= Ayrshire Collections **12.4**). Ayr.

Paterson, J 1852 *History of the County of Ayr*. vol II. Stevenson, Edinburgh.

Paul, J B 1904 *The Scots Peerage*. Douglas, Edinburgh.

Pollock, J 1882, 'Woodwork at Rowallan Castle' *Archaeological and Historical Collections relating to the Counties of Ayr and Wigton* **3**, 84–6.

RCAHMS 1956 *The County of Roxburgh*. HMSO, Edinburgh.

RCAHMS 1992 *Argyll. An Inventory of the Monuments*. Volume 7. *Mid Argyll and Cowal. Medieval and Later Monuments*. Stationery Office, Edinburgh.

Retours: *Inquisitionum ad Capellam Domini Regis Retornatarum . . . Abebreviatio*. Edinburgh, 1811.

Ritchie, J N G and Shepherd, A G 1973 'Beaker Pottery and Associated Artifacts in South-West Scotland', *Transactions Dumfries Galloway Natural History and Archaeology Society* **42**, 25–50.

Ritchie, P E 2002 *Mary of Guise in Scotland, 1548–1560; a political career*, Tuckwell Press, East Linton.

Robertson, G 1820 *Topographical Description of Ayrshire; more particularly of Cunninghame*. Cunninghame Press, Irvine.

Ross, A 2006 'Scottish environmental history and the (mis) use of Soums', *The Agricultural History Review*, **54**.2, 213–28

Rowallan 1976 *Rowallan: The Autobiography of Lord Rowallan*. Paul Harris, Edinburgh.

Sanderson, M H B 1997 *Ayrshire and the Reformation. People and Change, 1490–1600*. Tuckwell Press, East Linton.

Sanderson, M H B 2003 'The Lollard trial: some clues to the spread of pre-Protestant religious dissent in Scotland, and its legacy', *Scottish Church History Society* **33**, 1–33.

Savage, P 1980 *Lorimer and the Edinburgh Craft Designers*. Paul Harris, Edinburgh.

Scott J G 1989 'The Hall and Motte at Courthill, Dalry, Ayrshire', *Proc Soc Antiq Scot* **119**, 271–8.

Sheridan, A 1997 'Food Vessels from Westhaugh of Tulliemet', in Stewart, M E C and Barclay, G J, 'Excavations in burial and ceremonial sites of the Bronze Age in Tayside', *Tayside and Fife Archaeological Journal* **3** (1997), 37–41.

Simpson, D D A 1965 'Food Vessels in South-West Scotland', *Transactions Dumfries Galloway Natural History Archaeology Society* **42** (1965), 25–50.

Smith, J 1895 *Prehistoric Man in Ayrshire*. Stock, London.

Smout, T C (ed), 2003 *People and Woods in Scotland: a history*. Edinburgh University Press, Edinburgh.

Stace, C 1991 *New Flora of the British Isles*. Cambridge University Press, Cambridge.

Strawhorn, J 1975 *Ayrshire: The Story of a County*, Ayr, Ayrshire Archaeological and Natural History Society.

Thurley, S 2003 *Hampton Court. A Social and Architectural History*. Yale University Press, New Haven & London.

Timperley, L R (ed) 1976 *A Directory of Landownership in Scotland c 1770*. (= Scottish Record Society) Edinburgh.

Tough, W (ed) 1898 The *Works of Sir William Mure of Rowallan*. Edinburgh, Scottish Text Society **40**.

Thompson, M W 1987 *The Decline of the Castle*. Cambridge University Press, Cambridge.

Ubelaker, D H 1978 *Human Skeletal Remains*. Aldine, Washington.

Watson, C B B, 1929 *Roll of Edinburgh Burgesses, 1406–1700*. Scottish Record Society

Weaver, L 1913 'Rowallan, Ayrshire. The seat of Lord Rowallan', *Country Life* (**27**, 420–5.

Wells, C 1960 'A study of cremation', *Antiquity* **34** (1960), 29.

Whitehead, R 1996 *Buckles 1250–1800*. Greenlight Publishing, Chelmsford.

Whyte, I D 1979 *Agriculture and Society in 17th Century Scotland*. John Donald, Edinburgh.

Woodfield, C 1981 'Finds from the Free Grammar School at the Whitefriars, Coventry, c.1545–c.1557/58', *Post-Medieval Archaeology* **15**, 81–159.

Young, A 1997 *Robert the Bruce's Rivals: The Comyns, 1212–1314*. Tuckwell Press, East Linton.

Young, M D (ed) 1993 The *Parliaments of Scotland. Burgh and Shire Commissioners*. Scottish Academic Press, Edinburgh.

Primary Sources

ADCC 1 – Acts of the Lords of Council in Civil Causes, 1478–1494. 1839. Edinburgh.

ADCC 2 – Acts of the Lords of Council in Civil Causes, 1496–1501. Edinburgh.

ADCC 3 – Acts of the Lords of Council vol III 1501–1503 Calderwood, Alma B (ed) 1993. Edinburgh.

ADCP – Hannay, R K (ed) 1932, Acts of the Lords of Council in Public Affairs, 1501–1554. Edinburgh.

ALA –Acts of the Lords Auditors of Causes and Complaints 1466–1494 1839. Edinburgh. *CDS – Calendar of Documents Relating to Scotland* Bain, J (ed) 1881–8. Edinburgh.

CSP Scot – Calendar of State Papers Relating to Scotland and Mary, Queen of Scots. Bain, J (ed) 1898. Edinburgh.

ER – Exchequer Rolls of Scotland. Stuart, J (ed) 1878–1908. Edinburgh.

MW – Accounts of the Masters of Works for Building and Repairing Royal Castles and Palaces Paton, H M, Imrie, J and Dunbar, J G (eds) 1957. HMSO, Edinburgh.

RMS – Registrum Magni Sigilli Regum Scotorum: The Register of the Great Seal of Scotland, 1306–1688. Paul, J B and Thomson, J M (eds) 1882-1914. Edinburgh.

RPC – The Register of the Privy Council of Scotland. Burton, J H *et al* 1877. Edinburgh.

RRS – Regesta Regum Scottorum. Edinburgh.

RSS – Registrum Secreti Sigilli Regum Scotorum: The Register of the Privy Seal of Scotland. Livingstone, M (ed) 1908-82. Edinburgh.

Manuscript sources

AA – Ayrshire Archives

EACMAS – East Ayrshire Council Museum and Arts Service

Houghton Library, Harvard University – MS Hyde, letter of Flora MacLeod Mure-campbell of Raasay (http://oasis.lib.harvard.edu/oasis/deliver/~hou01776)

Laing MS – Edinburgh University Library, Special Collections, The Laing Collection

NAS – National Archives of Scotland

NLS – National Library of Scotland

RCAHMS – Royal Commission on the Ancient and Historical Monuments of Scotland

Ayrshire Archives (AA)

AA ATD41 – Rowallan Papers

East Ayrshire Council Museum and Arts Service (EACMAS)

EACMAS – Cessnock Papers

National Archives of Scotland, Edinburgh

NAS CC8 – Edinburgh Commissary Court Register of Testaments

NAS CC9 – Glasgow Commissary Court Register of Testaments

NAS CC9/7/9 – Testament of Jean Porterfield, spouse of William Mure, younger, 7/4/1614

NAS CS7/3 Register of Acts and Decreets of Court of Session, 1st series, 1542-64

NAS E69 – Hearth Tax Return

NAS E326/1/11–16 – Window Tax Return

NAS E326/3/4 – Inhabited Houses Tax

NAS GD1/19 – Miscellaneous charters

NAS SC6/44/10/235 – Testament of Flora Campbell Mure, 23/3/1840.

NAS GD3 – Papers of the Montgomerie Family, Earls of Eglinton

NAS GD8 – Boyd Papers

NAS GD25 – Ailsa Muniments

NAS GD25/1/1024 – Sasine arising from the matrimonial contract between Neil Montgomery and Marian Mure, 9 February 1592.

NAS GD26 – Leven and Melville Papers

NAS GD90 – Yule Collection

NAS GD148 – Papers of the Cuninghame Family of Craigends, Renfrewshire

NAS GD224 – Scott of Buccleuch

NAS GD237 – Earls of Glasgow

NAS GD39 – Earls of Glencairn Papers

NAS GD406 – Hamilton Muniments

NAS IRS – Inland Revenue Survey of houses and properties

MW/1/1383 – Ancient Monuments file, 1943–50

NAS RD – General Register of Deeds

NAS RH11/19 – Bailiary of Cunningham

NAS RHP – Maps and plans series

NAS RS – Register of Sasines

NAS SC6 – Ayr Sheriff Court Records

NLS MS 3416 – Mure of Rowallan MSS, 18th-century copies

NLS MS 3813 – Mure of Rowallan 16th-century manuscripts

NLS Adv MS4.1.7 – Mure of Rowallan correspondence

NLS Adv MS22.2.9 – Mure of Rowallan correspondence

National Library of Scotland (NLS)

NLS Adv MS54.1.7–54.1.8. Rowallan Papers. Letters of John Mure, 1548–93 (Adv MS22.9 ff 47–60 for transcription)

NLS MS3813 Letter signed by Earl of Arran as Regent in favour of John Mure of Rowallan, 1551

NLS Ch2042 Royal letter in favour of Mungo, son of John Mure, 1514

DRAWINGS AND CARTOGRAPHIC SOURCES

British Library
Military Survey of Scotland by William Roy, 1747–55, sheet 04/6b.

Glasgow City Archives
Photograph of Rowallan by Thomas Annan

Hunterian Art Gallery
Charles Rennie Mackintosh, pencil drawing, Rowallan Castle: corner of courtyard, c 1887 (Catalogue no 41417)

National Library of Scotland
Forman Armorial, c 1562 (NLS Adv MS31.4.2).
Map of 'Cuninghamia' by Timothy Blaeu, published 1654 (NLS WD3B/20).
Andrew Armstrong *A New Map of Ayrshire* 1775 (NLS EMS.s.515).
OS Ayrshire Sheet XVIII, scale1:10,560, surveyed 1856

Royal Commission on the Ancient and Historical Monuments of Scotland (RCAHMS)

Cowie and Seton Collection
AYD 58/13P – Bedroom floor plan, N Joyce, 1869

AYD 58/14P – Ground-floor plan, N Joyce, 1869

AYD 58/15P – Attic floor plan, N Joyce, 1869

AYD 58/16P – N elevation to court, N Joyce, 1869

AYD 58/18P – W elevation and section, N Joyce, 1869

AYD 58/19P – S elevation showing additions, N Joyce, 1869

Orphoot, Whiting and Lindsay Collection
AYD 58/5 – Mechanical copy of drawing showing ground-floor plan, Orphoot, Whiting and Lindsay, 1948

AYD 58/6 – Mechanical copy of drawing showing E elevation and sections, Orphoot, Whiting and Lindsay, 1948

AYD 58/7 – Mechanical copy of drawing showing elevations, Orphoot, Whiting and Lindsay, 1948

AYD 58/8 – Mechanical copy of drawing showing plan of attic and undercroft, Orphoot, Whiting and Lindsay, 1948

AYD 58/9: Mechanical copy of drawing showing plan of first floor and E elevation of courtyard, Orphoot, Whiting and Lindsay, 1948

Ex Blair Cadell MacMillan WS Collection
AYD 58/24 – Plan of basement, Leadbetter and Fairley, 1896

AYD 58/25 – Plan of ground floor, Leadbetter and Fairley, 1896

AYD 58/26 – Plan of first floor, Leadbetter and Fairley, 1896

AYD 58/27 – Plan of ground floor with additions, Leadbetter and Fairley, 1896

AYD 58/28 – Plan of principal floor with additions, Leadbetter and Fairley, 1896

AYD 58/29 – Plan of bedroom floor with additions, Leadbetter and Fairley, 1896

AYD 58/30 – Plan of attic floor with additions, Leadbetter and Fairley, 1896

AYD 58/31 – S and W elevations with additions, Leadbetter and Fairley, 1896

AYD 58/32 – N elevation and section of S wing, Leadbetter and Fairley, 1896

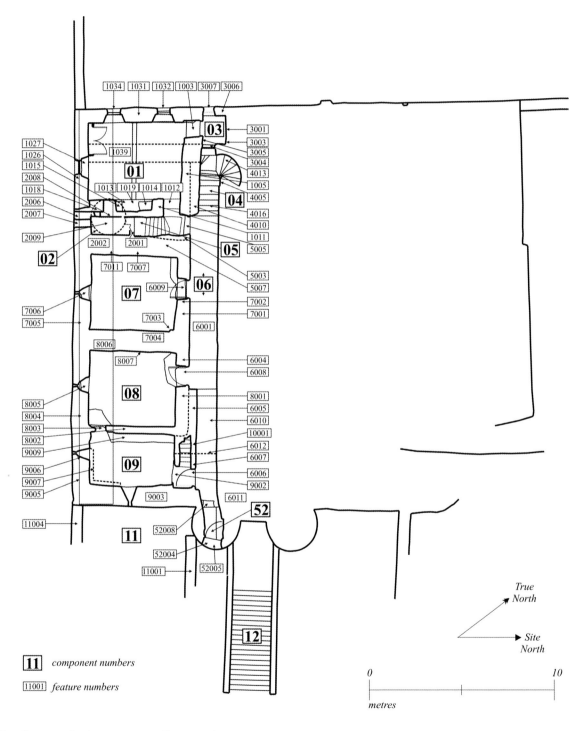

73 Plan of basement, showing component and feature numbers

TECHNICAL APPENDIX: ANALYSIS OF THE COMPONENTS OF THE BUILDING

Gordon Ewart

THE STANDING BUILDING SURVEY AND RECORDING METHODOLOGY

The upstanding building recording programme was based on the division of the upstanding structure in terms of components with due reference to all elevations, floors and ceilings via archaeological contextual referencing. It was important to establish a comprehensive coverage of the entire complex and consequently prioritisation of key features was inevitable. These included obviously major elements such as doors, fireplaces, windows, etc, but also any indications of breaks in build and structurally diagnostic elements such as mouldings, etc. Each component was assigned a unique number and the features within that component were recorded with reference to that unique number. A feature recorded during standing building survey can be identified by either a four- or five- digit number.

For example, **F4010** would be Feature 10 in Component 4, while **F40010** would be Feature 10 in Component 40. Any three-digit feature numbers (for example, **F123**) refer to excavation contexts.

Features were recorded on pro-forma record cards and later converted to a digital database. This database is not presented with this report but is available as part of the site archive. A summary analysis of the findings of the standing building recording programme is presented below in tabular form.

It should be noted that this was standing building record was completed on a site-specific basis and does not represent a complete record of every single structural feature. However, the evidence does demonstrate the main building periods of the castle from the 13th century to the present (Illus 73-76).

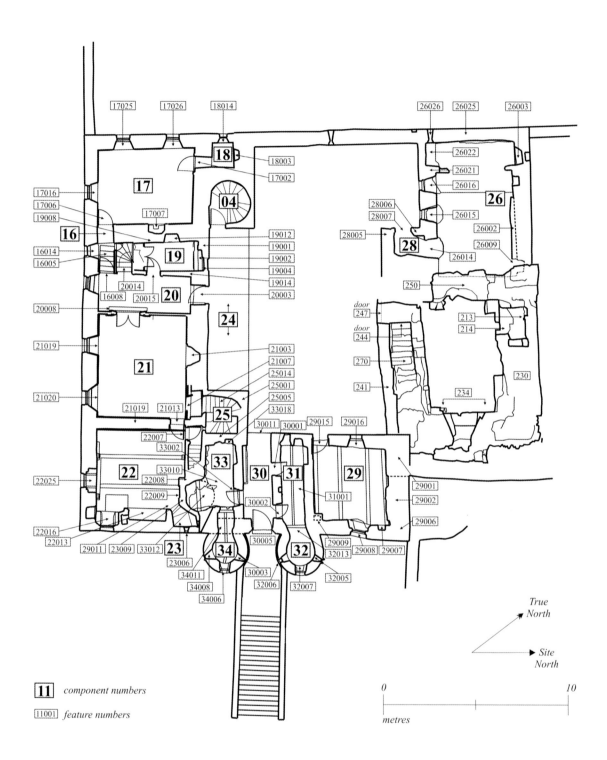

11 *component numbers*

11001 *feature numbers*

74 Plan of ground floor, showing component and feature numbers

PERIOD 1: HALL/TOWER HOUSE MID 13TH TO 15TH CENTURY

Period 1: The NE Tower – Ground Floor (Illus 18-21)

Ground floor: Chamber 1, Component 53	
Plan	3.8m by 6.1m
Access	Via S wall doorway (F247/F244)
Windows	E window (F232)
Discussion	The absence of a fireplace suggests that this was service space beneath the first floor hall.

Period 1: The NE Tower – First Floor

First Floor Hall: Chamber 1, upper floor Component 53	
Plan	C3.8m by 6.1 m
Access	From S via an intramural stair– door site likely to be towards the E end of the chamber
Windows	N wall window (F213), with probably a second in the E wall
Fireplace	W wall – fireplace (F250/F251)
Discussion	At first floor was a hall featuring a large fireplace, with 15th-century moulding, in the W wall and windows probably in the N and E walls. The doorway into the hall might be assumed to be located in the S wall, towards the E end of the chamber, opposite the top of an intramural stair, and furthest from the fireplace. First and ground floor were separated by a wooden floor supported within the gable walls (F253/F254).

PERIOD 2: E AND S COURTYARD RANGES: 1480s – EARLY 16TH CENTURY, MAINLY JOHN MURE

Period 2: The NE Tower – as Period 1

Period 2: The South Range – Basement (Illus 73 and 77)

The basement chambers of the S range and possibly the W courtyard wall survive from this period as standing structures. They comprise at least three chambers, although it is likely that the well that lies to the W of Chamber 1 would have been in a further room with its own window. The western limits of the Period 2 basement are not clear at present, but may have been close to those suggested for Period 3.

Chamber 1, Component 7	
Plan	Up to 5m by 4m
Access	A door in the N wall, slightly E of Period 4 version (F7002)
Windows	One centrally placed dumb-bell loop (F7006)
Discussion	The insertion of the vaults in Period 3 has caused some rebuilding of E and W walls as well as the relocation of its N door.

Chamber 2, Component 8	
Plan	5m by 4.2m
Access	From N door (F6008)
Windows	One centrally located dumbbell loop (F8005).
Discussion	This basement chamber has some evidence of earlier masonry in its W wall (F8007) where earlier walls have been thickened to accommodate the Period 3 vault. The location of the door towards the W end of the N wall is a consequence of the wall (Component 10) above. The door site is therefore largely original – however, the door itself appears to have been enlarged on the basis of a possible fragment of an earlier vault in the base of the existing W wall.

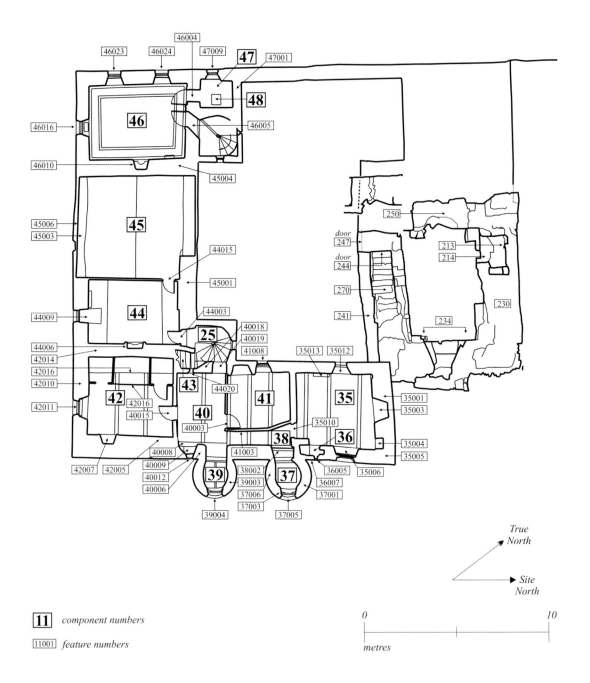

11 component numbers

11001 feature numbers

75 Plan of first floor, showing component and feature numbers

Chamber 3, Component 9	
Plan	The full extent of this space is not obvious, but appears to be some 4.75m N–S.
Access	A door linking with Chamber 2 (F9013) appears original and there may have been a through route towards the transe via doorway (F9002).
Windows	One centrally located dumb-bell loop (F9006).
Discussion	To the W is masonry (F9008), a possible storage bench

The Transe, Component 6	
Plan	Up to 3.75m wide by 19m long.
Access	From W and E ends, although precise details no longer survive. Doorway (F3004), at the extreme W end of the transe, may be a Period 3 access route, although it appears to open out beyond the defensive wall.
Windows	See access
Discussion	This access route is the result of the drop in level between the original building platform, as defined by the NE tower sequence, and the remaining available building platforms to the S. It is likely that the location of an extended range outwith the tower house complex had to be located well to the S of the original platform on the nearest available level ground. This resulted in the basement sequence of rooms for the S range linked only at ground level with the rest of the castle complex. The upper platform was extended to form the present courtyard surface, and the tipped deposits were revetted by the N wall of the transe. The transe appears to have been unroofed at this time and access to the ground floor was via the intramural stair at the E end of the range. The W end of the transe includes steps at a higher threshold, later integrated with a new Period 4 western basement chamber. This may in turn indicate that the natural ground level rose in this area of the site and that the Period 3 S range sat at the limits of raised ground on its W and N sides. A fragment of outer defensive wall, later defining the N side of Component 3 and its successors, contains a gun loop (F18003). This could be seen as an outer wall which was so angled as to retain the line of the transe before merging with the W wall of Chamber 1 (Period 3), although access to the exterior elevation of the W wall was not possible at the time.

Period 2: The S Range – Ground Floor (Illus 74 and 77)

All that survives is the intramural stair arrangement (Component 10) and its door (F22007) (Illus 78).

The Intramural Stair, Component 10	
Plan	0.75m by 4m
Access	Door (F22007) at the top of the stairs and doors (F9002) and (F6006) at the foot of the stairs
Windows	One loop in the N wall (F6007)
Discussion	This route was retained throughout the development of the S range. The limits of the associated hall or annexe at upper level are not obvious. It is noteworthy that the mouldings around the Great Hall E fireplace (F22013) date to c 1500 and as such pre-date the known building programme of Mungo Mure. This may represent the eastern limits of an earlier hall.

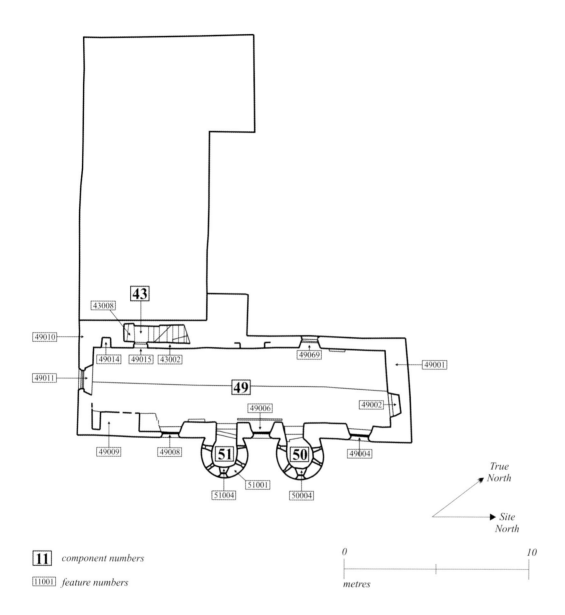

76 Plan of second floor, showing component and feature numbers

PERIOD 3: GREAT HALL AND COURTYARD COMPLEX, MUNGO MURE AND JOHN MURE 1513–50S

Period 3: The NE Tower – as Period 2

Period 3: The S Range – Basement (Illus 73 and 79)

The S range comprised four chambers aligned N–S, accessed via a covered transe to the N. The layout was based on much of the Period 2 S range at basement level.

Chamber 1, Component 1	
This chamber defined the W end of the range, although only the E and part of the N and S walls remain, the W wall having been removed in Period 4.	
Plan	4m by 5m internally
Access	From the N (door (F4011)
Windows	None survive, although window (F1027) may be a revision of an earlier opening in the S wall.
Discussion	This chamber is seen as the revision of the Period 2 equivalent and as such integrated earlier features. These include the well (F2009) and the higher floor level of the Period 3 chamber. The latter is indicated by short flights of steps (Components 4 and 5).

Chamber 2, Component 7	
This chamber is identical in plan to the Period 2 version.	
Plan	4m by 5m (max) internally
Access	Door in N wall (F6009)
Windows	One centrally located dumbbell loop (F7006)
Discussion	The N door appears to have been altered from the Period 2 version.

Chamber 3, Component 8 (Illus 80)	
Plan	4m by 5m internally
Access	N door (F6008) and E door (F8003)
Windows	One centrally located dumb-bell loop (F8005)
Discussion	This chamber was created by the relining of the E Period 2 equivalent wall by the addition of masonry (F8002) against Period 2 walling (F9008). The Period 3 E door appears to recycle the existing Period 2 door.

Chamber 4, Component 9 (Illus 81)	
Plan	2.5m by 4.75m
Access	W door leading to Chamber 3 (F8003). N door (F9002) to transe and stair (Component 10).
Windows	One S window dumb-bell loop type and one E window, dumb-bell loop (F9006) and (F9004) respectively)
Discussion	This chamber appears to be built over an earlier component from Period 2. Masonry (F9007) is evident, particularly under the Period 3 S wall (F9005). The N door is also a Period 2 survival (F9002) and access is the intramural stair (Component 10) and also the transe to the N.

The Transe, Component 6 (Illus 82)	
Plan	c 20m by 1.6m
Access	To the W via Period 2 steps (F4016) plus spiral stair to ground-floor courtyard level (Component 4). To E via door (F6004) to intramural stair (Component 10). Three further doors serve each of the remaining chambers (F6008, F6009 and F5005).
Windows	At the extreme W end a recycled Period 2 door (F3005) forms a new window (F3004).
Discussion	This passage dates at least from Period 2 and is the rationalisation of the steep drop in level between the main building terrace and the available building area outwith the early tower. This was further landscaped by the infilling of an as yet undefined area between the natural limits of the early building platform and the present transe floor, to form the present courtyard (Period 3 onwards). The transe may have been uncovered during Period 2 for most of its length, but was vaulted over with the advent of new spiral stairs. To the W Component 4 took the Period 2 flight of steps up to the new courtyard level, while to the E a new spiral stair was created at ground-floor level above the line of the transe (F33012, etc.).

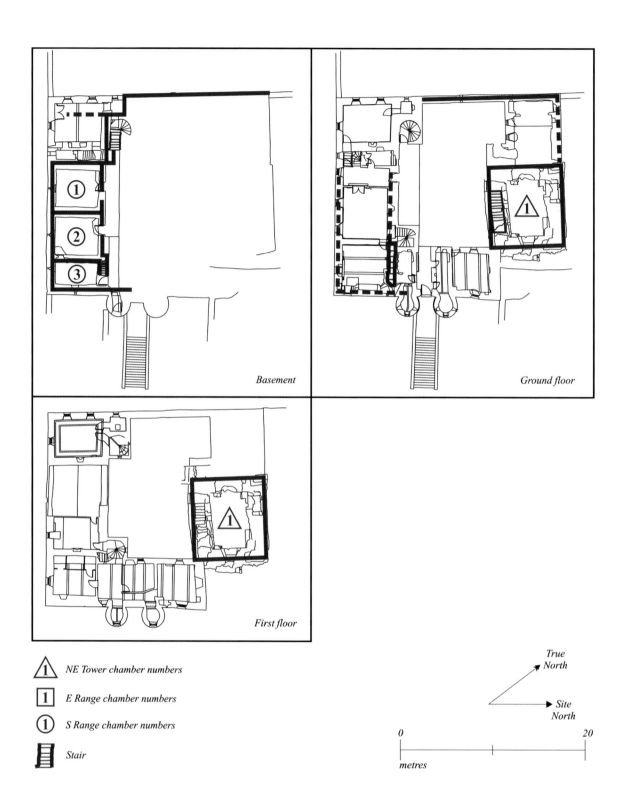

Basement

Ground floor

First floor

△1̲ NE Tower chamber numbers

□1 E Range chamber numbers

① S Range chamber numbers

▦ Stair

True North

Site North

0   20

metres

77 Period 2 plans

Period 3: The S Range – Ground Floor (Ilus 74 and 79)

This level comprises three chambers: an antechamber, hall and a solar apartment to the E.

Chamber 1, Components 17 and 19	
Plan	Later work has completely removed any obvious structural evidence for this chamber, but it arguably follows the footprint of the equivalent basement chamber below (4m by 5m).
Access	Presently blocked door from outer courtyard (to W of door, F19002) and a W door. Stair (Component 5) from basement
Windows	No surviving evidence; obscured by later additions
Discussion	This room is accessed from the courtyard and over the covered transe. The full extent and function of this room remain unknown; possibly a service area with access to well chamber below.

Chamber 2/Components 20 and 21, Hall	
Plan	The full dimensions of the maximum hall space, with screens passage, are 9.4m by 5m.
Access	Door in N wall, via screens passage (F19004). Access to Chamber 3 was via E door (F21013).
Windows	Three windows, existing in Period 4, may date from this period. Window to N (F21007) later replaced by a door.
Discussion	This is the hall possibly built by Mungo Mure. There was a fireplace in its N wall. A doorway leads to a chamber to the E; the mouldings of this doorway (F21003) are of 16th-century date.

Chamber 3, Component 22	
Plan	5m by 4.5m
Access	In W wall, door (F22103). In N wall, recycled Period 2 door (F22007). Also at E end, door (F22009) leading to E spiral stair.
Windows	Two original windows survive, S wall E end (F22025) and E wall (F22016). A further secondary light (F23006) lies in a recess (Component 23) N of fireplace (F22013).
Discussion	This is a private apartment or solar at the E end of the hall. There was a fireplace (F22013). The E spiral stair linked the E range and S range first-floor levels with the ground floor.

Period 3: The S Range – First Floor (Illus 75 and 79)

This comprises one chamber located at the E end of the range.

First Floor, Component 42	
Plan	4.5m by 5m
Access	Via N door (F40015) leading to E spiral stair
Windows	No original window survives.
Discussion	This is a private apartment or solar. There was a fireplace (F42007). The spiral stair linked the E range and S range first floor levels with the ground floor.

Period 3: The E Range – Basement

There is no basement level due to the rise in ground level between the primary building platform and the lower building terrace defined by the S range.

Period 3: The E Range – Ground Floor (Illus 74 and 79)

This probably comprises three chambers and represents the infill of a probable Period 2 E barmkin wall and the SE corner of the NE tower. It is likely that this area of the site has featured the main entrance from Period 2 onwards.

Chamber 1 (S),Component 33	
Plan	An irregular shape as it now combines spiral stair (F33012) within a narrow rectangular chamber. The latter measures 1.75m by 4.25 m.
Access	Via N door (F33002)
Windows	A small window is located in the W wall (F33018), later blocked in Period 4.
Discussion	This structure is built over the transe and accommodates a new spiral stair leading to upper floors in S and E range. It is also highly likely that the gate house arrangements embellished in Period 4 were broadly in place in Period 3 and that the main entrance to the castle lay to the N of this chamber. This building is critical to the effective rationalisation of the courtyard plan and the integration of S and E ranges.

N elevation

E elevation

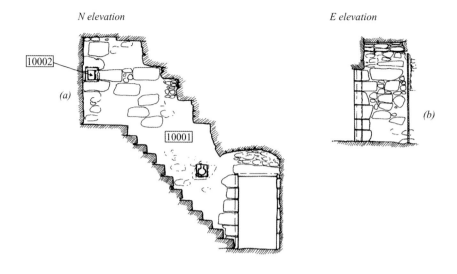

10002

10001

(a)

(b)

S elevation

W elevation

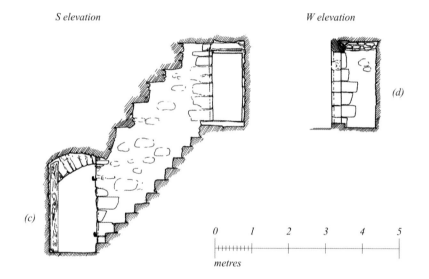

(c)

(d)

0   1   2   3   4   5

metres

78 Component 10

Chamber 2, Component 29	
Plan	This structure completes the E side of the courtyard circuit linking with the NE tower.
Access	Likely access from courtyard although original doorway does not survive.
Windows	The E wall window (F29008)
Discussion	The irregularity of the E wall of this chamber plus the presence of an integrated garderobe chute (F29009), both Period 4 features, indicate how the Period 4 N gatehouse tower was inserted into an existing E range. This probably featured the main entrance, but the details of range and entrance way are presently obscured.

Chamber 3, Components 29–31	
Plan	The Period 4 N gatehouse tower and chamber (Components 31 and 32) have obscured the southern limits of a Period 3 range linked to some form of entrance passage between Chamber 3 and the S chamber (Chamber 1). This structure is probably 4m wide (E–W), although its N–S dimensions are not clear.
Access	Period 3 access is difficult to discern and may incorporate earlier work, all of which could be obscured by Period 4 works.
Windows	Not identified
Discussion	This is probably the N side of a gatehouse entrance, the southern limits of which are not clear.

Period 3: The E Range – First Floor (Illus 75 and 79)

This possibly comprises two chambers of roughly similar dimensions, although a third chamber may have been in place, echoing the ground floor arrangements.

Chamber 1, Component 42	
Plan	6m by 4m
Access	Door in S wall (F4005) leading to first floor, S range chamber via spiral stair, Component 42. Door in the N wall (F35010) leading to Chamber 2.
Windows	W wall window (F40020), E wall window (F40012)
Discussion	This chamber is part of the private solar or suite of rooms linked with the S range.

Chamber 2, Component 35	
Plan	4.5m by 4m
Access	S door (F35010) linked to Chamber 1. Also door (F38002) to garderobe, Component 36.
Windows	Small garderobe window (F36005) and part of Period 4 window (F35006). It is possible that the present window (F35012) was a revision of a Period 3 window site.
Discussion	There is a fireplace in the N gable (F35003) along with a recess (F35004), suggesting domestic accommodation.

Period 3: The E Range – Second Floor (Illus 76 and 79)

The layout of the upper floors has been completely obscured by the Period 4 gallery. However, it is likely that there was some form of garret accommodation at this level leading to wall head access, all later enclosed by Period 4 when the wall head was raised.

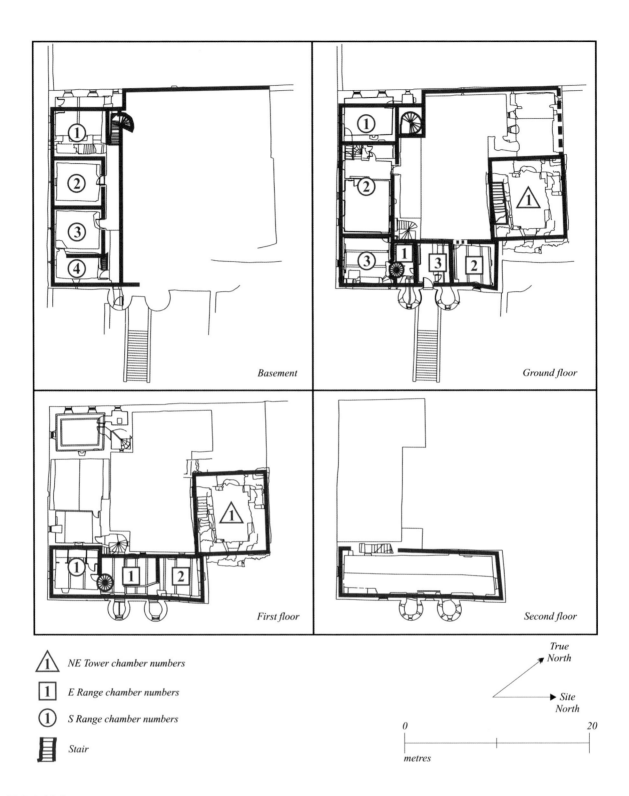

Basement

Ground floor

First floor

Second floor

NE Tower chamber numbers

E Range chamber numbers

S Range chamber numbers

Stair

True North

Site North

0   metres   20

79 Period 3 plans

PERIOD 4: FOREWORK, BACK WORK, WOMAN HOUSE AND GALLERY, JOHN MURE 1550s–81

Period 4: The NE Tower – as Period 2

Period 4: The S Range – Basement

The S range comprised seven chambers. (Illus 73 and 83)

Chamber 1 (W), Component 1	
Plan	4.25m by 5.25m
Access	In the N wall, door (F1003) to annexe (Component 3). In E wall, door (F1012) leading to Chamber 3 (Component 5).
Windows	Three main windows – one in S wall (F1027), two in W wall (F1034) and (F1032). An aperture exists linking newly formed well chamber (Component 2) in SE corner of Chamber 1 (F1018).
Discussion	This kitchen is created by the insertion of a new E wall (F1011) with a fireplace and flue above. The old W wall has been removed and a new line established further W (F1031). This was intended to tie in with the line of an existing Period 2 barmkin wall and in so doing create the annexe (Component 3). The creation of E wall (F1011) necessitated a new door (F1012) and limited access to the well chamber (Component 2). The floor level has been altered (lowered) to generally harmonise with the general floor level of the transe and other basement rooms. This has necessitated the blocking of the N door.

Chamber 2, Component 2	
Plan	2.25m by 1m
Access	Via a recess/doorway (F1018), 1m in height, 820 mm wide and 620 mm deep. The jambs are of well-dressed sandstone. The lintel has a check in its lower face.
Windows	One barred window in S wall (F2007) with splayed reveals and a double sandstone lintel.
Discussion	The well (F2009) is at least Period 2 in date. It does however feature a N wall of similar vintage to Period 2 wall (F2002). The explanation may in turn be linked to the change in levels enacted in Period 4 where the Period 2 floor levels for Chamber 1 were higher. Consequently the wall forming the N side of Chamber 2 (F2001) respects the threshold, or the top, of some form of limited enclosure with winding mechanism, etc, for the well itself. There is no precise evidence for how the well was incorporated within the Period 2 basement, but the new wall (F1011) clearly altered some earlier access arrangement.

Chamber 3, Component 5	
Plan	3.5m by 1m
Access	N door (F5005) and W door (F1012)
Windows	None
Discussion	This space was created by the insertion of wall (F1011) and became a stair passage, although the stairs may relate to Period 3. This ultimately links with Period 4 access to the first floor. The stair was part of the Period 3 arrangements for service access from ground-floor/courtyard level.

Chambers 4, 5 and 6
Exactly the same as in Period 3

Chamber 7, Component 52	
Plan	1m by 1.6m
Access	Present door (F52008) from transe dates from Period 5.
Windows	Possible window in W wall (F52005), altered in Period 5
Discussion	Possible room in base of new drum towers of gatehouse. It is possible that this room was not accessible until Period 5.

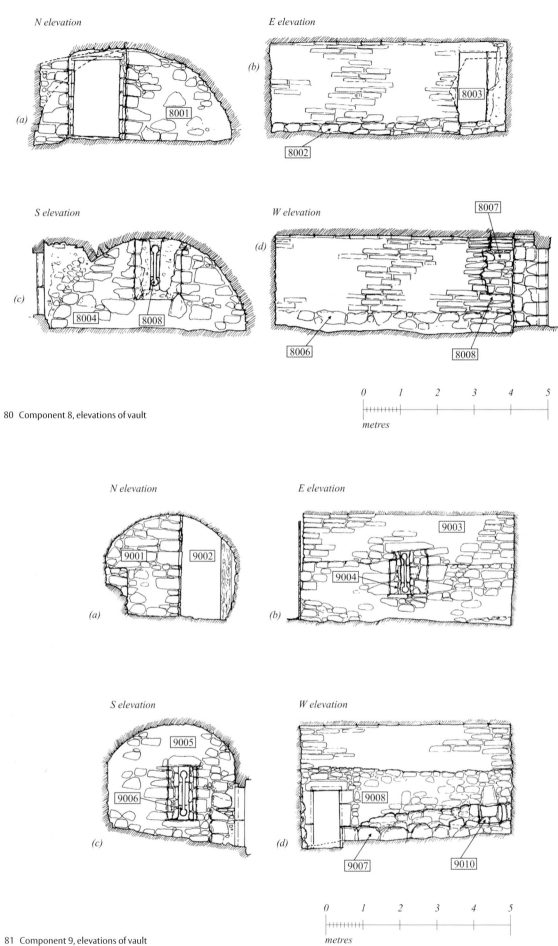

80 Component 8, elevations of vault

81 Component 9, elevations of vault

Chamber 8, Component 3	
Plan	1.5m by 1.5m
Access	S door (F1003)
Windows	W wall (F3007)
Discussion	This small space resulted from extension of the earlier W courtyard wall by the addition of a new W wall for Period 5 Chamber 1 (F3006) and (F1031). On the evidence of a gun loop (F18003) visible at ground-floor level, the N wall (F3001) was at one time an external wall. A blocked door (F3004) in its E wall is Period 2 access to the W end of the Period 3 transe. This space is retained throughout the S range sequence of building as a small annexe to the main W chambers.

Period 4: The S Range – Ground Floor (Illus 74 and 83)

This comprises six chambers.

Chamber 1, Component 17	
Plan	5.5m by 4m
Access	Door (F17006) in E wall leading to Stair 16. Door (F17002) in N wall leading to Chamber 6 (Component 18).
Windows	Three main window sites – S wall (F17016) and W wall (F17025 and F17026)
Discussion	Fireplace in E wall (F17007). The S and W walls have both been rebuilt, most likely during Period 6. It is assumed that this work reinstated earlier features.

Chamber 2, Component 16	
Plan	1m by 2.5m
Access	Door at W end (F17006) leading to Chamber 1 and at E end (F16008) leading to Chamber 3. Narrow door in N wall leading onto stair (Component 5).
Windows	S wall (F16014)
Discussion	This room is intended for access between the retained Period 3 ground-floor levels and the new lower W end chamber. Along with Stair 5 this represents access down to the kitchen via a secondary service door in the N wall (F16005). The access routes for both Components 16 and 5 date from Period 3, but may well have been reconstructed in Period 5.

Chamber 3, Component 21	
Plan	5m by 8.5m
Access	From the N via outer door (F19004) and from the E via door (F2103). New door (F21007) in N wall converted from window.
Windows	Three surviving main windows in S wall (F2012), (F21019) and (F21020)
Discussion	The fireplace in the N wall (F21003) is obscured by the present Period 5 panelling. This chamber retains the Period 3 courtyard entrance. The N window (F21007) was enlarged to form a door to a new E stair (Component 25).

Chamber 4, Component 22	
Plan	5m by 4.5m
Access	In W wall, door from hall (F2103). In N wall, Period 2 door (F22007). Period 3 E spiral stair removed.
Windows	As in Period 3

Chamber 5, Component 19	
Plan	3m by 1.5m
Access	Via outer door to the N (F19002)
Windows	None
Discussion	This small space (Component 19) survives along with the adjacent stairs as a Period 5 structure, but is likely to have been reflected in the Period 4 layout as the screens passage or antechamber before entering the main hall space (Chamber 3). The general symmetry of the fenestration in the S wall of Chamber 3 also suggests some form of N–S subdivision at this point.

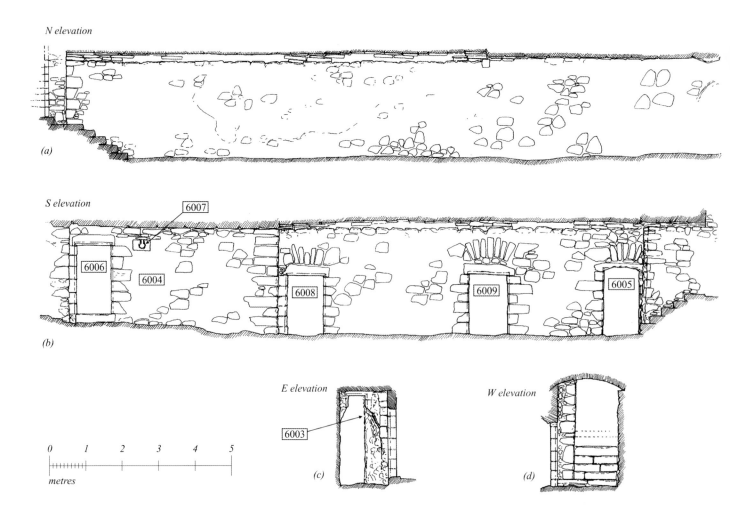

N elevation

(a)

S elevation

6007

6006

6004

6008

6009

6005

(b)

0   1   2   3   4   5

metres

E elevation

6003

(c)

W elevation

(d)

82 Component 6, elevations of transe

Chamber 6, Component 18	
Plan	2.25m by 1.25m
Access	S door (F17002)
Windows	W wall (F18014). N wall blocked Period 2 gun loop (F18003).
Discussion	This is created by the extension westwards of the Period 4 S range. The significance of the blocked gun loop is described above.

Period 4: The S Range – First Floor (Illus 75 and 83)
This comprises a single space at the E end of the range.

Chamber 1, Component 42	
Plan	5m by 4.5m
Access	Via door (F4008) in N wall (Period 3 former stair access)
Windows	In S wall (F42011)
Discussion	This room has a fireplace in its E wall. The possible blocked garderobe chute (Period 2) noted in the E wall may have been retained into Period 4.

Period 4: The E Range – Ground Floor (Illus 74 and 83)

This comprises five chambers.

Chamber 1
E spiral stair now removed. Chamber is now of reduced importance and it has no direct access to S range. The loss of its window (F25005) may have resulted in the linking with Chamber 2 if only to provide extra light.

Chamber 2, Components 33 and 34	
Plan	Rounded, 1.5m in diameter
Access	Doorway at W (F34011)
Windows	Three loops, symmetrically disposed
Discussion	This is the ground-floor chamber of the S gatehouse tower, built against the face of the E of the Period 3 E range. The towers are rounded in plan and ornamented with decorative moulding. They form part of an elaborate façade leading to an entrance way between the two tower elements.

Chamber 3, Component 30 (Illus 84)	
Plan	1.5m by 5.5m
Access	From W and E. Main outer door (F30005).
Windows	None
Discussion	This is the entrance passage between the towers and comprises a vault, the slight asymmetry of which at its E end may indicate the recycling of a similar Period 3 passage.

Chamber 4, Components 31 and 32	
Plan	Irregular – single space integrating rounded tower and narrow gate chamber. Width: 1.5m. Overall length: 6.5m.
Access	Two doors in the S wall (F3001) and (F3006), although the former appears slightly later than its partner.
Windows	None
Discussion	This is created on the footprint of a Period 3 chamber, possibly defined by wall (F29010). It is the twin for Chambers 1 and 2. Possible porter's lodge.

Chamber 5, Component 29	
Plan	4m by 4m
Access	Via W wall door (F29015)
Windows	E wall (F29016) and reworked Period 4 window to create (F29008)

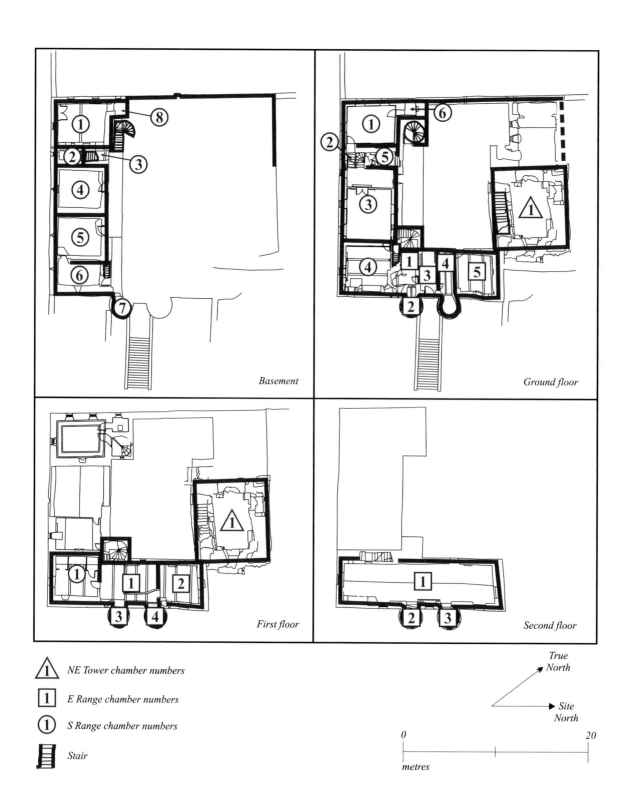

Basement

Ground floor

First floor

Second floor

△ 1 NE Tower chamber numbers

☐ 1 E Range chamber numbers

① S Range chamber numbers

▤ Stair

True North

Site North

0   20

metres

83 Period 4 plans

Period 4: The E Range – First Floor (Illus 75 and 83)

Four chambers in total – two as for Period 3 and two additional gatehouse towers (Components 39 and 37).

Chambers 1 and 2	
As for Period 3, but spiral stair (F33012) removed. New door in W wall leading to new E stair.	

Chamber 3, Component 39	
Plan	Irregular, subcircular, 1.5m N–S by 2.25m E–W
Access	From W.
Windows	One central window in E face (F39004). The present window is Period 5 in construction, but original window may well have been as lavish.

Chamber 4, Component 37	
Plan	Irregular, vaguely rounded, 1.5m N–S by 2.25m E–W
Access	From W
Windows	One central window in E face (F37004)
Discussion	The size of this chamber (Component 37) has been affected by the presence of the garderobe (Component 36) immediately N and has constrained the entranceway slightly. This has resulted in a rather irregular plan.

Period 4: The E Range – Second Floor (Illus 76 and 83)

The upper floor consists of a single space forming a long gallery with two with smaller chambers/closets (Chambers 1 and 2) off at the head of the gatehouse towers.

Chamber 1, Component 49	
Plan	17m by 4m (average)
Access	Via new door in W wall (F49015), leading to stair (Component 43)
Windows	Three in E wall (F49004, F49006 and F49008), one in S wall (F49011) and one in the W wall (F49069)
Discussion	Fireplace (F49002) in the N wall

Chamber 2, Component 51	
Plan	Irregular – 2.5m by 1.5 m
Access	From W
Windows	Four small loops and one large loop (F51004)
Discussion	Chamber off long gallery

Chamber 3, Component 50	
Plan	Irregular – 2.5m by 1.5m
Access	From W
Windows	Four small loops, and one single window in the E wall (F50004)
Discussion	Chamber off long gallery

Period 4: The Stairs

The E stair (Component 25) (Illus 85) has been built in the re-entrant angle of the S and E ranges, and replaces the earlier turnpike stair. The construction of this stair necessitated the enlargement of an earlier ground-floor window (F21007) as a door; a further stair (Component 43) gave access to the second-floor gallery.

Period 4: The NW Range

This comprised the outer defensive wall (F26025) with loops, for example F26026.

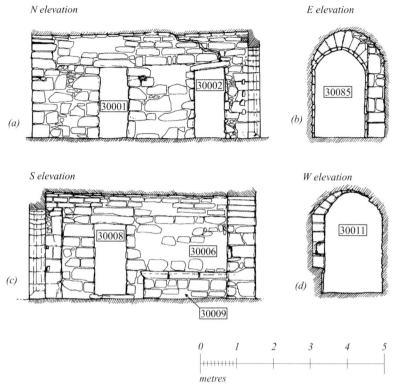

84 Elevations of gateway passage, Component 30

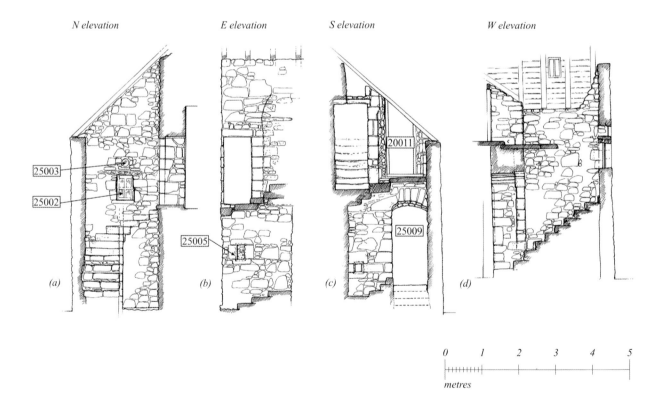

85 Stair, Component 25

Period 5: Courtyard complex, early- 17th–early 18th century

Period 5: The NE Tower – Ground Floor (Illus 74 and 86)

This comprises a single chamber.

Plan	As Period 2
Access	Same arrangements as Period 2
Windows	E window reduced in size
Discussion	The Period 2 first- and ground-floor chambers were altered by the lowering of the floor levels by some 0.4m. The basement E window (Period 2) was reduced in size and the N window (Period 2) may have been converted to a hearth. In turn a vault (F208) was constructed to support the new first-floor chamber. The NW range was built and the NE tower was integrated within a courtyard plan.

Period 5: NE Tower – First Floor (Illus 75 and 86)

This comprises a single chamber.

Plan	Probably same as Period 2
Access	Period 2 stair retained with additional access from new NW range
Windows	None survive.
Fireplace	Period 2 window (F213) possibly recycled as a small hearth in N wall
Discussion	The new upper floor is thought to be linked with the flooring arrangements in the adjoining NW range.

Period 5: S Range – Basement (Illus 73 and 86)

This comprises seven chambers and is the same as in Period 4 except for Chamber 2 where new windows were added (F1027), (F1034) and (F1032). Elsewhere a new door was added into the E end of the transe via the basement of the S gatehouse tower.

Period 5: S Range – Ground Floor (Illus 74 and 86)

This comprises eight chambers and five stairs.

Chamber 1, Component 17	
Plan	As Period 4
Access	As Period 4
Windows	New windows added (F17016), (F17025) and (F17026)
Discussion	This chamber was upgraded by the addition of panelling and new windows, possibly for use as a lower parlour. The exterior S and W walls have been rebuilt, probably during Period 6.

Chamber 2, Component 16 (Illus 87)	
Plan	As Period 4
Access	As Period 4
Windows	The surviving stairs date from this period and have the added access to Component 5, Chamber 3, via door (F16005).
Discussion	This is part of the final arrangement for separate access between domestic access at ground floor and above linking the chamber to the W and the hall, etc. Door (F16005) allows service access to Service Stair 5 (Chamber 3) leading ultimately to the kitchen at basement level.

Chamber 3, Component 20	
Plan	1.75m by 1.5m
Access	In E wall, door (F20014)
Windows	No windows
Discussion	As in Chamber 2, this recycled stairway arrangement has been rationalised to its present form with wooden risers. It represents service access between ground floor and basement.

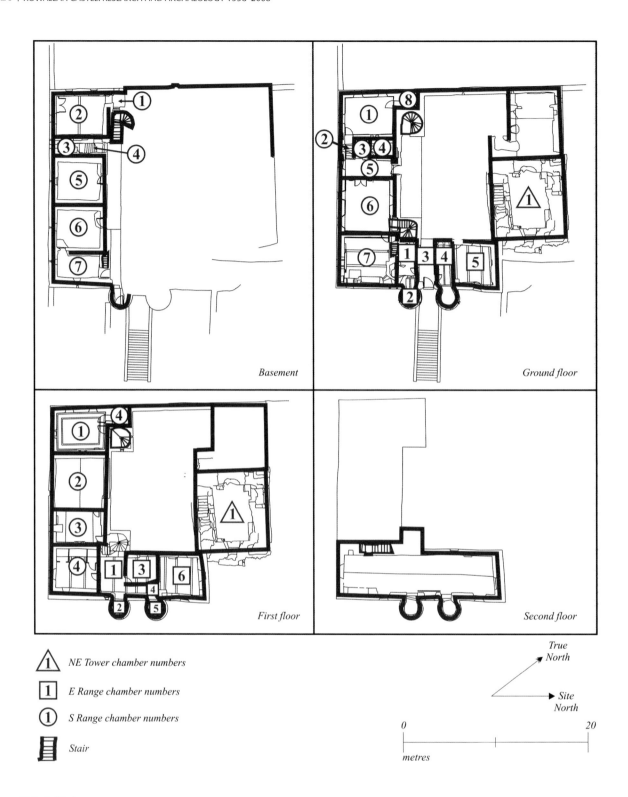

Basement

Ground floor

First floor

Second floor

NE Tower chamber numbers

E Range chamber numbers

S Range chamber numbers

Stair

True North

Site North

0   20

metres

86 Period 5 plans

Chamber 4, Component 19

Plan	3.5m by 1.5m
Access	Door (F20015) in E wall
Windows	Window (F19004) formed from Period 3 door (F19002) (now blocked)
Discussion	This room is created from the need to combine the two stair elements, Chambers 2 and 3, resulting in part of the earlier screens passage being converted to a closet. The main access to the hall from courtyard level was via door (F19002) up until this time. The latter is now partially blocked and converted to a window. New access to the hall, etc, is now via door (F20003).

Chamber 5, Component 20

Plan	5.25m by 2m
Access	New N door (F20003). W wall door (F16008), leading to Chamber 1. Door (F20014) leading down to basement and door (F20015) leading to Chamber 4. In E wall, door (F20008) leads to Chamber 6 (Component 21).
Windows	No new windows
Discussion	This chamber defines the new lobby or antechamber for access throughout the ground floor, replacing in function the former screens passage.

Chamber 6, Component 21

Plan	5m by 5.5m
Access	From W via doorway in new partition wall (F2008). Otherwise as Period 4.
Windows	Window openings as Period 4 (F21019) and (F21020)
Discussion	This chamber is panelled with the addition of a new W partition wall. There is a new fireplace (F21003) in the N wall.

Chamber 7, Component 22

Plan	As for Period 4
Access	Period 4 door in W wall retained. Also Period 2 door in N wall retained.
Windows	As for Period 4
Discussion	This chamber featured elaborate panelling, as reported by MacGibbon and Ross (1887–92), but which is now absent. This included an internal porch and screened a closet

Chamber 8, Component 18

Plan	As for Period 4
Access	As for Period 4
Windows	As for Period 4
Discussion	As for Period 4

Period 5: S Range – First Floor (Illus 75 and 86)
This comprises five chambers.

Chamber 1, Component 46

Plan	5.7m by 4.1m
Access	N wall door (F46004) leading to Chamber 5. Also door (F46005) leads to extended W circular stair (Component 4).
Windows	New window openings set in possible Period 4 embrasures (F46016), (F46023) and (F46024)
Discussion	This chamber necessitated the extension of the existing W circular stair. It is not accessible from the remainder of the S range. It is panelled and has a fireplace in its E wall (F46010). The panelling appears to be 18th-century, but may be associated with the partial rebuilding of the S and W walls. The room may have served as an upper parlour.

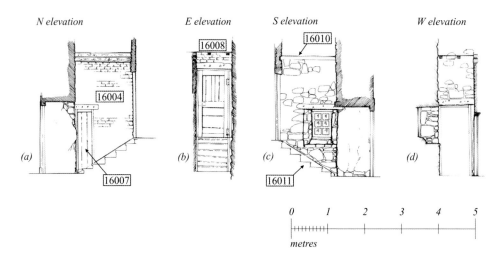

N elevation   *E elevation*   *S elevation*   *W elevation*

16008

16010

16004

16007

16011

(a)   (b)   (c)   (d)

0   1   2   3   4   5

metres

87 Stair, Component 16

Chamber 2, Component 45	
Plan	5.75m by 5.6m
Access	W door (F44015)
Windows	Blocked window in S wall, shown open on MacGibbon and Ross (1887–92, 375)
Discussion	Probable use as a bedchamber as part of an apartment with Chamber 3. Only access through Chamber 3 (Component 44).

Chamber 3, Component 44	
Plan	5.75m by 3.4m
Access	N door (F44003) on to stair
Windows	S wall (F44009)
Discussion	Bolection-moulded fireplace in its E wall (F44006). This room is likely to have served as an antechamber for bedchamber in Chamber 2.

Chamber 4, Component 42	
Plan	5m by 4.5m
Access	New door (F40015) in N wall leading to E range
Windows	As for Period 4
Discussion	This room is linked directly with the E range first floor and, on the evidence of surviving timber partitions for a bed alcove, it is a bedchamber with closets. The earlier fireplace in the E wall (F42007) has been reduced (F42009). This was the most prestigious of the bedchambers and was likely to be part of an apartment that extended the length of the E range.

Chamber 5, Component 47	
Plan	2m by 1.6m
Access	Door (F46004) in S wall leading to Chamber 1, noticeably wider on the outside than the opening into the chamber
Windows	As for Period 4.
Discussion	This is a small room, or closet, off Chamber 1.

Period 5: S Range – Second Floor (Illus 76 and 86)

At this stage the S range is merged effectively with the E range in Period 4. This space is therefore discussed as the E range, second-floor gallery.

Period 5: E Range – Ground Floor (Illus 74 and 86)

This comprises five chambers.

Chamber 1	
Plan	As for Period 4
Access	As Period 4
Windows	As Period 4
Discussion	As for Period 4

Chamber 2, Component 34	
Plan	As for Period 4
Access	As for Period 4
Windows	As for Period 4
Discussion	This chamber may have been merged with Chamber 1 to form a single space in view of a new role for Chamber 1 as storage/service space.

Chamber 3, Component 34	
Plan	As for Period 4
Access	As for Period 4
Windows	As for Period 4
Discussion	The entranceway remained as for Period 4. The formal approach stair (F13006) may date to this period.

Chamber 4, Component 31	
Plan	As for Period 4
Access	As for Period 4
Windows	As for Period 4
Discussion	As for Period 4

Chamber 5, Component 29	
Plan	As for Period 4
Access	As for Period 4
Windows	As for Period 4
Discussion	As for Period 4

Period 5: E Range – First Floor (Illus 75 and 86)

This comprises six chambers.

Chamber 1, Component 40	
Plan	2.75m by 4m
Access	Door in W wall (F40019) leading to stair (Component 25). Door in N wall (F4003) leading to Chamber 3. Door leading to Chamber 4. Door in S wall (F40015) leading to Chamber 4, S range.
Windows	Recycled Period 3 window (F4008) and also light via window (F39004), Chamber 2
Discussion	This chamber represents a possible subdivision of a larger Period 4 space.

Chamber 2, Component 39	
Plan	As for Period 4
Access	As for Period 4
Windows	New window inserted (F39004)
Discussion	This chamber opens directly into Chamber 1 and was probably upgraded at some time after Period 4 and prior to construction of Chamber 3 via window enlargements.

Chamber 3, Component 41	
Plan	3.6m by 3m
Access	Via S door (F4003)
Windows	As for Period 4 (F41008)
Discussion	This represents an internal partition within the larger Period 4 Chamber 1 using lighter construction techniques for the S and E walls (F41006 and F41003 respectively). It forms a closet between Chambers 1 and 6. It may have been used as a dressing room.

Chamber 4, Component 38	
Plan	4m by 1m (average)
Access	From S linking directly (no door fitting) with Chamber 1. At N wall via doorway (F35010), leading to Chamber 6. Open access into Chamber 5.
Windows	Borrowed light from Period 4 E wall fenestration
Discussion	This forms a corridor between Chambers 1 and 6. This arrangement saw abandonment of the original access into the garderobe in the E wall of Chamber 6 and simply provides access for the newly subdivided E range apartments.

Chamber 5, Component 37	
Plan	As for Period 4
Access	As for Period 4
Windows	As for Period 4
Discussion	This space provided light and closet space (?) during Period 5.

Chamber 6, Component 35	
Plan	As for Period 4
Access	Via new door in S wall (F35010)
Windows	As for Period 4
Discussion	The Period 3 garderobe (Component 36) in the E wall continues in use during Period 5, although access arrangements have been modified with the abandonment of a S aperture (F38003).

Period 5: E Range – Second Floor (Illus 76 and 86)

This comprises a single space.

Plan	17m by 4m (average)
Access	Via new door in W wall (F49015), leading to new stair (Component 43)
Windows	As for Period 4
Discussion	This period saw the use of the gallery for religious services.

Period 5: The Stairs

The W circular stair (Component 1) has been extended upwards to permit access from courtyard level to first-floor S range Chamber 1.

The E stair (Component 25) remains as Period 4.

Period 5: The NW Range – Ground Floor (Illus 74 and 86)

Access restricted during survey due to safety considerations.

Component 26	
Plan	4.2m by 7.4m
Access	Via door (F26014) in S wall, leading to outer doorway (F28007)
Windows	In S wall two new windows (F26015 and F26016)
Discussion	This is interpreted as the 'New wark in the north syde of the close' of Sir William Mure. The structure is built into the NW angle of an earlier outer wall and fills the gap between the NE tower and this outer wall, thus completing the existing courtyard plan. The surviving ground floor is some form of undercroft, its upper floors accessed via a stair arrangement (F28004) within the outer passage (Component 28).